NAGEL'S

ENCYCLOPEDIA-GUIDE

AWARDS
ROME, 1958   PARIS, 1961   VIENNA, 1968, 1972

RUMANIA

400 pages
36 pages of plans in black and white
4 maps and plans in colour

Fourth edition

NAGEL PUBLISHERS
GENEVA · PARIS · MUNICH

ISBN 2–8263–0738–X

CONTENTS

MAPS AND PLANS

PUBLISHER'S NOTE

When, several years ago, we decided to undertake the preparation of this guidebook there was no guide to present-day Rumania in existence. The success of our guides to Czechoslovakia, Hungary, Poland and the U.S.S.R. showed that large numbers of people were anxious to visit Eastern Europe; and now Rumania, which for so long stood out of the tourist movement of the post-war years, has entered the field with considerable success.

Rumania has, in fact, great tourist assets, and it is surprising that they have been so long neglected. It has a great variety of attractions to offer visitors: a wide range of beautiful scenery, from the wooded Carpathians to the marshes of the Danube Delta— the ancient ruins of the Dacian and Greco-Roman civilisations—its innumerable monasteries with their astonishing wealth of architecture and art—its marvellous beaches along the Black Sea coast—its traditional culture and folklore preserved intact. From every point of view Rumania is undoubtedly one of the most rewarding countries in Europe for the visitor.

It is also one of the most hospitable and the closest to the West. This is the result of its Latin culture, and wherever he goes the visitor will find traces of western influence. He will have no feeling of being lost in a foreign country: everywhere, without effort, he will feel at home.

Note to Fourth edition

The present edition of this Guide has been thoroughly revised and brought up to date. We are grateful to the Rumanian authorities for the help they have continued to give us in the preparation of this new edition, and also for the suggestions and comments by users of earlier editions. As always, we welcome criticisms and comments which enable us to make each successive edition an improvement on its predecessors.

We add our usual reminder that the Nagel Guides contain no advertising matter, so that the information they contain can be relied upon as being entirely objective and unbiassed.

GEOGRAPHY

Rumania is situated in the south-east of Europe, between 43° 37' 07" and 48° 15' 06" N and 20° 15' 44" and 29° 41' 24" E, extending for some 300 miles from north to south and for some 400 miles from west to east. The country occupies a special geographical position: lying astride the arc of the Carpathians in the north, it extends southward to the lower Danube basin and the shores of the Black Sea, both the river and the sea providing good communications with other countries.

Physical Features

Rumania has a total area of 91,400 square miles. Its frontiers extend over 1,970 miles — 669 miles of land frontiers, 1,148 on rivers and 153 on the sea. It has common boundaries with the U.S.S.R., Bulgaria, Hungary and Yugoslavia.

The area of the country is almost equally divided between plains (roughly 33 % of the total), hills and plateaux (36 %) and mountains (31 %).

The concentric arrangement of the main physical features gives Rumania the aspect of a natural fortress. In the centre is the massive arc of the Carpathians, covered with great forests of deciduous and coniferous trees. Within this "Carpathian redoubt" is Transylvania, and outside it is a range of lower mountains, the Subcarpathians, which in turn have a fringe of hills. Finally come the plains and the great rivers of the periphery, and then, linking this fortress to the Black Sea, the Dobrogea (Dobrudja). Perhaps it would be fairer to say that there are two Dobrudjas: one formed by a plateau and the other by the eroded remains of a chain of Palaeozoic mountains.

The Carpathians. The geography of Rumania is dominated by the Carpathians, a continuation of the Alps. They are the most sinuous chain of mountains in Europe, punctuated by numerous extinct volcanoes. Like the Alps, they were formed in the Tertiary period, and are composed of a great variety of types of rock (metamorphic, volcanic and sedimentary). In the course of time these rocks have taken on the most fantastic shapes, giving rise in the popular imagination to all kinds of legends. The Carpathians attract both tourists and scientists by the picturesqueness and wild beauty of their scenery as well as by their geological diversity.

There are few peaks (Rodna, Căliman) higher than 2,000 metres (6,560 feet), and peaks above 2,500 metres (8,200 feet) are exceptional (Bucegi, Făgăraş, Parîng and Retezat). They show a great variety of shape. The highest mountain in Rumania (Moldoveanu, 8,346 feet) is in the very centre of the Carpathians, in the Făgăraş Mountains. Most of the peaks range between 1,000 and 1,500 metres (3,300 and 4,900 feet). Here and there are mountain corries and moraines left by Quaternary glaciers, now almost entirely covered by forest. Glaciers are no longer to be found in the high valleys, but the marks left by their passage have contributed to the picturesqueness of the Southern Carpathians, the Rodna Mountains and the Maramureş Carpathians. Here there are considerable numbers of hollows excavated by the ice, now often occupied by limpid mountain lakes.

In certain places the massive wall of the Carpathians is interrupted by wide depressions, and some of these, having in the past formed separate economic and even military units, are known as "countries"—the *Maramureş Country*, the *Oaş Country*, the *Dornas Country*, the *Bîrsa Country*, the *Olt Country* and the *Motzi Country*.

In addition to these depressions, which played an important part in the ups and downs of Rumanian history, there are many passes and defiles providing a passage through the mountain chain. Among these are the famous Iron Gates in the Danube valley, which are unique of their kind in Europe, the defile of Turnu Roşu in the Olt Valley, the Urde pass which takes the road from Novaci to Sebeş over the Parîng range at a height of over 2,000 metres (6,560 feet), the Predeal pass at over 1,000 metres (3,280 feet), etc.

The sedimentary and volcanic rocks have a solid and massive appearance, but the conglomerates and limestones, particularly the latter, have taken on the most varied and picturesque shapes. Thus the long narrow corridor of the Bicaz Gorges, the most imposing in Rumania, has been carved by water out of the limestone mass of Suhard, behind Mount Ceahlău. The wild beauty of the gorges and the thunder of the water at the bottom of this huge cleft in the mountains form an unforgettable spectacle. The Turda Gorges in the Apuseni Mountains are remarkable for the fantastic shapes into which water and wind have carved the limestone, and also for the unusual plant life found here, the result of a particularly favourable microclimate.

The Carpathians are rich in picturesque scenery, for their geological structure has offered scope for external agencies to create the most bizarre landscapes. Many of these areas are now nature reserves (Retezat, Bucegi, Ceahlău, Scărişoara, etc., see page 51).

Nature has been generous to this region, which possesses iron and non-ferrous metals, precious metals, etc. Its gold mines were already being worked in the time of the Dacians and the Romans.

The Subcarpathians. The transition from the mountains to the hills is a gradual one. The height and the geological structure vary from place to place. A chain of hills and depressions girdles the outside of the Carpathians, leading gradually down to the plateaux or the plains. This is the Subcarpathian range. In general it has the same characteristics as the Carpathians, except that the rock is more friable, the mountains are completely covered with forest and the soil is even richer in minerals.

The Subcarpathians can be considered as high hills, reaching 700 to 800 metres (2,300 to 2,600 feet) or even more. At one point where the range forms an angle is a region of vineyards, orchards and forests, the Măgura Odobeştilor, where the hills rise to 1,000 metres (3,280 feet). The main wealth of the Subcarpathians is formed by coal, salt and above all by oil: in this area oil derricks are a very common feature of the landscape.

The Plateaux. The Carpathians then merge into large plateaux on a lower level. Here the landscape is more regular, with rivers flowing between long hills or through high table land. Depending on their position in relation to the Carpathians, their altitude and the rocks of which they are formed, these plateaux are classified as *internal plateaux* like the Transylvanian Plateau or the Someş Plateau or as *external plateaux* like the Moldavian Plateau, the Getic Plateau, the Western Hills and the Dobrudja Plateau, each one having its own specific characteristics. There are many villages, and the towns are populous. The valleys are wide, with gently sloping sides.

The soil is rich in minerals—oil under the slopes of the Getic Plateau, salt and methane gas in Transylvania, mineral water and building stone in the hills of Moldavia and the Dobrudja— as well as fertile in crops: forests of beech and oak, vines (Cotnari, Odobeşti, Huşi, Nicoreşti, Segarcea, Drăgălani, Murfatlar, Tîrnave, etc.), and orchards of apples, plums and other fruit trees, alongside large fields of wheat and maize.

In this area, therefore, Rumania possesses not only great variety of landscape, from the Subcarpathians with their rugged hills to the long slopes of the plateaux, but also great scope for the development of a diversified economy.

The Plains. Rumania contains the largest plain in the lower Danube basin, the *Rumanian Plain* (Wallachia), and the eastern part of the plain of the middle Danube basin, the *Western Plain* (Banat). Although in general it lies at a height of between 40 and 100 metres (130 and 330 feet), the Rumanian Plain resembles a plateau as a result of the deep valleys which the Danube and its tribunaries have hollowed out of its surface.

Extending from Drobeta-Turnu Severin to Galaţ and reaching a maximum width of 85 miles, the Rumanian Plain (Oltenia in the west, Muntenia in the east) occupies the whole area between the hills and the Danube, ending in a steep slope into the Danube valley. For the most part it is formed of alluvial soil and a thick layer of lœss. Apart from the valleys, the monotony of the plain is broken here and there by sand dunes and, in the east, by small depressions, most of which contain lakes, sometimes salt (Amara, the Salt Lake, Strachina, Ianca, etc.). The sand, mostly found along the rivers, was formerly given to drifting but is now held in place by forests of acacia, vineyards and orchards. There are fields too, and the steppe—a favourite haunt of bustards—has been converted into cultivable land which produces abundant harvests. A network of roads and railways covers the plain, and the pattern is completed by the new buildings, the silos and the rows of oil derricks.

On the left bank of the Danube below Calafat is what is known as the *Valley*, an area varying in width from 6 to 15 miles built up from alluvial deposits which is the youngest part of the Danube plain. Between the two arms of the river are the areas known as the "Marsh of Ialomiţa" and the "Marsh of Brăila", a verdant landscape sprinkled with picturesque lakes and lagoons where thousands of acres of fertile land have been reclaimed from the waters. The mild damp climate produces abundant crops.

The *Danube Delta*, covering an area of over 1,500 square miles, is the lowest-lying plain in Rumania—a plain still in process of formation. It is a type of scenery which stands quite by itself, a corner of nature which is unrivalled for the abundance and variety of its vegetation and of its land and water fauna. There is nothing like it anywhere else in Europe.

Climate

Rumania's geographical situation and physical configuration give it a varied climate, appropriate to an area of transition between Central Europe, Western Europe and Mediterranean Europe. The damp sea air from the west, the dry continental air from the east and the mild Mediterranean air from the south mingle to form a balanced climate, so that Rumania does not suffer from the mists which are so prevalent along the Atlantic coasts of Europe and is less subject to the long periods of severe drought which sometimes occur in the eastern part of the Continent.

In general the climate of Rumania is a continental one: relatively uniform, without any great differences between one part of the country and another in spite of its geographical diversity. A number of local variations can be explained by particular physical features—the general pattern of the mountain chains, the width and orientation of particular valleys, the morphology of certain enclosed depressions, etc.

The highest mean annual temperatures are recorded in the low-lying areas in the south, south-east and south-west of the country (the Dobrudja, the Rumanian Plain, the Banat plain), the lowest on the Carpathian peaks and in some of the depressions within the Carpathians.

The coldest month is January, the warmest July (except in the alpine areas of the Carpathians, where February is the coldest month and August the warmest). In January the mean temperature ranges between −5° and −10 °C. in the mountains and between −2° and −5° in the plains; in July it reaches 23° along the Danube and in the Dobrudja, 20° in Moldavia and Transylvania, 10° to 12° in the high mountains (only 8° in the Retezat, Făgăraş and Bucegi Mountains). The extreme temperatures so far recorded are 44.4 °C. (in 1951, near Brăila, in the Bărăgan) and −38.5 °C. (in 1942, in the Braşov depression).

The movements of the air masses are extremely irregular, varying considerably in direction and speed, and are influenced locally by the varying pattern of the Carpathian mountains. In Transylvania the prevailing winds are west, in Moldavia north and north-east, in the Bărăgan and the Dobrudja north-east and south-east.

The rainfall varies from area to area, the lowest rates (14–16 in. annually) being recorded on the Black Sea coast, the highest

(40–60 in.) in the mountainous areas. There is much rain in spring; less in summer and autumn.

The combination of these various meteorological features from season to season in the different geographical conditions of different parts of the country gives rise to some striking local variations. Thus, particularly in the hills and the plain areas, the autumn is warm and lasts a very long time, so that quite often the trees put out fresh leaves at the end of September.

In the southern Dobrudja and the south-west of Rumania the influence of the Mediterranean climate begins to make itself felt, with mild winters and warm, dry summers.

Hydrography

As a result of the complexity of its rock structure and its contorted tectonic pattern the soil of Rumania contains a great variety of mineral waters. Altogether there are more than 2,000 mineral sprigns, some of which have remarkable therapeutic properties (Herculane, with water at a temperature of over 50 °C., Vatra Dornei, Băile Felix, Tuşnad, Sovata, etc.). Most of these are in the sub-mountainous areas where the climate is particularly pleasant, and this has led to the growth of many health resorts in these areas. These resorts, well provided with amenities, give Rumania a high place among European countries in this field.

The main rivers are the Someş, the Mureş, the Jiu, the Olt, the Argeş, the Dîmboviţa, the Ialomiţa, the Siret and the Prut. All of them flow, directly or indirectly, into the Danube, which has a total length within Rumania of over 670 miles, finally dividing into three arms and flowing into the Black Sea. Like the other countries bordering on the Danube, Rumania makes the most of the resources offered by the river. A new dam at the Iron Gates feeds a powerful hydro-electric station, brought into service in 1972, which has considerably increased the water-power potential of Rumania and Yugoslavia and improved navigation in this part of the river.

Fauna and Flora

The pattern of the fauna and flora, and their distribution in the different natural regions, are a consequence of the complexity of physical and geographical conditions, largely due to variations in the configuration of the country.

From the Alpine peaks, the haunt of the chamois and the bearded vulture, to the reedy country of the Delta, providing a paradise for birds, Rumania has a very varied fauna and flora. In certain areas specific physical features or peculiarities of climate or hydrography have led to the formation of local variations, known as "endemic elements" (for example plants of the *Hieracium* type in the *Compositae* family), which are found only in Rumania. There are not many of them, but they are of great scientific interest.

The Rumanian forests—found mainly in the mountains and hills, and covering an area of 25,000 square miles—contain a variety of game. Deer, roe-deer, bears, wolves, lynxes, martens, squirrels, black grouse, etc.—all these are found in abundance. The steppe is the haunt of hares and bustards.

The Danube basin possesses more than 70 species of fish. In the mountain streams there are trout, and rarer species like the grayling and the salmon trout; in the rivers of the plains and the lower hills there are perch, carp, and barbel. And finally there is the sturgeon, which makes its way up the Danube from the Black Sea in the spawning season.

HISTORY

The Origins

The territory in which the Rumanian people was formed and developed over the centuries was inhabited from the remotest times. Favourable natural conditions and a rich and varied fauna and flora encouraged continuity of human settlement from the early Palaeolithic period onwards. Large numbers of remains bear witness to the existence and development of the various stages of culture—Palaeolithic, Mesolithic, Neolithic, Bronze Age, and so on.

The earliest written record of the peoples who lived north of the Danube is contained in Herodotus. In his account of the expedition mounted in 514 B.C. by Darius, King of the Persians, against the Scythians who had just settled on the banks of the Danube, Herodotus notes that this area, like the centre of the Balkan peninsula, was thickly peopled by Thracian tribes, who herded cattle, grew grain and vines, and kept bees. Among this mass of related tribes the Daco-Getae, occupying the territory of present-day Rumania, gradually achieved an individuality of their own during the second half of the first millennium and entered into contact with the Scythians, the Celts, the Sarmatians and the Greek cities established at the beginning of the 7th century B.C. along the Black Sea coast.

The Period of Romanisation

When the Romans reached the Danube the Dacians had founded a kingdom which attained its maximum extent and power in the reign of Burebista, a contemporary of Caesar. The Dacian kingdom broke into pieces after his death, but was partly reconstituted in the reign of *Decebal* (87–106), who inflicted a series of defeats on the Roman legions in the time of the Emperor Domitian. In 101–102 and 105–106, however, the Emperor Trajan led two great expeditions against the Dacians and after much hard fighting finally succeeded in subjugating the country.

The people of Dacia, now incorporated in the Empire, suffered the same fate as other nations conquered by the Romans. The country was covered with roads and fortifications, and became a bulwark against the migrating barbarian peoples who were threatening the Empire to the east and north of the Carpathians. The increasing pressure of the barbarians against the frontiers of the Empire, however, led in the year 271 to the withdrawal of the Roman army and administration. The main result of the intensive process of romanisation to which Dacia was subjected for 165 years was that the language of the Romans became the language of the native peoples as well as of the settlers who were brought here from every province of the Empire.

The Middle Ages

In spite of the varying influences exercised over a period of almost a thousand years by the migrant peoples who passed in successive waves over the territory of Rumania during their advance into western or southern Europe, or sometimes even settled there for a time, the Daco-Roman population—as there is an abundance of archaeological, epigraphical, linguistic, ethnographical and other evidence to show—continued in uninterrupted occupation of the territory. About the year 1000, as a result of their progressive assimilation of the various groups of migrant peoples who had remained in the area, and particularly the Slav elements, the Rumanian people and the Rumanian language came into being in the country north of the lower Danube valley. Their nucleus was in the mountain and hill regions of Dacia (Transylvania, Oltenia and Northern Wallachia) which were less exposed to the final waves of invasion. The basic vocabulary of Rumanian, the fundamental structure of its syntax and its morphological pattern make it a Romance language, one of the present-day descendants of Latin.

It was during this period, about the 10th century, that the first germs of feudal society gradually developed. Then in the following century the historical sources record the existence of actual feudal states in different parts of the country. Thus, according to the anonymous chronicler of King Bela III, the Hungarian kings succeeded in conquering Transylvania only after overcoming the resistance of a series of Rumanian voivodes (Glad, Menumorut, Gelu, etc.).

In the 13th and 14th centuries two larger feudal states were formed—*Wallachia*, extending from the Carpathians to the Danube, and *Moldavia*, covering the whole area to the east of the Carpathians and the north of the Danube. Transylvania meanwhile retained a special status within the Hungarian kingdom. Wallachia and Moldavia were involved in conflict both with Hungary, which was trying to extend its control east and south of the Carpathians, and with the Mongols from Asia who frequently launched devastating raids into Europe. Nevertheless the two states gradually succeeded in consolidating their position, at time when in other parts of Europe there was a tendency to split up into smaller feudal units.

The Modern Period

The appearance of the Turks on the Danube after their rapid conquest of the Balkan peninsula involved the Rumanian people in a difficult and unequal struggle against the expansion of the Ottoman Empire. Under the leadership of a series of voivodes — Mircea the Old (1386–1418), Iancu of Hunedoara (1441–56), Vlad the Impaler (1456–62), Stephen the Great (1457–1504), Ion the Terrible (1572–1574), Michael the Brave (1593–1601), etc. — who are mentioned with admiration in the Polish, Hungarian and Italian chronicles, the Rumanians won a number of victories over the Turkish invader during the 15th and 16th centuries. Thus they helped to slow down the Turkish advance towards central Europe at a time when the West, torn by internal disturbances, was in no state to offer any organised resistance to this expansion.

Although in the end they were compelled to submit to Turkish domination the Rumanians maintained their autonomy and were not formed into Turkish pashaliks. At the beginning of the 18th century Turkish control was strengthened when the native princes were replaced by Phanariot princes appointed by the Sublime Porte from Greek families of the Phanar (a district in Constantinople) who sought to make their careers in the Turkish administration; and it was not finally broken until 1877. The systematic plundering of the country by the Turks delayed for several centuries the appearance and development of a modern society in Rumania.

After the battle of Mohacs (1526), which marked the end of the Hungarian state, Transylvania passed under Turkish control until 1699, when it fell into the hands of the Habsburgs. Throughout the whole of the Middle Ages — which, for the reasons just noted, continued in Rumania until the middle of the 19th century — the Rumanian people was engaged in bitter struggles to shake off the Turkish domination in Wallachia and Moldavia and the Hungarian and Habsburg domination in Transylvania. There were also innumerable peasant revolts against the feudal system—as, for example, the risings in Transylvania in 1437, 1514 and 1784 and the rising led by Tudor Vladimirescu in Wallachia in 1821.

The 19th Century Liberation

From the second half of the 18th century, and particularly at the beginning of the 19th, the crumbling of the feudal system and the appearance of structures of capitalist type coincided with the spread of the ideas of the French Revolution and the Romantic movement. All these causes combined to produce a recrudescence of the liberal and national movement in the 1820s, when the neighbouring countries of Serbia and Greece succeeded in throwing off the Ottoman yoke.

The idea of the union of all Rumanian territory was now gaining ground among leaders of Rumanian thought, and the poet Assaki called for the union of all Rumanians under Austrian or Turkish domination. The temporary occupation of the Moldavian and Wallachian principalities by the Russians after the treaty of Adrianople in 1829 resulted, paradoxically, in an attempt at liberalisation under the influence of the military governor *Kiseleff*. Kiseleff granted the principalities an "organic statute", an embryo constitution worked out with the help of Rumanian men of letters. Since, however, this statute favoured the nobles it did not satisfy the townspeople and peasants, and as a result there grew up a democratic movement under the leadership of Nicolae Golescu, Nicolae Bălcescu, Ion Radulescu and others.

In 1848 revolutionary movements broke out simultaneously in Moldavia, Wallachia and Transylvania. Although they failed, these movements played an important part in forging the moral unity of the Rumanian people and mark an important stage in the advance towards national and social liberation. A prominent role was played in these movements by N. Bălcescu, who died shortly afterwards in exile at Palermo.

In 1856 the Congress of Paris after the Crimean War decided that while the Principalities should remain under the suzerainty of Turkey they would be protected by the collective guarantee of the signatory powers. The two principalities of Moldavia and Wallachia, however, remained separate. Then support for their union came from the Emperor Napoleon III, in spite of opposition from the Austrians, fearing Transylvanian separatism; and in 1859 the Moldavians and Wallachians elected the same prince,

Alexandru Ioan Cuza. The Great Powers accepted the *fait accompli* and the new state took the name of the United Principalities, and later that of Rumania. With the help of intellectuals of liberal views, Alexandru Ioan Cuza decreed a series of social and political reforms. The most important of these was the agrarian reform of 1864, which abolished serfdom and shared out some of the nobles' land among the peasants, subject to the payment of compensation by the peasants to the former owners.

In spite of the limited nature of the reforms and social and political measures carried out under the aegis of Prince Alexandru Ioan Cuza, the Prince met with resistance from conservative forces, and on 11 February 1866 was compelled to abdicate. The conservatives — anxious to protect the interests of the large landed proprietors and the middle classes, who were seeking to attract foreign and particularly German capital — then put on the throne a representative of the Hohenzollern family (Carol I).

The "Compromise" of 1867 between Austria and Hungary brought Transylvania finally under Hungarian domination. The Austro-Hungarian Empire carried on a policy of oppression against the Rumanians in Transylvania, who formed a majority of the population of this area.

Having fought alongside Russia in the Russian's war against Turkey, Rumania obtained in the treaty of Berlin (1878) its national independance and the final ending of Turkish control; it also recovered the Dobrudja, a former Rumanian territory which had been conquered by the Turks at the beginning of the 15th century.

Meanwhile Transylvania was being subjected to a harsh process of "magyarisation". In the Budapest Parliament, however, Hungarian policy was opposed by a Rumanian National Party, which lodged an energetic protest in a Memorandum of 1892. This attracted much support in Western Europe. The resolute action of the Rumanians of Transylvania — led by such men as Ion Ratiu and Vasile Lucaciu, the principal authors of the 1892 Memorandum, Octavian Goga, Vasile Goldis, Aurel Lazar and Iuliu Maniu — was supported in Bucharest by the Rumanian Cultural League under the leadership of the great historian Nicolae Iorga. But the presence on the trone of a prince of German origin, committed to supporting the Triple Alliance, made all hopes of unification vain.

Since 1914

Carol I—whose wife, Queen Elizabeth, achieved some literary fame under the pseudonym of Carmen Sylva—died in October 1914 and was succeeded by his nephew Ferdinand, husband of Queen Marie. At first neutral, Rumania decided on 28 August 1916—under the influence of Brusilov's offensive and the French defence of Verdun—to join the Allies. Unfortunately, after a short-lived advance, the Rumanian army was forced to retreat, evacuate Bucharest and fall back to the Sereth (Siret). The Russian Revolution left this army isolated, and a French mission under General Berthelot was sent to help it to reorganise. The Rumanian army was thus able to break von Mackensen's offensive at Mărăşeşti in August 1917.

In March 1918 Bessarabia, which had declared itself a republic independent of Russia in December 1917, voted for union with Rumania; but soon afterwards pressure from the Central Powers obliged Rumania, isolated from its allies, to sign the treaty of Bucharest (7 May 1918), under which it lost all economic independence.

The position was completely restored, however, by the Allied victory over Germany and Austro-Hungary. On 27 October 1918 Bukovina was united with Rumania. There was a vigorous agitation for national emancipation in Transylvania, at a time when the Habsburg monarchy was falling apart; and on 1 December 1918 the Great National Assembly of Alba Iulia proclaimed the union of Transylvania with Rumania. The peace treaties of Saint-Germain, Neuilly and Trianon gave formal recognition to this reunification of Rumania, and in 1922 Ferdinand I was crowned king of all Rumanians in the cathedral of Alba Iulia.

Rumanian political life between the two world wars took the form of a democracy of Western type, at first under the predominance of the Liberal Party, and from 1928 onwards of the National Peasants' Party. The Communist Party was banned in 1924 and went underground. Although the agrarian reform carried out in 1921 had partly satisfied the aspirations of the peasants, who were granted 6 million hectares of land, the demands of industrial workers were left unfulfilled, and indeed were aggravated by the consequences of the world economic crisis which began in 1929. There were serious disturbances at he beginning of 1933, with strikes by railwaymen and oil workers.

In 1930 King Carol II, who had been excluded from the sucession in 1926, came to the throne, and the trend towards the exercise of personal power became more marked. Nicolae Titulescu, the brilliant Minister of Foreign Affairs who had promoted the policy of independence for the smaller nations and defended the system of collective security, was dismissed under pressure from the Fascist powers. The example of Mussolini's Italy and Hitler's Germany was imitated by Fascist groups within Rumania, like Codreanu's "Iron Guard". Finally in 1938 Carol abolished all political parties, established a personal dictatorship and reduced the country's parliamentary institutions to virtual impotence.

The second world war had unhappy consequences for Rumania. At the end of June 1940, after the defeat of France, the Soviet Union compelled Rumania to hand back Bessarabia and to cede Northern Bukovina; and soon afterwards, on 30 August 1940, the Vienna arbitration imposed by Hitler and Mussolini transferred Northern Transylvania to Horthy's Hungary. This national disaster, combined with pressure from pro-Hitler groups, obliged Carol to abdicate; and his son Michael was compelled to grant wide powers to Marshal Antonesco, who became *Conducator* or "Leader". The new regime, totally subservient to German policy, then declared war on the Soviet Union on 22 June 1941.

After some initial victories, which enabled Rumania to annex temporarily the territory of Transnistria, between the Dniester and the Bug, the defeats suffered from 1943 onwards led to a dramatic change in the situation. On 23 August 1944 — still the Rumanian National Day — when Soviet armies were reaching the country's frontiers, a national rising broke out, in accordance with plans prepared by Resistance forces, particularly the Communists, and accepted by King Michael's advisers. The Antonesco government was overthrown, and the Rumanian army turned against the Nazis and took an active part, alongside the Soviet army, in the liberation of the country and of Hungary and Czechoslovakia.

On 6 March 1945 Petru Groza formed a government which represented a transition towards a "people's democracy", and this was finally established after King Michael's abdication on 30 December 1947 and the elimination of the lest bourgeois members of the government. The Rumanian People's Republic was then proclaimed, and a Great National Assembly was elected in 1948. In the following month the Assembly adopted a new constitution, and in June 1948 the principal means of production were nationalised.

The frontiers of the country had been fixed by the treaty of Paris in 1947. The whole of Transylvania returned to Rumania, but Bessarabia and Northern Bukovina remained in Soviet hands, while the Southern Dobrudja fell to Bulgaria.

After various episodes during the years 1948-65 the Rumanian People's Republic — the most notable President of which was Gheorghe Gheorgiu-Dej, who died in 1965 — became in August 1965 the Socialist Republic of Rumania.

In 1965 the Great National Assembly decided that the Secretary-General of the Central Committee of the Rumanian Communist Party, Nicolae Ceauşescu, should also become President of the Council of State. In 1968 was established the Socialist Unity Front, a permanent political formation on which are represented, in addition to the Rumanian Communist Party — the country's political directing force — the principal mass organisations both public and professional, together with the Workers' Councils belonging to the various nationalities within Rumania.

The Tenth Congress of the Rumania Communist Party (1969) worked out a programme for the comprehensive development of Rumania from 1971 to 1975 together with guidelines for development until 1980. Measures for putting these decisions into effect were adopted at a National Conference of the Party held at Bucharest in 1972.

LITERATURE, SCIENCE AND ART

Literature

The Rumanian people has always possessed a characteristic culture of its own, in which oral poetry (usually secular), the oldest forms of dramatic performance, legends, heroic epics, ballads and tales, lyrical poems and songs, and proverbs gave artistic expression to the aspiration towards beauty. The appearance of written literature in the 16th century (the first work printed in Rumania, the *Missal of Macarie*, dates from 1508), the development of music and drama in the 18th and 19th centuries and of the cinema in the early part of the 20th (the first Rumanian feature film dates from 1911), and the whole evolution of these forms of expression are closely associated with the conditions in which the national culture of the Rumanian people was established and developed.

In the 17th and 18th centuries Rumanian culture already has some outstanding names, like the learned chronicler Miron Costin (1633–91), the talented story-teller Ion Neculce (1672–1745) and above all Prince *Dimitrie Cantemir*, a writer, historian and philosopher. Then in the 19th century there is Nicolae Bălcescu, the leader of the 1848 revolution, whose historical and philosophical works made such a valuable contribution to Rumanian literature. Nor must we forget *Vasile Alecsandri* (1821–90), poet and dramatist, the founder of Rumanian dramatic literature.

The traditions of Rumanian culture found lofty expression in the poetry of *Mihail Eminescu* (1850–89), in the prose writings and plays of *Ion Luca Caragiale* (1852–1912), whose satirical comedy, "A Lost Letter", brought him a considerable reputation abroad; and in the works of classical writers like *I. Creangă* (1837–1889), *I. Slavici* (1848–25), *G. Coşbuc* (1866-1918), *A. Vlahuță* (1858-1919) and A. Macedonachi (1854-1920), one of the first great European Symbolists. The Rumanian theatre, too, can point to producers and actors like Matei Millo (1814-96), Mihail Pascaly (1830-82), C. I. Nottara (1859-1935), Eufrosina Popescu (1821-1900) and Aristizza Romanescu (1854-1918).

Rumanian music has always remained in close contact with the traditions of folk music—given brilliant expression in the works of composers like Ciprian Porumbescu (1853–83),

Gavril Muzicescu (1847–1903), Iacob Mureşianu (1857–1917) and Gheorghe Dima (1847–1925)—while assimilating the best that classical music had to offer.

In the 20th century Rumanian literature and art sought answers to the great problems of the day. The difficulties of present-day society, the tragic fate of millions of human beings have found in them sensitive interpreters and passionate advocates. In prose there are realist writers like *M. Sadoveanu* (1880-1961) and *Liviu Rebreanu* (1885-1944). In poetry a new star rose into the firmament in the second decade of this century — *Tudor Arghezi* (1880-1967), whose prodigious career culminated in the publication in 1956 of the "Hymn to Man". Among the outstanding writers who so vigorously resisted the rise of Fascism must be mentioned the talented prose writer *Alexandru Sahia* (1908-37). And the list would not be complete without the names of the fiery poet *Octavian Goga*, George Bacovia (1881-1957), Ion Minulescu (1881-1944) and Mihai Codreanu (1876-1957), who wrote sonnets in the Parnassian manner.

A whole generation of writers and poets between the wars — for example Lucian Blaga (1895–1961), Victor Eftimiu (born 1908), Demostene Botez (born 1893), Geo Bozga (1889–1972), Camil Petrescu (1894–1957), Cezar Petrescu (1892–1961), G. Călinescu (1899–1965), Maria Banuş (born 1914), Zaharia Stancu (born 1902), Eugen Jebeleanu (born 1911), Marcel Breslaşu (born 1903) and Mihai Beniuc (born 1907)—continued their careers after the last war. To them must be added a whole galaxy of young poets and novelists: Mihu Dragomir (1919–64), Marin Preda (born 1922), Titus Popovici (born 1931), Eugen Barbu (born 1924), V. E. Galan (born 1921) and N. Labiş (1935–56).

Finally mention must be made of a number of Rumanian writers who lived in France between the wars and wrote in French: Panait Istrati (1884-1935); Tristan Tzara (1896-1963), a leading figure in the Dadaist movement and one of the founders of Surrealism; B. Fundoianu (1898-1944), who wrote under the name of Benjamin Fondane and took part in the French Resistance; and Ilarie Voronca (1903-46), who, like Fundoianu, was a representative of the Surrealist avant-garde.

The last hundred years have seen the birth of a great movement forward in the theatre, with great actors like Grigore Manolescu (1857–92), Ion Brezeanu (1869–1940) and Aristide Demetriad (1872–1930), and talented producers like Paul Gusty (1859–1944),

Ion Sava (1900–44), Victor Ion Popa (1895–1954) and others. The contemporary Rumanian theatre continues to develop in every field and has achieved an international reputation through guest performances in various other countries. Rumania now possesses 39 theatres and 42 companies of actors.

Among the best known Rumanian dramatists are *Eugène Ionesco* (born 1912), who left Rumania just before the second world war, G. M. Zamfirescu (1898-1939), Mihail Sebastian (1907-45), Tudor Muşatescu (1903-70), Alexandru Kiritescu (1888-1961), Mircea Stefănescu (born 1898), Lucia Demetrius (born 1910), Mihail Davidoglu (born 1910), Horia Lovinesco (born 1917), Aurel Baranga (born 1913) and A. Mirodan (born 1927). We must mention also producers and talented performers such as *Elvire Popesco* (born 1895), who had remarkable success in France, Sică Alexandrescu (born 1896), Liviu Ciulei (born 1923), Radu Beligan (born 1918), Costache Antoniu (born 1900), George Calboreanu (born 1896), Ion Fintesteanu (born 1900), György Kovacs (born 1911), Aura Buzescu (born 1894) and Alexandru Giugaru (born 1897); and great actors and actresses like Lucia Sturdza Bulandra (1873-1961), N. Bălţăţeanu (1893-1956), G. Timica (1886-1954), George Vraca (1896-1964), Maria Filotti (1883-1956), Jules Cazaban (1903-1963), Gr. Vasiliu-Birlic (1905-70) and Constantin Tănase (1880-1945).

In the field of music one name stands above all the rest—that of the celebrated composer, violinist, pianist and conductor *George Enescu* (1881–1955), to whom Rumanian music owes its international reputation. The development of contemporary Rumanian music has helped to introduce to an international public composers and performers like Mihail Jora (1891–1971), Paul Constantinescu (1908–63), Theodor Rogalski (1901–54), *George Georgescu* (1887–1964), *Dinu Lipatti* (1917–50), Stan Golestan (1875–1956), Ion Voicu (born 1912), Valentin Gheorghiu (born 1928), Ştefan Ruha (born 1931), Nicolae Herlea (born 1926), Arta Florescu (born 1921), Maria Tănase (1913–63), Tiberiu Brediceanu (1877–1968), Sabin Drăgoi (1894–1968), Martian Negrea (born 1893), Mihai Andricu (born 1894), Ion Dumitrescu (born 1913), Sigismund Toduţă (born 1908), Antonin Ciolan (1883-1971), Egizio Massini (1894-1966), Mircea Basarab (born 1921), Petre Ştefănescu Goangă (born 1902) Zenaida Pally (born 1919), Ion Dacian (born 1911) and many others, like the conductors *Constantin Silvestri* (1913-69) and *Ionel Perlea* (1900-70).

The status of Rumanian music is also demonstrated by the success of the George Enescu Festival and Competition organised by the State, which not only offers young performers an opportunity of making their mark but also secures a wide audience for music played by established artistes from all over the world.

Rumania now possesses 6 opera houses, 13 operetta and variety houses, 17 symphony orchestras, 20 folk orchestras and 10 song and dance groups.

The *Rumanian cinema* has made great progress since the last war, following the building of the new Buftea studios, and has achieved a series of successes which have made it internationally known: for example the films "Danube Waves", "Thirst", "Tudor", "Codine", "The Forest of the Hanged", "The Dacians", "Michael the Brave" and "On Sunday at Six", and the cartoons of Ion Popesco-Gopo, particularly "A Short Story".

Science

Among the outstanding writers of earlier centuries are *Nicolae Milescu* (1636–1708), who visited China ("Description of China", "Journal of a Visit to China"); *Constantin Cantacuzinu* (1650–1716), a former student of the School of Padua (which provided him with a model for the establishment of the Prince's Academy of Bucharest), author of historical works and of the first maps of Wallachia; and *Dimitrie Cantemir* (1673–1723), a member of the Berlin Academy and the author of excellent histories of the Ottoman Empire and of Rumania, as well as works of philosophy, literature, music, etc.

Then from the 18th century to our own day there has been a great upsurge of scientific activity, thanks to historians like G. Sincai (1754–1816), *N. Bălcescu* (1819–52), *M. Kogălniceanu* (1817–1891), B. P. Hasdeu (1838–1907), A. D. Xenopol (1847–1920), author of "Theories of History" (Paris, 1900) and "History of the Rumanians", D. Onciul (1856–1923), V. Pârvan (1882–1927), author of "Getica" (1927) and "Dacia" (1928) and *N. Iorga* (1871–1940), author of many works which have attracted attention outside Rumania, to linguists like Timotei Cipariu (1805–1887), Ovid Densuşianu (1873–1938), Moses Gaster (1856–1939) and Sextil Puşcariu (1877–1948), to lawyers like *Nicolae Titulescu* (1882–1941), Rumanian representative at the League of Nations, and many others.

From the second half of the 19th century onwards there was also a great development of mathematics, with E. Bacaloglu (1830–91), S. Haret (1851–1912), G. Tiţeica (1873–1939), one of the creators of differential geometry, T. Lalescu (1882-1929) one of the founders of the theory of integral equations, and D. Pompei (1873-1954); of geology, with G. Cobălescu (1831-1892), G. Ştefănescu (1836-1941), L. Mrazec (1867-1944) and G. Munteanu-Murgoci (1882-1925); and of medicine, with V. Babeş (1854-1926), one of the founders of modern microbiology, Ion Cantacuzino (1863-1934), N. Ionescu-Sisesti (1888-1954), Gh. Marinescu (1863-1938), C. I. Parhon (1874-1969), author of the first treatise on endocrinology, and N. Paulescu (1869-1931), a forerunner of the discovery of insulin. In the 20th century there have been great scientists like D. Hurmuzescu (1865-1954), who produced the electroscope with which Pierre and Marie Curie, along with Henri Becquerel, carried out their research into radioactivity, A. Proca (1897-1955), who discovered the meson, and S. Procopiou (born 1890), who discovered the existence of atomic magnetism at the same time as the great Niels Bohr, in physics; C. l. Istrate (1850-1918), C. G. Longinescu (1869-1939) and L. Edeleanu (1861-1941) in chemistry; and D. Voinov (1867-1951), G. Antipa (1867-1944), E. Teodorescu (1866-1949) and Tr. Săvulescu (1880-1963) in biology.

In our own day scientific research is carried out under the auspices of the Rumanian Academy (which was reorganised and had new sections added to it after 1948), the Academy of Medical Sciences, the Academy of Agricultural and Silvicultural Sciences, the Academy of Social and Political Sciences, various higher educational institutions and the National Council of Scientific Research. Some 10,000 scientists and technicians are employed in the hundred institutes of scientific research, which are provided with modern laboratories and equipment. The various Academies also maintain close relationships with corresponding establishments in other countries. Their work is supplemented by the institutes run by the various Ministries, each specialising in a particular branch of the national economy; while the Academies themselves are mainly concerned with the study of the fundamental problems raised by the development of science and technology.

Contemporary Rumanian *mathematicians*—led by S. Stoilov (1887–1961), G. Moisil (born 1906), Miron Nicolescu (born 1903), G. Vrînceanu (born 1900), O. Mayer (1895–1966) and

Tiberiu Popoviciu (born 1906)—have made valuable contributions to the theory of complex functions, the theory of spectral decomposition, the algebra of automatic mechanisms, the theory of elasticity, etc. The first Rumanian electronic calculating were machines produced in 1958–59.

In *physics*, G. Constantinescu (1881-1965), who originated the theory of sonics, H. Hulubei (1896-1972), S. Țițeica (born 1908), E. Bădărău (born 1887) and others have remarkable achievements to their credit. In 1957 a nuclear research centre was established with an atomic reactor of 3,000 kilowatts and a cyclotron of 12.5 mega-electron-volts. Research has been undertaken into high energy physics, nuclear physics, the separation of radioactive isotopes and beta spectroscopy, and results achieved which have been immediately applicable in the oil industry.

In *chemistry* activity has been concentrated in recent years on the development and the proper use of the natural resources of Rumania. Contributions have been made to the physical chemistry of fused electrolytes, the structure of organic substances and certain complexes has been studied, and considerable advances have been made in the study of synthetic polymers. In addition the synthesis of cyclobutadiene has been achieved, thus solving a problem which had remained in suspense for 50 years. In the field of theoretical and applied chemistry a considerable reputation has been achieved by Academicians Ilie Murgulescu (born 1902), G. Spacu (1883–1955), Radu Cernătescu (1894–1958), C. D. Nenițescu (1902–71), Raluca Ripan (born 1894), I. Tănăsescu (1892–1958), E. Macovschi (born 1906) and others.

In the *technical sciences*, outstanding work has been done by Anghel Saligny (1882-1913), who designed the bridge over the Danube at Cernavodă (the longest in Europe at the end of the 19th century), Traian Vuia (1872-1950), inventor of the first airborne craft to fly under its own power, Aurel Vlaicu (1882-1913), one of the pioneers of aviation, and Academicians H. Coandă (1886–1972), father of the jet aircraft and discoverer of the "Coandă effect", C. I. Budeanu (1886-1959), I. S. Gheorghiu (1885-1968), E. Carafoli (born 1901), S. Bălan (born 1913), Remus Răduleț (born 1904) and their fellow-workers. The Institute of Energetics of the Rumanian Academy carries on research directed to the more effective utilisation of the country's power supply resources. Excellent results, with an industrial application, have been obtained in the study of fuels and in the production of metallurgical coke from Rumanian coal. Research has also been done in aerodynamics under the direction of Academician E. Carafoli, in the mechanics of fluids under the direction of Academician C. Iacob (born 1912), in the hydrodynamics of lubrification under the direction of Professor N. Tipei, a corresponding member of the Academy, etc.

In the field of *agricultural research* much work has been done, in collaboration with the National Geological Committee, on studies of land use, re-afforestation, the control of erosion and the rehabilitation of poor land. In recent years scientists like G. Ionescu-Sişesti (1885–1967), G. Obreja (born 1911) and A. Priadcenco (born 1902) have produced improved varieties of winter and spring wheat, hybrid maize, oats and barley, and have also improved certain breeds of stock.

In *medicine*, specialists are familiar with the work done in Rumania in the field of geriatrics by Professor Ana Aslan, in physiopathology by Academicians D. Danielopolu (1884-1955) and G. Benetato (1905-72), in the study and treatment of endemic goitre by St. Milcou (born 1902), in epilepsy by A. Kreindler (born 1900), and in parasitology, microbiology and inframicrobiology by M. Ciucă (1883-1969), Ionescu-Mihăiesti (1883-1962) and S. S. Nicolau (1896-1970). Rumanian scientists have also carried out research into cardiovascular and respiratory conditions, the action of hormonocytostatic compounds in experimental cancer, etc.

In the *natural sciences* noted names include E. Racoviţa (1868-1947), founder of bio-speleology, and G. Antipa (1867-1944), founder of the Rumanian school of hydrobiology and ichthyology.

In the *social sciences*, important work has been done by Academicians A. Joja (1904-72), M. Ralea (1896-1964), C. Radulescu-Motru (1868-1957), Dimitrie Gusti (1880-1955), founder of the Bucharest school of sociology, and C. I. Gulian (born 1914) in the field of philosophy, P. Constantinesco-Iasi (born 1892), C. Daicoviciu (born 1898), P. P. Panaitescu (born 1900), C. Giurescu (born 1901), A. Oţetea (born 1894) and E. Condurachi (born 1912), in history, and Tudor Vianu (1897-1964) and G. Călinescu (1899-1965) in aesthetics and literary history.

Important works have also been published in the fields of philosophy, psychology, economics and linguistics. The linguistic works of Academicians I. Iordan (born 1888), E. Petrovici (1899–1968), A. Graur (born 1900) and A. Rosetti (born 1895) have made considerable contributions to the progress of this discipline.

The various publishing houses attached to the Academy—scientific, political, technical, medical, etc.—publish every year hundreds of scientific works by Rumanian or foreign authors; and the scientific institutes and societies also produce a large number of journals and specialised publications.

Rumanian science keeps in close touch with what is being done in other countries. Rumanian scientists take part in international scientific meetings and in the work of many international cultural and scientific organisations; and similarly many foreign scientists have taken part in conferences in Rumania. Rumania also exchanges publications with over 3,000 institutes in a hundred different countries.

Art

The origins. The oldest traces of art in Rumania date from the Neolithic period. The people who occupied the country thousands of years ago created a distinctive art style, based on a great variety of geometric ornament, which is still found in the traditional folk art of the present day. Excavation at Cucuteni in the Iaşi region and at Hamangia in the Dobrudja has yielded objects of great historical and artistic value dating from this period. The discovery at the foot of the Southern Carpathians, in Oltenia, Transylvania and the Bărăgan, of objects dating from the Bronze and Iron Ages has shown that the people of these later periods also had artistic leanings and could produce decorative work of high quality, with ornamental motifs which clearly show the unity of the culture developed by the people who lived throughout this territory.

In the last centuries before the Christian era Thracian and Geto-Dacian art developed, producing objects of striking originality in which zoomorphic and anthropomorphic sculpture play a considerable role. Long before the Roman conquest a local artistic tradition had grown up in the territory of present-day Rumania, a tradition expressed particularly in the decoration of pottery, in the production of terracotta statuettes and in metalwork. On this tradition were superimposed influences from Greek civilisation, which were felt particularly along the Black Sea coast. At Tomi (now Constanţa), Histria and Callatis (now Mangalia) there was a flourishing local art in which local elements were often found mingling with features taken from Greek art to produce a distinctive regional style. Thus excavation at Tomi in 1959 revealed a coloured mosaic covering 21,000 square feet and a number of marble statues which showed this symbiosis of southern and native influences.

In this period—the period of direct contact with Greek culture, extending roughly from the 7th century B.C. to the 4th century A.D.—architecture also achieved great distinction. The buildings discovered in the cities on the Black Sea coast are strongly influenced by Greek classical architecture, just as in other parts of the country, particularly in Transylvania and Oltenia, Roman culture makes its influence felt both in architecture and in sculpture.

The Middle Ages. In the early Middle Ages historical circumstances were not favourable to the flourishing of art. Thus archaeology has yielded less interesting results for this period than for the ancient period. In certain parts of Rumania, however, remains have been found which demonstrate the continuity of the artistic tradition, a tradition enriched by elements contributed by the Germanic, Mongol and Slav peoples who passed through the country in their drive toward western and southern Europe.

From the 14th century, with the establishment of the first Rumanian principalities, the number of buildings increases, and we find a very individual assimilation of Byzantine influence. Monasteries like those at Tismana (14th century) and Curtea de Argeş (16th century), the Prince's Church at Cîmpulung (15th century), and the ruins of the Catholic Church of Sîn Nicoară (late 13th century) in Wallachia show the mingling of a local tradition with influences from the south and west. In Moldavia, particularly in the reign of Voivode Stephen the Great (1457–1504), the Gothic style—seen particularly in the pointed arches found in buildings in the north of the country, associated in an individual way with local elements—produced buildings in a rather severe style of architecture, as at Voroneţ, Humor, Arbore, Dragomirna and Moldoviţa. The most striking characteristic of these buildings is the use of the *external fresco*, showing a riot of fancy which goes far beyond the canons of the Byzantine style. The artists who painted these frescoes—most of whom are anonymous—were masters of their craft, for after 500 years, in spite of their exposure to the weather, the colouring is as fresh as the day it was painted.

The 17th century. This was the golden age of architecture, particularly in the reigns of the Moldavian Prince Vasile Lupu (1633–52) and the Wallachian Prince Constantin Brîncoveanu (1688–1714). The finest achievement of the earlier period is the Church of the Three Hierarchs in Iaşi, a supreme masterpiece decorated with a tracery of sculptural ornament showing inexhaustible imagination. The Brîncoveanu period produced, both in architecture and in decoration, a characteristic style—the *Brîncoveanu style*—marked by light arcades supported by richly ornamented pillars. The church in the Hurez Monastery, in northern Oltenia, and the princely palace at Mogoşoaia near Bucharest are among the most celebrated buildings of this period.

From this period also date the first frescoes signed by the artist, and these painters (Pîrvu the Dumb, Radu the Painter) are accepted as being the founders of the Rumanian school of painting. Both in the principal towns and in many country areas there were active schools of painting, the forerunners of the art schools of the present day, and under their influence the art of painting flourished. At the same time we can see an increasing tendency towards the development of a secular art, even within the field of religious painting; and the same tendency is shown in the art of illumination, the oldest specimens of which date from the 14th and 15th centuries. The pervasive influence of Rumanian folk art is seen in the wealth of ornament, the subtle harmony of the colouring and the constant effort to achieve a faithful representation of the model.

For throughout the whole of this long period we can trace the development of a *folk art* which shows common features over the whole of Rumanian territory. Throughout the centuries the Rumanian peasant has demonstrated his skill in ornamenting his tools and domestic implements, achieving a very individual synthesis between tradition and the influence of the other peoples with whom he is in contact. The pillars of the veranda, the distaff, the shepherd's pipe, carved or decorated in pokerwork with a great variety of ornament—the carpets in their elaborate patterns of carefully blended colours—the costumes, the paintings on glass, the crosses in the churchyards, the pottery: all these things show a great diversity of styles in the different parts of the country, but they also demonstrate the remarkable unity of Rumanian art as a whole. And if Rumanian artists are excellent colourists this is no doubt because they have never lost contact with the traditions of folk art.

The modern period. *Theodor Aman* (1831–91), who was mainly interested in peasant life and the history of Rumania, founded the first art school in Rumania. *N. Grigorescu* (1838-1907) and *I. Andreescu* (1850-82) are distinguished representatives of the Rumanian school, which — partly as a result of contact with French art — achieved great expressiveness with a generous use of colour. *Ş. Luchian* (1868-1916) gave this tradition a personal note, a dramatic content and a deep seriousness. With *N. Toniţa* (1886-1940), F. Sirato (1877-1953), S. Dimitrescu (1886-1933), I. Iser (1881-1958), J. Al. Steriadi (1880-1957) and C. Ressu (1880-1962), Rumanian painting joined the mainstream of European art, though its exuberant but sensitive colouring still kept it within the distinctive Rumanian tradition. The strong individuality of *Theodor Pallady* (1877–1956), a friend of Matisse's, and *G. Petraşcu* (1872–1948) gave it still greater brilliance and even greater expressive force.

Contemporary Rumanian painting has achieved a considerable reputation abroad as a result of exhibitions held in a number of foreign countries. Among its outstanding representatives are *I. Ţuculescu* (1910-62), whose work, tending increasingly towards an abstract expressionism, achieves powerful decorative effects, in which his interpretation of traditional plastic ornament plays a predominant part; *D. Ghiaţă* (born 1888), an artist with an unusual feeling for the distinctive features of folk art, which he interprets in a profoundly personal style; *A. Ciucurenco* (born 1903), a delicate colourist; H. Catargi (born 1894); and *C. Baba* (born 1906), a painter of robust realism. And in their train a generation of younger artists are turning their attention to the realities of contemporary life.

The starting point of Rumanian *graphic art* was the old book illustration of the 16th to 18th centuries; and thus at a time when Rumanian printers were producing books for the Orthodox world of the Near East and the Balkans the art of engraving developed on a considerable scale. At the end of the 19th century, thanks to the scope it offered for illustrating current political and social events, graphic art achieved still greater popularity, particularly in the field of journalism, with the work of C. Ressu, F. Sirato, I. Iser, N. Toniţa, N. Cristea(1907–36), G. Popescu (1866–1937), A. Jiquidi (1896–1962) and others.

Rumanian *sculpture* was founded in the 19th century by I. Georgescu (1856–1898), a classical artist who produced the first works bearing the name of a Rumanian sculptor, and S. Ionescu-Valbudea (1856–1918), who belonged to the Romantic school. In D. Paciurea (1875-1932) it gave the measure of its creative possibilities. C. Brâncuşi (1876-1957), an artist of world fame and one of the great sculptors of modern times, still preserved in his work the characteristic features of the folk art of the country in which he was born. And the tradition of Rumanian sculpture has been enriched by a whole galaxy of other artists: *C. Medrea* (1889-1964), I. Jalea (born 1887), O. Han (born 1891), G. Anghel (1904-66), I. Irimescu (born 1903) and B. Caragea (born 1906). R. Ladea (1901-71) and Gheza Vida (born 1913) have given fresh expressiveness and an almost dramatic feeling to the art of sculpture in wood, in which there is an old folk tradition.

Finally *modern Rumanian architecture*, now active on a large scale, is based on solid foundations laid down by its fore-runners, the founders of the Rumanian school of architecture such as I. Mincu (1851-1912). Monumental art has also attracted the interest of the most talented painters and sculptors.

THE RUMANIAN ECONOMY

The nationalisation on 11 June 1948 of the principal means of production in the industrial sector, all mines and transport, and banking and insurance established the conditions for a planned economy and the industrialisation of the country on a socialist basis.

Industry

General. The industry of Rumania is notable for the rapid pace of its development and for the priority given to the growth of heavy industry, which conditions the development of all the other branches of industry. Industry has become the key element in the Rumanian economy, whereas before 1940 agriculture had a considerable preponderance. Over the past twenty years total industrial production has increased at an average annual rate of over 12.6%.

Public investment in machinery and plant has increased considerably. At the same time the use of automation in production has increased. In numerous plants all the principal operations are automatically controlled. In the electric power industry certain sections have been automated and operate under remote control; in the chemical industry some plants are now operating with a high degree of automation; and automatic and semi-automatic production lines have been introduced in other branches of industry.

The volume of industrial production in 1972 was 21 times what it was in 1938. It is particularly significant that industry (including building) now provides over 61% of the total national income, whereas before 1939 the highest proportion of the national income was provided by agriculture, and industry contributed only a third.

Power. Rumania possesses a variety of sources of power: oil deposits, natural gas, coal, hydro-electricity.

The soil of Rumania contains considerable deposits of *coal* (black coal and lignite). The largest reserves are concentrated in the Jiu valley, which supplies some 50% of the total output of coal; the lignite deposits are in Oltenia, Muntenia and Crişana As a result of the establishment of new mining centres, the introduction of new machinery and the high degree of mechanisation underground—the largest pits have been entirely mechanised—the production of coal in Rumania reached 23 million tons in 1970 (2,826,000 tons in 1938).

The successful completion of the plan for the *electrification* of the country has brought the production of electric power to some 40,000 million kilowatt hours against 1,100 million in 1938. Over this period the production of electric power per head of population has increased more than 10 times. Among the new plants brought into service in recent years are the thermo-electric stations of Doiceşti (Dîmboviţa region), Sîngeorgiu de Pădure (Mureş region), Paroşeni (Hunedoara region), Brazi (Prahova region), Ovidiu (Constanţa region) and Borzeşti (Bacău region), and the hydro-electric stations on the Bistriţa (Neamţ region), at Moreni (Dîmboviţa region), Sadu (Constanţa region), on the Argeş and the Lotru. Recently the Rumanian hydro-electric stations have been linked in a national grid, and a link (220 kilovolts) has been established between Rumania and Czechoslovakia. In addition the 110 kilovolt line between Chichinda Mare and Timişoara makes it possible to establish a local link with the Yugoslav power system. The large hydro-electric installation at the Iron Gates—a cooperative effort between Rumania and Yugoslavia completed in 1972—makes it possible to use the potential of the Danube and improve navigation on this stretch of the river. The station is one of the largest in Europe, with an output of 10,000 million kilowatt hours—the same as Volgograd, or five times the output of Donzère-Mondragon on the Rhône.

Rumania possesses large deposits of *oil*, with the second largest output of oil in Europe, after the Soviet Union (13 million tons of crude oil annally, compared with 6.6 million in 1938). In addition to the old-established oil producing areas round Ploieşti and Bacău, new oil centres have been appearing on the map of Rumania in recent years, the largest being in the Dîbomviţa, Argeş and Dolj regions. The development of the oil industry is based on careful husbanding of the country's reserves of oil and on the proper planning of refinery production to take account both of internal demand and of the quality and range of products required on the world market.

In parallel with the increase in the extraction of oil, the refinery installations have been reconstructed and developed. New refineries have been built and equipped with modern plant, most of it produced within Rumania. The petro-chemical industry has come into being at the same time, and an ultra-modern petro-chemical plant has recently been brought into service at Borzeşti, near Gh. Gheorghiu-Dej (Oneşti).

Alongside the production of oil the production of *natural gas* (methane) has developed considerably. This is being used on an increasing scale as an industrial raw material (producing, among other things, lamp-black, ammonia, nitrate fertilisers and plastics).

Iron and steel. The iron and steel industry, one of the fundamental branches of the economy, has developed considerably in the last twenty years. Older centres like Hunedoara and Reşiţa have been rebuilt and modernised, new metalworking plants have been established (including a tube factory at Roman with an output of 300,000 tons annually and a factory at Bucharest producing welded tubes), and the latest equipment has been installed on a large scale. A large steelworks at Galaţi will have an output of 4 million tons when working at full capacity. As a result of these developments the Rumanian iron and steel industry produced in 1970 over 6,5 million tons of steel (more than 23 times as much as in 1938), some 4,2 million tons of cast iron (30 times as much as in 1938) and over 4,5 million tons of sheet steel. Great attention has been paid to extending the mining of iron ore, and at the same time the extraction of non-ferrous metals and rare metals has been developed, leading to the growth of the non-ferrous metals industry.

Engineering. This industry, which was relatively backward before 1940, has advanced rapidly in the past twenty years, achieving an output in 1970 which was 48 times greater than in 1938 and 2.6 times greater than in 1959. The average annual rate of growth between 1951 and 1963 was 20.5%. This sector includes a number of new forms of industry such as oil and mining equipment (at Ploieşti and Tîrgovişte), machines and equipment for the electrical and electricity supply industries (at Bucharest, Timişoara, Craiova and Braşov), tractors and agricultural machinery and equipment (at Braşov, Bucharest and Craiova), and machine tools (at Arad, Oradea, Rîşnov, Sibiu, etc.).

In the past Rumania had to import 95% of the machinery and equipment it needed; today it produces equipment for the oil industry, ships, electric locomotives, tractors and agricultural machinery, lorries, machine tools, machinery for the mining, metalworking, chemical and foodstuffs industries and for light industry, ball bearings, etc. The engineering industry (with an output which in 1970, along with the metal processing industries, represented 25% of total industrial production) supplies something like two-thirds of the machinery and equipment required by Rumanian industry in addition to increased quantities of products for export.

Chemical industry. Rumania possesses considerable stocks of raw materials necessary to a modern chemical industry. This is in striking contrast with the position before 1940, when Rumania had to depend on foreign countries for its supplies.

Between 1960 and 1967 the average annual rate of growth of the chemical industry was 22%, and production in 1964 was no less than 92 times greater than in 1938. Among the many new factories built are a factory at Govora making sodium products, a synthetic fibre factory at Săvineşti, a nitrate fertiliser plant at Roznov, a factory at Năvodari producing sulphuric acid and superphosphates, a plant near Brăila for producing paper and cellulose from the reeds of the Danube Delta, chemical plants at Borzeşti and Victoria, a factory at Popeşti-Leordeni (near Bucharest) producing synthetic rubber and petro-chemical products, with an output of 1,6 million tyres a year, etc. The pharmaceutical industry manufactures some 700 preparations, including a wide range of antibiotics, which are sufficient to meet internal needs and are also exported to many other countries.

Timber industry. With its wealth of forests, Rumania has a well developed timber industry. The construction of a large number of modern plants (at Vatra Dornei, Gura Humorului, Rîmnicu Vîlcea, Bucharest, Tîrgu Jiu, Timişoara, Tîrgu Mureş, Brăila, etc) ensures that full use is made of the country's resources of timber. Large quantities of products are now made from wood (plywood, hardboard, flooring, high class furniture, boats, sporting equipment, musical instruments, etc.). In 1970 the timber and wood-processing industries had a total output more than 14 times as great as in 1938.

The **building materials industry** has become in recent years an important branch of the national economy. Rumania now produces (at Medgidia, Bicaz, Turda, Fieni and other places) 14 qualities of high grade cement, which find a ready market both in Rumania and abroad. There are some 200 brickworks and tileworks and 11 glassworks (producing nearly 2,000 different items). The production of prefabricated elements in concrete and reinforced concrete supplements the output of the traditional building materials. The total output of building materials in 1970 was 14 times the 1938 output.

Light and foodstuffs industries. Between 1938 and 1970 there was and eleven-fold increase in the output of the textile industry; the output of the clothing industry was 23 times as great, the leather industry 11 times, boots and shoes 11 times, furs 11 times, the glass and china industry 25 times, and the foodstuffs industry 5 times. New factories were brought into use in the consumer goods industry. The new worsted mill in Bucharest, the Intex factory at Păuleşti for the weaving and finishing of linen, the flour mill and bakery at Constanţa, and the sugar refineries at Bucecea, Luduş and Tîrgu Mureş are a few examples of recent developments.

Agriculture

Favourable natural conditions, the development of agricultural cooperatives, the measures taken to provide incentives for the peasant and the heavy capital investment by the State: these are the main features of the agricultural sector in Rumania. Out of the 59,000,000 acres which the country contains, 36,000,000 are in agricultural use, including some 25,000,000 acres of arable land. In 1970 there were 107,000 tractors employed in agriculture, 50,000 harvesters and much other equipment.

In 1967 the average annual production of cereals for the whole country exceeded 13,5 million tons, compared with 8 million tons for the years 1934–38. The 1971 cereal crop was the largest ever achieved in Rumania (14,5 million tons). At the same time the level of stock-rearing also increased. Rumania now has 5,2 million cattle, 6,4 million pigs, 13,8 million sheep and 54 million poultry.

Nearly 27% of the surface of the country, or about 16,000,000 acres, is covered by forest, representing about 84 of an acre per head of population. A large-scale re-afforestation programme has been undertaken during the last few years. Between 1960 and 1963 over 2,500,000 acres were planted with species of high productivity.

Transport and Trade

The total volume of goods transported reached 430 million tons in 1970. As a result of work carried out in recent years the total length of the Rumanian railways is now 7,000 miles and of the roads 48,000 miles. In 1970 the number of passengers carried by rail and by road reached 690 million.

The Friendship Bridge (7,200 feet) across the Danube between Giurgiu (Rumania) and Ruse (Bulgaria), one of the largest of its kind in Europe, provides an international road and rail link between the Balkan peninsula and the countries north of the Danube. The most important highway in Rumania cuts diagonally across the country from Episcopia Bihorului to Giurgiu on the Danube and Constanţa on the Black Sea coast, providing a direct connection between central and south-eastern Europe. The increased construction of merchant and passenger ships has made it possible to develop the river and sea trade of Rumania; and the ports on the Danube and the Black Sea are also transit points on international traffic routes.

In the field of air transport, the Rumanian national airline TAROM, flies 10 main routes and a number of secondary routes connecting Bucharest with 16 of the principal towns in the country. International services are provided by direct flights between Bucharest and other capitals or large cities: Paris, Moscow, London, Brussels, Zurich, Frankfurt, Copenhagen, Berlin, Vienna, Budapest, Prague, Warsaw, Sofia, Belgrade, Athens, Istanbul, Rome, Beirut and Tel Aviv.

Rumanian *internal trade* is carried on through a network of shops belonging either to the State or to cooperatives (the latter being mainly in rural areas). In 1971 there were a total of some 62,000 establishments engaged in the retail and food trades in Rumania (shops displaying and selling goods, restaurants, consumer cooperatives, etc.). Retail sales in 1970 amounted to almost 97,000 million lei.

Rumania maintains commercial relations with more than 110 other countries. While extending its economic relations with the socialist countries within the framework of COMECON (of which it has been a member since its establishment in 1949), it continues to develop economic cooperation with other countries. It takes part in the work of international economic bodies like GATT, the International Monetary Fund, the International Bank for Reconstruction and Development and the European Economic Commission of the United

Nations, in international trade fairs and exhibitions, and in other organisations like UNESCO, etc. It has also developed commercial contacts with the Common Market. A law on foreign trade passed in 1971 provided a legal framework for the establishment of varied forms of cooperation with other countries, including the creation of joint production or consumption agencies either in Rumania or in other countries.

An increasing share of Rumanian exports is constituted by machinery and complete plants, semi-fabricated products, chemical products and finished articles. The greater part of Rumania's imports consists of industrial plant, equipment required for power stations, the chemical industry, light industry, etc.

55% of the total volume of Rumanian foreign trade is with the Communist countries; 25% with the Soviet Union. In recent years considerable contacts have been made with the West, Rumania's most important trading partners among the Western countries being the German Federal Republic, Italy, France, the United Kingdom, Austria, the United States and Switzerland. The Rumanians are also seeking to develop a "productive cooperation" with the countries of Africa, Asia and Latin America.

POPULATION AND TRADITIONS

Demography

Rumania is the ninth country in Europe in terms of population, with 20 million inhabitants. In 1861, for the same area, the population was 8.6 million; in 1900 11.1 million; in 1948 15.9 million. The average density of population over the country as a whole was over 215 per square mile in 1970.

At the 1956 census the Rumanians represented 85.8% of the population; and there were a number of national minorities—Magyars, Germans, Ukrainians, Russians, Serbians, etc. The constitution of the Socialist Republic of Rumania guarantees absolute equality to all citizens, without distinction of nationality, sex or creed, in all fields of economic, political and cultural life.

There have been profound changes in the distribution of the population between town and country. The urban population now represents 38.4% of the total, compared with 21.4% at the 1930 census. In 1930 there were only four towns. (Bucharest, Cluj, Iaşi and Galaţ) with more than 100,000 inhabitants: there are now 16 (the additional ones being Braşov, Ploieşti, Timişoara, Constanţa, Craiova, Arad, Brăila, Oradea, Sibiu, Tîrgn Mureş, Rietşti and Bacău).

Language

The great majority of the population speak Rumanian, a language of Latin origin. In addition to the words inherited from Latin the vocabulary of Rumanian includes many elements borrowed from other languages, but its grammatical structure remains almost entirely Latin. And if we look at the vocabulary carefully, considering only words regularly used throughout the whole country, we shall find that it is not so variegated as it may appear to be at first sight. Most of the essential words are of Latin origin; and for the rest only the words of Slav origin amount to a significant percentage of the total.

Brought to Dacia and the areas bordering it on the south by settlers from every corner of the Roman Empire, the Latin language was enriched by elements borrowed from the language of the native population. It was then subjected to Slav and Hungarian influences. Later it assimilated certain Turkish and

Greek elements, having already been exposed to Greek influence at a much earlier stage by way of Latin or Slav.

From the earliest times neologisms of Latin origin made their way into Rumanian by a variety of different routes, their number increasing with the development of culture in Rumanian territory. In addition, from the 19th century onwards Rumanian has had a massive influx of words in international use (technical and scientific terms, etc.) by way of Greek, Russian, French or other languages. These words now make up a large proportion of the vocabulary.

Education

In Rumania the educational system consists of the following four stages:

Pre-school education, i. e., kindergartens providing training and education for children from 3 to 6.

General education, divided into compulsory general education (classes I to X) and middle or secondary education (classes IX to XII). General schools with a special teaching programme (music, art, dancing, sport, etc.) have been established for children with particular aptitudes for the arts or sport.

Professional and technical education for the training of the operatives and technicians required for industry and agriculture. This is open to pupils who have completed their compulsory general education or their secondary education, depending on the particular training they wish to take.

Higher education, covering a range of different institutes (agricultural, medical, teachers' training, etc.), universities, polytechnic schools, art schools, etc.

In Rumania education at all stages is provided for all pupils free of charge, without regard to social status, creed, sex or nationality. Another characteristic feature is that each stage offers its pupils the opportunity of passing on to the next stage. According to their knowledge and aptitudes pupils who have completed the 8 years of general education can continue their studies in any other school in the next higher stage. This ready availability of education finds its expression in the fact that there are now more than 500,000 pupils in the general schools and more than 120,000 in the specialised schools, compared with a total af 29,000 in 1938; in addition some 155,000 students are receiving higher education in 195 faculties.

Evening classes and correspondence courses. These forms of education are intended for those who want to continue their studies without interrupting their work.

This extension of education has been accompanied by a substantial increase in the number of teachers. Thus during the school year 1966–67 the teaching staff in post (including those engaged in higher education) amounted to over 235,000.

It should be noted also that in addition to the teaching establishments under the control of the Ministry of Education there are in Rumania 30 "People's Universities" with 25,000 students.

Customs and Traditions

Although based on the same essential elements, the popular customs of Rumania nevertheless show a wide range of local variations: this is, indeed, what gives them their interest and picturesqueness.

Among these popular customs the most interesting, both for their scale and their beauty, are the **New Year customs.** In Rumania the celebrations which mark the passage from one year to the next are spread over the period between 24th December and 7th January, thus including Christmas, New Year and the Epiphany (Twelfth Night). According to tradition it is the young lads of the village who organise the celebrations. As early as 6th December the young men meet in groups to rehearse all the details of the programme—miming plays, hymns, songs and New Year greetings. In Rumanian folk tradition these ceremonies have retained their ancient secular character, the few religious elements in them being a later addition.

On New Year's Eve the children form themselves into bands (which in Oltenia may include as many as 70 or even 100 children) and go from house to house wishing abundance and prosperity to each family in simple, naive verses. The ceremonial and the words of these greetings are reminiscent of those sung by Roman children on the Calends of January. On Christmas Eve and the three following days, during the New Year celebrations and also, in certain places, on Twelfth Night the young men also go from house to house singing *colinde*. These are allegorical songs for the New Year, wishing prosperity to the master and mistress of the house, the girls and young men of marriageable age, the children, the shepherds, and so on, and are therefore varied according to the recipients of the greetings.

In consequence the repertoire of greetings is remarkable wide and varied. The *colinde* welcome the New Year, offer greetings in traditional form, sing of family life, of heroic deeds and of love, wish young people a good marriage, and so on.

In addition to the children's greetings and the *colinde* the New Year customs include games of tip-cat, the goat dance (also known in other countries in Europe), and the *"Little Plough"*, in which the young boys parade through the village singing and addressing greetings to all the inhabitants. The Little Plough and the game of tip-cat which are played in certain parts of Transylvania are in fact reminiscences of the "story of bread"—the story of the farming year, from the sowing of the grain to the baking of the traditional ring-biscuits. In Moldavia, Transylvania and the Banat, however, the New Year celebrations also include masked processions like those of the Carnival, hymns to the Star, mime plays of the Three Wise Men and folk plays. Finally at the Epiphany horse races are held in certain parts of the country, particularly in the Wallachian plain and the Dobrudja.

Among the **spring celebrations** two in particular must be mentioned—the *Ariet*, or shepherds' festival, and the *Ploughman's Festival*.

The *Ariet* or *Gathering of the Ewes* is a celebration marked by copious eating and drinking, singing and dancing, in honour of the traditional practice of collecting all the sheep of the village into a single large flock which is then taken into the mountains. The *Ploughman's Festival* was a traditional ceremony in which the young man who began ploughing first was recognised as leader of the young men of the village, with the right to punish those who did not do their work properly. This custom, once found throughout the country, now survives only in a few villages in southern Transylvania. Another ancient custom, the *Drăgaica*, is now practised only in a few districts in Wallachia on Midsummer Day: on this day girls wearing crowns and hoods go into the fields, singing and dancing, to see whether the wheat is ready for harvest. On Midsummer Day in Transylvania the girls go into the fields, weave circlets of flowers, and then throw them over the roofs of the cottages to bring luck to the people of the village.

Withsun is marked by ceremonies at which the *Căluş* ("little horse") is danced—though this custom is now found only in the plain of Oltenia. The *Căluş*—an ancient initiation and fertility dance, also regarded as securing the cure of illness—is now a very popular spectacle, a skilled performance by expert dancers. Rumanian teams dancing this dance have won many international competitions.

Until quite recently the peasants in certain parts of the country danced magic dances designed to bring rain to the parched fields—the *Paparude*, danced by gipsy girls, the *Scaloian* (the "thin little man") and the *Mumulită* ("Little Mother Rain").

In Transylvania until the first world war the **harvest festival** was a great occasion. The ceremonies were based on the practice of doing the farming work of the village in common (so that, for example, the whole village went out together to reap the fields of each peasant in turn). First a crown was woven from the finest heads of grain, and this was then borne in procession, to the accompaniment of ceremonial songs, to the house of the farmer whose field had just been reaped. From time to time during the procession the crown was sprinkled with water. When the party reached the farmer's house they danced round the crown and then hung it up in a place of honour; and finally the grain from the crown was mingled with the grain set aside for sowing in order to ensure a good harvest.

Among the customs associated with the most important occasions of family life, special mention must be made of the customs connected with the **marriage ceremony**, both for their beauty and as examples of folk tradition handed down from the remote past.

The traditional period for marriages used to be between New Year and Lent; nowadays autumn is the favourite time. There are a number of stages of great significance—the betrothal, the ceremony in which the engaged couple take their leave of the young people of their own age, the marriage itself, and finally the ceremony marking the entry of the bride and groom into the ranks of the married. In Rumania the marriage ceremony is a picturesque occasion, an occasion for good humour and for singing and dancing. Particularly interesting are the songs sung in honour of the young couple when they take their leave of the young men and girls of their own age, the ceremony of the decoration of the fir tree or the banner (which is made in the bridegroom's house and then carried by a "fir-tree-carrier" to the bride's), and the pretended fight between the bridegroom's procession and the bride's when the bridegroom comes to claim his bride for the marriage. The "speech" which is recited on this occasion is a long allegorical poem.

4

Some other features, too, deserve mention for their beauty and their lyrical character—the songs sung to the bride when she leaves her parent's house, the dance which is danced after the ceremony, the ballads and the old epic songs sung at the great wedding feast, the bride's dance, and the song sung in her honour at the putting on of the veil which marks her new status as a married woman. In many areas comic dances or masked dances are danced to amuse the wedding party. In general the traditional wedding as celebrated by the ordinary people of Rumania is a considerable occasion, a cheerful and colourful spectacle with much singing and dancing.

As for **funerals**, the most striking features are the keening (*bocete*), the wake and the special funeral songs—the *Dawn*, the *Fir Tree*, the *Great Song* and so on. In many places the women of the dead man's family, along with neighbours and women friends, make a great show of weeping and wailing (professional "keeners" are unknown). The *bocet* is a lament improvised on a traditional pattern and composed of a series of stereotyped formulas. In the Wallachian plain and in Oltenia the *bocet* is entirely improvised: it is in fact a kind of conversation with the dead man, full of psychological and social interest.

The funeral wake, accompanied in some places by masked dances, represents the last farewell to the dead man before the village takes its leave of him. Until quite recently, in southern Moldavia and the Vrancea Country, the masked figures who took part in the wake danced an ancient dance in which they jumped over a fire lit in the farm steading as a sign of purification. *Dawn* and the *Fir Tree*, which are sung all over Subcarpathian Oltenia, southern Transylvania and the Banat, are ancient traditional songs which comment in allegorical form on the different stages of the burial ceremony—the preparation of the dead man for his last journey, the ceremony in which the family and the village take their leave of him, and so on.

A study of the words of these songs brings out the Rumanians' ancient and traditional conception of death as a long journey into another world, which is seen in the image of the real world and takes no account of the duality of Hell and Paradise which is peculiar to Christianity.

The constant process of transformation to which popular traditions are exposed inevitably, of course, leads to considerable changes in the pattern and function of traditional customs. Some customs associated with the yearly round of farming work, such as the invocation to rain, have died out completely;

others have considerably altered their character. The real meaning of the old beliefs tends to disappear, while the purely formal aspect of the old customs becomes more marked and the element of spectacle becomes preponderant. Thus these ancient traditional observances, surviving into quite different conditions of life, add a touch of picturesqueness and variety to the routine of everyday life.

Folk Art

The characteristics of folk art differ from region to region, sometimes even from village to village. Thus the interiors of peasants' houses offer a series of varied and very individual patterns: often they are real works of art, not only in their architectural features but in their wealth of decoration and their tasteful furnishing.

The cloths and embroidery in traditional style, remarkable both for the harmony of their colouring and their decorative patterns, are works of art whose merits have been recognised at international exhibitions of folk art.

The famous **carpets** of Oltenia (brightly coloured in red and blue, with elegantly stylised patterns of flowers and animals), of Moldavia (soberly coloured in black, grey and brown) and the Maramureş (with geometric patterns) are among the finest achievements in this field.

Folk art has also achieved the most brilliant effects in Rumanian **traditional costumes.** These costumes differ considerably from region to region and are remarkable for their variety, for their archaic style, and for the beauty of their very decorative embroidery and the richness of their ornament in gold and silver thread. It is fairly general throughout the country to indicate by the colours used in a costume the age of the person wearing it—brighter colours for young people, darker for older ones. As a rule, too, young married women wear a special kind of headdress to distinguish them from unmarried girls.

The women usually wear a delicately embroidered blouse, a *fota* (a kind of apron-skirt worn on top of a white underskirt), a *marama* (an embroidered veil of natural silk) and a cap ornamented with pearls. The men wear a shirt (long in the south and east of the country, short in the north and west), and trousers of coarse handmade wool (long and narrow in the south and east, still longer and narrower in the rest of the country) supported by a belt of hand-woven cloth or leather. In autumn and spring both men and women wear warm garments of cloth or wool. In winter they wear waistcoats and fur cloaks, varying in length from one region to another.

The traditional skill in making these costumes is shown both by the work done by the peasants at home and by the fine examples which the cooperatives send to the shops selling craft goods.

Rumanian **pottery** goes back to an age-old tradition and is notable for the variety of its shapes and ornament. Many villages specialise in the production of pottery whose wealth of ornament reflects the most varied aspects of everyday life.

A particular reputation is enjoyed by the pottery of Hurez (Argeş region), decorated with horns and with jays, and with geometric ornament covering the vases with a web of gossamer. The black pottery of northern Moldavia, following a Dacian tradition, is decorated in a luminous grey, or in a range of shades going from grey to black.

Equally sought after is the pottery of Transylvania, particularly for the dishes, plates and jugs in brilliant colourings under a transparent glaze which are much used for decorative purposes in the house. There are also pottery models of toys, instruments, small figures of birds and animals, butterflies, or scenes from everyday life.

Carved wooden objects are a very widespread form of folk art, ranging from the pillars of a balcony to distaffs, spoons, ladles, etc. The characteristic decorative themes, like the sun or braided cords, show a distinctive stylisation and have frequently been imitated by Rumanian sculptors.

Rumanian **painting on glass,** of which the most notable examples are the famous glass icons of Transylvania, shows striking realism and a highly skilled use of colour. The colours are well preserved in the fine painted churches of northern Moldavia, which demonstrate the skill of the folk painters.

PROTECTION OF NATURE
(NATURE RESERVES)

The Rumanian national parks comprise "general nature reserves" (which are preserved as they are) and "controlled nature reserves" (which are used for study).

Of all the Rumanian nature reserves the largest, the completest and the most beautiful is the Retezat National Park.

The *Retezat National Park* is in the Retezat Mountains, 35 km (22 miles) from the small town of Hațeg. It has been under statutory protection since 1935 and covers an area of 25,000 acres, of which over 4,700 acres (the Zlata valley, Lake Gemenele and Lake Negru) form a nature reserve devoted exclusively to scientific research.

In this park—a landscape of high corries, mountain lakes, fields of scree and boulders, and Alpine peaks—there is a rich natural flora, consisting of forests of firs and larches, beech forests, and a variety of Alpine plants with many endemic species (including *Hieracium*, of the *Compositae* family).

The fauna of the Retezat reserve is no less rich than its flora. Here are found—to mention only the most interesting animals—the chamois *(Rupicapra rupicapra)*, the lynx *(Lynx lynx)*, the wild boar and, among the birds, the capercailzie *(Tetrao urogallus)*, the golden eagle *(Aquila chrysaetus)* and various species of vulture including (though this is rarely seen) the bearded vulture *(Gypaetus barbatus)*. The trout *(Salmo fario)*, which abounds in all the mountain streams, has also been acclimatised in certain Alpine lakes (Bucura, Zănoaga, Galeș, Gemenele) situated at an altitude of 6,200–6,600 feet, which nevertheless provide the food it requires.

Plant reserves. After the Retezat National Park the largest reserve in Rumania is the Bucegi Mountains Reserve (12,500 acres). Lying between Sinaia (2,770 feet) and Mount Omul (8,225 feet), it contains a varied Alpine flora (over 1,000 species), large numbers of birds, and some of the most striking scenery in Rumania.

On the edge of the Bîrsa Country, not far from Brașov (22 miles away), is the ridge of Piatra Craiului (over 7,200 feet high), edged with steep precipices. In this Alpine area is a nature reserve (scenery and flora), noted for its rich endemic flora, including a pink of outstanding beauty, the pink of Piatra Craiului, *Dianthus callizonus*.

The glacial basin of Lake Bîlea (6,768 feet) in the Făgăraş Mountains has also been made a reserve in order to protect the Alpine flora.

Above the hot springs of Herculane, in the Banat, towers Mount Domogled, with its plant and forest reserve containing rare species from southern areas (eastern Balkans, the Illyrian and Mediterranean countries). Another reserve in the Banat is the Beuşniţa Forest, a plant and forest reserve which provides a home for many warmth-loving species.

There are also important plant reserves containing endemic flora in the wild country of the Apuseni Mountains (Turda Gorges, Scărişoara, Belioara).

One of the most popular reserves in Rumania is on Lake Peţea and the Peţea River at the thermal resort of 1 Mai, near the town of Oradea. The warm water of the lake and the river, at a temperature of over 30 °C., provides a suitable environment for a magnificent relic of the Tertiary period, the scallop-leaved water lily *(Nymphaea lotus* var. *thermalis)*, a subtropical plant unique in Europe which grows naturally only in this area.

The principal plant reserves in the Dobrudja—Agigea and the Letea Forest—are also of considerable importance. The Agigea reserve contains plants which live on the shifting sand of the sea *(Ephedra dystachya)* and plants usually found in warmer areas such as *Convolvulus persicus*. In the Letea Forest are found the grey oak and the hairy ash *(Fraxinus holotricha)*, the vine, and a Mediterranean plant named *Pariploca graeca*.

Forest reserves. Among the ancient forests in the larch and fir areas the most important reserves are the *Slătioara Forest* on the slopes of Mount Rarău in the Suceava region and the *larch forest on Mount Ceahlău*. In the deciduous forests the main reserves are those of *Snagov* (4,200 acres), near Bucharest; *Bejan*, near the town of Deva; *Valea Fagilor* (the "Valley of Beeches")at Luncaviţa, in the northern Dobrudja; and *Hasmacoul Mare* (or Letea), in the Danube Delta.

Geological reserves and fossiliferous areas; speleological reserves. Among the main geological and palaeontological features protected by the law are the great accumulations of basalt prisms at Detunata Goală and Detunata Flocoasă in the Apuseni Mountains, the Roman citadels at Roşia Montana in the Cluj region with their remains of Roman gold workings, the fossiliferous limestones of Valea Mare and Ampoiţa in the Hunedoara region, the granite and nummulitic limestones of Albeşti, the fossiliferous lake of Mărlăuz-Suslăneşti in the Muscel district, the salt mountains of Slănic Prahovei, the mud volcanoes of Pîclele Mari and Pîclele Mici in the Ploieşti region, and Repedea Hill near Iaşi.

Particular attention is given to the preservation of the caves and other features of the karst country. The sites protected by law include the Scărişoara Glacier, the cave of Pojarul Poliţei, the magnificent Citadels of Ponor, the tumultuous Galbena valley, the cave and defile of Vadul Crişului—all in the Apuseni Mountains—as well as a number of caves in Oltenia (the Cloşani Cave, the Cioaca Cave, etc.), the Hunedoara region (the Tecuri Cave) and the Cluj region (the cave of Izvorul Tăuşoarelor). All these places are of interest both for the variety of their limestone concretions and for their cave-dwelling fauna.

Plants and animals protected by law. The picking of edelweiss *(Leontopodium alpinum)*, found on the limestone crags of the Alpine zone, and of the rare and graceful lady's slipper orchid *(Cypripedium calceolus)* is strictly prohibited throughout the whole of Rumania. In the Bucegi range and the Prahova valley the two species of nigritella found in these areas *(Nigritella nigra* and *Nigritella rubra)* are also protected; as are the Rumanian peony *(Paeonia romanica)* which is common in the forests near Bucharest and the snake's head lily *(Fritillaria meleagris)* which grows round Sibiu and in northern Moldavia. Among trees and shrubs, the *Taxus baccata* is protected thoughout the country, and the white ivy *(Daphne blagayana)* is protected in the Bucegi Mountains, on Postăvarul, the Piatra Mare, etc.

In order to ensure the preservation and reproduction of the species, the shooting of chamois is prohibited in the Bucegi Mountains and the shooting of lynx is permitted only within certain limits.

All the members of the eagle family found in Rumania— including the bearded vulture *(Gypaetus barbatus grandis)*, the black vulture *(Aegypius monachus)* and the golden eagle *(Aquila chrysaetus)*, the largest representative of the family in Rumania—are protected by law. The females of the capercailzie *(Tetrao urogallus)*, the great bustard *(Otis tarda)* and the little bustard *(Otis tetrax orientalis)* are similarly protected. The shooting of the black grouse *(Lyrurus tetrix)* is strictly prohibited.

In the Danube Delta and its lagoons the shooting of the pelican *(Pelecanus crispus* and *Pelecanus onocrotalus)*, the white heron *(Egretta alba alba)*, the spoonbill *(Platalea leucorodia)*, the shelduck *(Tadorna tadorna)*, the ruddy shelduck *(Casarca ferruginea)*, etc., is prohibited. Two species of tortoise are protected by law, the *Testudo graeca ibero*, which lives in the Dobrudja, and the less common *Testudo hermanii*, found only in southern Oltenia and the Banat.

Two large additional reserves are to be established in the near future to protect the flora and fauna of the Danube Delta. It is also proposed to designate a second national park in the Apuseni Mountains.

1. BUCHAREST

Character of the Town

Bucharest, *(Bucureşti)*, capital of the Socialist Republic of Rumania, is the political, administrative, economic and cultural centre of the country. It contains the headquarters of the central institutions of government and administration (Council of State of the S. R. of Rumania, National Assembly, Council of Ministers, Ministries, etc.) and of political, trade union and cultural organisations.

Bucharest occupies a place of prime importance in the economy of the country. Between 1965 and 1970, 50 new factories were built and 50 existing establishments enlarged and modernised. Today the industry of Bucharest produces machinery, equipment for the oil and mining industries and for agriculture, electrical apparatus, consumer goods, etc. Bucharest's industrial establishments account for 17,6% of the industrial production of Rumania (a third of the production of chemicals, over a quarter of the production of machinery and the metalworking industries, roughly a third of the production of textiles and the building industry, more than 70% of the printing and publishing industry, etc.).

Bucharest is also the scene of intense scientific and cultural activity. The Rumanian Academy, the principal scientific and cultural institution of the country, has its headquarters here.

An important University centre, Bucharest possesses 12 institutes of higher education, with 58 faculties and more than 68,000 students, Rumanian and foreign.

The artistic life of Bucharest reflects the interest of its citizens in the pleasures of the mind. The performances given in the city's 17 theatres are seen by several million people every year, and its 50 cinemas are frequented by tens of millions of people. Bucharest's very active musical life puts it among those European capitals with high traditions in this field. Three symphony orchestras (the George Enescu Philharmonic Orchestra, the Orchestra of Rumanian Radio and Television and the Conservatoire Orchestra) give frequent performances in the Palace Hall, the Rumanian Athenaeum, the Concert Hall of Rumanian Radio and Television, and other halls. Every three years the

George Enescu Festival and International Competition is held in the capital.

Bucharest also possesses over 40 museums, art collections and house-museums associated with well known people. The most popular of these are the Art Museum and the Village Museum.

There is intense sporting activity in the seven large stadia (the largest of which, the 23rd of August Stadium, can accommodate over 80,000 spectators and the 200 or so sports grounds (football, volleyball, handball, rugby) and gymnasia.

Geography and History

Bucharest lies in latitude 44° 24' N. and longitude 26° 06' E., roughly half way between the Danube and the Sub-Carpathians. The town has an area of 380 square miles, divided into eight administrative districts or wards, and a population of over 1,500,000.

Situated in the middle of a plain, at an altitude between 175 and 315 feet, Bucharest enjoys a delightful natural setting, with an attractive pattern of parks, woods and forests varied by rivers and lakes. The River Dîmbovița flows through the town, and its tributary the Colentina winds through the northern outskirts, frequently broadening out to form lakes fringed with trees and grass.

The large number of parks and open spaces, along with the lime trees and horse chestnuts which line most of the streets, give Bucharest its distinctive atmosphere. Another characteristic feature of the city is the large number of new buildings which have been erected in the centre and more particularly in the outskirts, replacing the older areas and untidy patches of waste ground.

Bucharest is a city with a long history. The archaeologists have discovered in various parts of the town remains which bear witness to the continuity of life here since the Palaeolithic period.

The "citadel on the Dîmbovița" is mentioned in documents of 1368, but the name of *Bucharest* appears for the first time in a document dated 20 September 1459 in the reign of Prince Vlad the Impaler. According to one of the legends about the origin of the town, the name of Bucharest comes from a shepherd called Bucur who was attracted by the beauty of the banks of the Dîmboviţa and settled in this area, formerly covered by the Vlăsia Forest.

For two centuries the residence of the Princes Regnant of Wallachia alternated between Tîrgovişte, the old capital, and Bucharest. From 1659, however, Bucharest became the capital of the country and its main political and economic centre. Round the Prince's palace, which occupied the geographical centre of the town, groups of traders and craftsmen came to settle, leaving their mark in street names which have been preserved into our own day: *Lipscani* (the street occupied by shopkeepers selling goods from Leipzig—in Rumanian Lipsca), *Blănari* (the street of the furriers), *Şelari* (the street of the saddlers) etc.

Bucharest also developed because of its situation on a busy trade route linking Central Europe with Constantinople and the Near East.

Side by side with the new buildings, both public and private, which give Bucharest the atmosphere of a modern capital city, there are many buildings of great architectural interest to bear witness to its eventful past.

A. THE OLD CENTRE

The geographical centre of the town (the starting point from which the roads from Bucharest to the various parts of the country are measured) is the **Piaţa 1848,** which was also the centre of the mediaeval town.

Along the south side of the square ran the wall of the **Prince's Palace,** built about the middle of the 16th century. The wall, in which there were only two gates, enclosed a considerable area, corresponding roughly to Str. Lipscani, Str. Şelari, Str. 30 Decembrie, Str. Bărătiei and Calea Moşilor in the present-day town.

The Prince's Palace—which the people of Bucharest called the *Old Palace* (**Curtea Veche**) from the 18th century onwards— was reduced to a state of ruin after a series of fires and earthquakes, and was replaced by another residence, the *New Palace,*

BUCUREȘTI

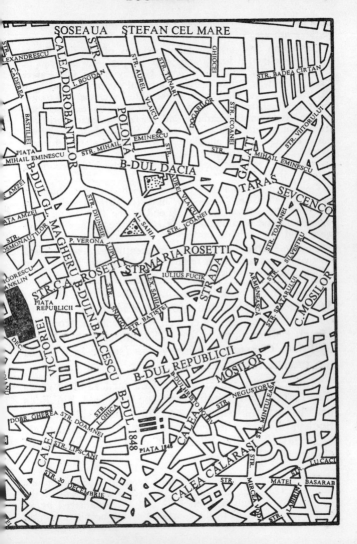

built by Alexandru Ypsilanti in 1776 on the hill of Dealul Spirei to the south-west of the town.

Excavation has revealed a few remains of the Old Palace — walls, cellars, a loggia and some paving — which can be seen in the *Old Palace Museum.* Nearby is the **Old Palace Church,** built by Prince Mircea Ciobanul about the middle of the 16th century. The church — the oldest architectural monument in Bucharest — although several times restored, has retained its original appearance, with the features characteristic of Rumanian architecture of the period (façade with horizontal bands of facing bricks alternating with areas of plaster; rows of small niches under the cornices; specially shaped bricks forming the plinth). The stone *doorway* of the church, richly decorated, dates from 1715.

Opposite the Old Palace Church a rich Armenian business man and politician, Manuc-bey, built (in 1818) a well known inn which bore his name. At the end of the 19th century this was rebuilt and became the *Dacia Hotel,* where many meetings were held by militant workers of the Bucharest proletariat. *Manuc's Inn* (Hanul lui Manuc) has recently been restored, and now comprises a hotel, a restaurant, a pâtisserie and a shop selling handicraft articles.

In the small park in the Piaţa 1848 is the *Church of Sf. Gheorghe Nou*, built in the middle of the 19th century on the site of a church which was destroyed in March 1847 by a great fire. The church was founded by Prince Constantin Brîncoveanu (statue in front of the present church.)

Going northward along the Bulevard 1848 towards the Piaţa Universitătii, we see two old buildings just before the square, one on each side of the boulevard. On the right is the **Colţea Hospital,** built in 1708 by Michael Cantacuzino, uncle of Constantin Brîncoveanu.

The hospital was enlarged and altered in 1888 when the Bulevard 1848 was laid out, involving the demolition of the Colţea Tower (built between 1709 and 1715, damaged by an earthquake in 1802.) In the courtyard of the hospital, with an entrance from the boulevard, is the **Colţea Church,** an interesting example of old Rumanian architecture. It was founded at the beginning of the 18th century by Michael Cantacuzino. The statue of the founder in the courtyard of the hospital is by the sculptor Karl Storck (1869).

Opposite the Colţea Hospital is the former *Suţu Palace*, in the neo-classical style of the first half of the 19th century, now containing the valuable collections of the **Museum of the History of the City of Bucharest.** The exhibits include material illustrating the different stages in the development of Bucharest.

The palace has recently been restored. Until 1914 it was the scene of receptions and parties for the high society of Bucharest; then from 1919 to 1939 it was occupied by banks. Since 1959 it has housed the collections of the Bucharest Historical Museum, previously displayed in the Municipal Museum in the Calea Victoriei. The number of items has risen from 25,000 in 1949 to over 100,000 today.

The Museum contains some twenty rooms, arranged in four sections—ancient history, mediaeval history, the capitalist era and the socialist period.

Among the things which must be seen in a short visit—a detailed visit would take several hours—may be mentioned the prehistoric section, the tools of the Getic and Dacian period, the material from the Roman occupation, the parchment found at Snagov in which the name of Bucharest is mentioned for the first time (in Old Slavonic; 1459, in the reign of Prince Vlad the Impaler), prints and maps showing the gradual extension of the city, Tudor Vladimirescu's proclamation of 1821, the first newspapers in the Rumanian language, material relating to the revolution of 1848 and the union of Rumania in 1859, the war of 1877–78, the industrial and urban development of the 19th century, and the two world wars.

In Str. Ion Ghica, to the south-west of the Historical Museum, is the *Russian Church* (1909), and opposite it is a wing of the Ministry of External Trade. On the same side of the street, at the corner of Str. Doamnei, is a neo-classical building erected in 1910 to the design of the architect Ştefan Burcuş, the *State Central Library*.

This contains some 2 million volumes, 5,000 rare books (incunabula, first editions), over 4,000 manuscripts and, in the music section, a large collection of gramophone records and tape recordings, with the necessary apparatus for listening to them.

On the other side of Str. Doamnei is a massive building in the classical style which contains the Ministry of Finance, built on to the older structure of the *National Bank*. This latter building, in the French Renaissance style, was erected in 1883 by the architects C. Bernard and A. Galleron, on the site formerly occupied by the *Şerban-Vodă Inn*, the first and the greatest of the inns of old Bucharest.

B. THE NORTHERN DISTRICTS

Itinerary: Piaţa Universităţii – Bd Bălcescu – Bd Magheru – Bd Ana Ipătescu – Şoseaua Kiseleff – Şoseaua Băneasa.

The **Piaţa Universitaţii**—named after the building on one side of the square which contains most of the faculties of the University of Bucharest—is one of great junction points of the town, the starting point of the main streets which lead to the different districts of Bucharest.

On the north-east side of the square are the National Theatre, a major work of modern architecture, and the 25-storey Intercontinental Hotel.

To the north is a succession of wide boulevards lined with buildings which for the most part have been erected within the last few decades: institutes, blocks of flats and, on street level, shops and restaurants. Shops and public buildings follow one another almost uninterruptedly from the Piaţa Universităţii to the Piaţa Romană, along the **Bd Bălcescu** and the **Bd Magheru.**

In this stretch there are three exhibition galleries: the *Dalles Hall* (18, Bd Bălcescu), recently enlarged by combining the premises of the Ion Dalles Foundation, erected in 1930, with two neighbouring art galleries, the "Orizont" (23 A Bd Bălcescu) and the "Simeza" (20 Bd Magheru).

Two of the largest hotels in Bucharest, the Ambasador and the Lido, stand opposite one another in the Bd Magheru. Near the latter are the offices of the Ministry of Tourism and the National Tourist Office (Carpaţi). Also in this area are two of the largest cinemas in Bucharest — the Scala at 2, Bd Magheru and the Patria at 12-14, Bd Magheru — and the Constantin Nottara Theatre at 20, Bd Magheru.

A short distance north-east of Bd Magheru, at 51, Bd Dacia, is the *Nottara House and Museum*, commemorating the great actor Constantin Nottara (1859–1935) and his son Constantin (1890–1951), a distinguished musician.

Bd Magheru ends at the **Piaţa Romană.** This square, an important traffic junction, is dominated by the imposing building of the Lenin Institute of Economic Science (the former Commercial Academy, built in 1926 by the architects G. Cerchez and Van Saanen). The **Bd Ana Ipătescu** is a wide and very busy main street.

It is divided into two by lawns and flower beds, and on each side are rows of lime trees and horse chestnuts. The buildings are almost entirely dwelling houses; some of these are modern, others in the style of the beginning of this century.

On the west side of the street, at Nº. 21, is the *Rumanian Astronomical Museum*, with an observatory, astronomical instruments and much other material. At Nº. 28 is the *Coandă Scientific Museum*, devoted to the great Rumanian scientist who invented the jet aircraft.

Bd Ana Ipătescu ends at the **Piaţa Victoriei,** called until 1878 "Capul Podului" (the Bridgehead), since it was the end of the "Mogoşoaia Bridge" (now Calea

Victoriei), a roadway paved with large timber baulks which connected the Old Palace with the princely residence of Mogoşoaia (p. 91).

To the east of the large Piaţa Victoriei is the *Palace of the Council of Ministers*, a monumental modern building erected in 1936–38 to the plans of Duiliu Marcu.

At the corner of the Bulevard Aviatorilor and the Şoseaua Kiseleff is the *Monument to the Soviet Forces*, by the sculptor Baraschi. Behind it, at 2, Şos. Kiseleff, is a building (erected 1906, in the neo-Rumanian style, by the architect Ştefanescu) containing collections of minerals, rocks and fossils found in Rumania. Only part of the material is on show.

At the corner of Şos. Kiseleff (N°. 1) and the Piaţa Victoriei is the **Museum of Natural History** named after *Grigore Antipa*, the founder of Rumanian ichthyology and marine biology, who established the museum and was its director until his death in 1944. It was one of the first natural history museums to be established anywhere in the world. Arranged on Darwinian principles, it demonstrates the development of life, from the simplest organisms to man, in a clear and attractive way. The 300,000 items in the museum include the complete skeleton of a *Deinotherium gigantissimum* 15 feet high discovered in Moldavia and a collection of 82,000 butterflies and moths which is one of the largest in Europe.

Close to the museum is an imposing structure in decorative brick, an interesting essay by the architect Ghica-Budeşti in monumental building in the Rumanian style. Partly built between 1912 and 1939, completed in 1951 and added to in 1963 and 1964, it now houses the *Museum of the History of the Rumanian Communist Party and of the Revolutionary and Democratic Movement in Rumania.*

The Museum contains a rich collection of material on the revolutionary struggle in Rumania, the strikes, the foundation of the Social Democratic Party in 1893, the peasant revolts of 1907, the establishment of the Rumanian Communist Party in 1921, the bloody strikes of 1933, the anti-Nazi resistance in 1941–44 and the rising of 23 August 1944, the abolition of the monarchy and the proclamation of the Republic.

In a small street immediately to the west of the Şoseaua Kiseleff is a courtyard containing a church dating from 1789.

The *Şos. Kiseleff* is a wide avenue with several lines of trees, mostly limes. At the first cross road (Str. Mincu) is a graceful building of medium size in the Rumanian style, the *Buffet*, designed by the architect Ion Mincu and occupied by a restaurant.

From here to the Triumphal Arch the Şos. Kiseleff passes through one of the finest residential districts in Bucharest, in which are situated the Soviet and Swedish embassies.

The **Triumphal Arch** stands in the middle of the third crossing on the Şos. Kiseleff.

The arch was erected in 1922 in temporary form (in wood and stucco), and rebuilt in stone and reinforced concrete in 1935–36 to the design of Petre Antonescu, based on the same general plan as the Arc de Triomphe in Paris. It is decorated with carvings by such talented sculptors as Jalea, Medrea, F. Storck, Paciurea, Späthe, Măcăoanu and Baraschi.

To the east is one the entrances to the large **Herăstrău Park of Culture and Rest.** This surrounds the lake of the same name, one of the 12 lakes, with a total surface area of 3,500 acres, formed by the River Colentina to the north of Bucharest.

The Herăstrău Park, covering an area of 460 acres, is a pleasant expanse of grass and flower beds, with its paths lined by slender poplars and majestic chestnut trees. Scattered about the park are a number of buildings containing exhibitions, libraries and a club. There is also an open air theatre with seats for 3,000, a stage for performances by amateur artistes (500 seats), and three restaurants—the Pescăruş, the Mioriţa and the Parc—with terraces giving a magnificent view over the lake. The lake is always busy with boats and yachts of all kinds, and is also popular with water skiers.

In the northern part is an amusements park. Its Big Wheel, like the one in the Prater in Vienna, can be seen a long way off, and offers its patrons a fine view of the city.

In a bay in the southern part of the lake is a charming little island connected to the shore by gently curving bridges. It has flagstone paths, and along these are beds containing a multitude of roses in many varieties. This is the "*Island of Roses*", and from the island can be seen one of the other attractions of the Herăstrău Park, a village in the heart of Bucharest—the Village Museum.

The **Village Museum**—one of the most interesting and unusual not only in Rumania but in the world— covers an area of 22 acres between Lake Herăstrău and the Şoseaua Kiseleff, from which a small path leads to the main entrance to the Museum.

The Museum was established in 1936, and considerably developed after reorganisation in 1947. At the present time it contains more than 200 buildings from all the different regions of Rumania, faithfully rebuilt by craftsmen from the various regions. The 15,500 items in the Museum (furniture, carpets, textiles, household objects, tools, etc.) are shown in their proper surroundings in the different houses and associated buildings. In addition to the houses with their furnishings the Museum contains windmills from the northern Dobrudja, a small building used for processing and preserving fish from the Danube Delta, a mill for crushing the gold-bearing rock of the Motzi Country, ironworkers' and potters' workshops, and two churches entirely built in wood: one from the Maramureş dating from 1727, a slender building with a graceful tower which rises proudly above the surrounding trees, and another from Moldavia (the Ceahlău area), an 18th century building which is remarkable for the quality of its ornament and the fine Byzantine paintings on its interior walls.

On the other side of the Şos. Kiseleff, opposite the Museum, is the *Youth Stadium*, reserved for school-children and students. Next to it is the Young People's Swimming Pool, with baths for racing and diving-boards.

On the east side of the Şos. Kiseleff, after the Village Museum, another entrance to the Herăstrău Park leads to the exhibition pavilion situated on the same side. Soon after this the Şos. Kiseleff runs into the **Piaţa Scînteia,** where it ends. The square has recently been re-planned in order to provide a better flow of traffic from the various streets which run into the square.

To the west one of these streets leads to the central pavilion used for industrial exhibitions, an imposing circular building mainly constructed of metal and glass.

Another street which runs north to Scînteia House contains a statue of Lenin by B. Caragea, erected in 1960. The massive structure of *Scînteia House* contains the headquarters of the State Committee for Culture and Art, a large printing works which can produce 2,200,000 newspapers and brochures daily, and the editorial offices of the main daily and weekly journals, publishing houses and the Rumanian Press Agency (Agerpress). To the west of this building, which catches the eye of the visitor arriving in Bucharest by road, can be seen the blocks of flats of a new housing area; to the east is a continuation of the Herăstrău Park.

On the far side of the square, to the north, the **Şoseaua Băneasa** runs north to Otopeni Airport, and beyond this to Ploieşti, Braşov and Cluj (D.N. 1). The avenue soon widens to form a small square, in the middle of which in the elegant *Miorita Fountain*, erected in 1936 to the design of O. Doicescu, with two mosaics by Milita Petraşcu representing scenes from the traditional legend of Miorita.

To the east of the little square is another entrance to Herăstrău Park. To the west is the **Villa of Dr Minovici,** a striking building in traditional Rumanian style.

Built in 1905 to the plans of C. Cerchez, the villa belonged to *Dr Nicolae Minovici* (1868–1941), founder of Casualty Hospital and the Ambulance Society of Bucharest (1906), who presented it to the State in 1936. It has now been turned into a museum containing 5,300 items from Dr Minovici's collection: furniture, objects in wood, pottery, icons on glass and on wood, clothing, carpets, and a fine collection of eggs with painted decorations in traditional regional patterns.

The house is built in a style similar to that of the fortified dwellings found throughout Rumania. On the first floor is a *foişor* (a kind of loggia) in the Brîncoveanu style; at the top of a square tower of feudal type is a carillon of bells.

In the vestibule is a display of cloths, embroidery (particularly from northern Moldavia), skirts, belts, shirt-fronts, waistcoats, Transylvanian pottery, etc. The reception room also contains fine specimens of these folk arts. On the staircase are wooden objects such as spoons, distaffs, sticks, etc.

On the first floor is a room containing musical instruments (Pan pipes, bagpipes, shepherds' pipes, flutes, etc). Another room displays a bride's trousseau (cloth, carpets, a trunk, etc.). In the main hall are many specimens of old pottery and old clothing. A small room contains some fine icons of the 18th and 19th centuries. In the bedroom is a portrait of Dr N. Minovici. The dining room is furnished and decorated with objects of traditional type.

Near the villa is a building in the English Tudor style. It was erected in 1940 for *Dr D. Minovici*, an engineer, who in 1944 bequeathed it to the Rumanian Academy. The Academy has organised an **Art Museum** in the building; it contains a number of interesting items:

Delft ware (17th century), Meissen (18th century), porcelain from Britain and China, Baroque statues in wood (15th and 16th centuries), paintings of the Flemish and Florentine schools, rare 16th century manuscripts, specimens of early printing (16th–18th centuries), etc.

Near the two villas is Băneasa station, on the Bucharest–Constanţa line.

Farther along on the left, after passing under the railway bridge, the visitor sees the *Church of Sf. Nicolae-Băneasa* (1792), founded by one of the first Rumanian poets, Ienăchiţa Văcărescu.

After crossing the bridge over the Herăstrău Lake, the Şos. Băneasa is joined on the right by the *Şos. Nordului* (the Northern Avenue), which runs round the northern part of the Herăstrău Park, and then comes to the *Bucharest (Băneasa) Airport*.

Now return to the Şos. Nordului, continue along it first in an easterly and then in a southerly direction, and cross the bridge over Lake Floreasca, near which is the Bordei ("Cottage") Restaurant and a large beach, to enter the **Bulevard Aviatorilor,** a fine wide avenue.

Immediately on the left is the Alexandru Sahia Studio where documentary and news films are produced. Near here, in the large Piaţa Aviatorilor, where mass demonstrations take place on special occasions, is the main entrance to Herăstrău Park.

A little farther on, turn off the boulevard into the Str. Muzeul Zambaccian to see the **Zambaccian Museum,** established by the collector and art critic K. H. Zambaccian (1889–1962) and presented by him to the State in 1947. The Museum contains almost 250 paintings, engravings and drawings and over 40 works of sculpture by great Rumanian painters like *Grigorescu, Andreescu, Luchian, Petraşcu, Pallady* and *Toniţa,* and sculptors like *Han* and *Medrea.* Note particularly a "Child's head" by *Constantin Brâncuşi.* The Zambaccian Museum also contains an interesting collection of paintings of the French school *(Corot, Delacroix, Sisley, Cézanne, Matisse, Utrillo, Picasso,* etc.).

In a street near the Zambaccian Museum (14, Str. Ştefan Gheorghiu) is a modern building containing the headquarters of the General Union of Rumanian Trade Unions.

Returning to the Boulevard, we pass on the left the Institute of Endocrinology and come to the square dominated by the *Monument to the Heroes of the Air.* Continuing towards the Piaţa Victoriei, we pass the *Nicolae Iorga Institute of History,* with the house in which the famous historian lived and worked, and return to the Piaţa Victoreii (p. 65).

Continuation below, Itinerary C.

C. THE CALEA VICTORIEI

The Calea Victoriei (the Street of Victory) is the busiest street in Bucharest. It is a one way street, with traffic going from north to south. It is described, therefore, in this direction.

This was formerly the road from the Prince's palace to his summer residence at Mogoşoaia. It was laid out at the end of the 17th century by Prince Constantin Brîncoveanu and was long known as the "Mogoşoaia Bridge" on account of the timber baulks with which it was paved. It was given the name of **Calea Victoriei** in 1878 to mark the return of the victorious Rumanian forces from the war against the Turks.

The street contains a number of houses formerly belonging to the old boyars, many of them converted into museums, administrative and official buildings, and many shops.

The *Disescu House*, at N⁰. 196, was built between 1910 and 1912 to the design of G. Cerchez. It is in the Rumanian style with the type of loggia characteristic of the Brîncoveanu period.

At N⁰ 153 is the *Numismatic Exhition*, with a rich collection of coins and medals.

The **George Enescu Museum,** at N⁰. 141, a building with a monumental façade erected in 1898-1900 to the design of I. D. Berindei, also contains the headquarters of the Composers' Union.

The George Enescu Museum was opened in 1956, soon after the death of the famous Rumanian composer (1881–1955). It contains a wealth of material on the life and activities of this great musician as composer, conductor, violinist, pianist and teacher.

At N⁰. 133 are the **Ministries of Metalworking and of the Engineering Industry,** in a massive building in the functional style.

At N⁰. 127 is the **Vernescu House,** built in the late 19th century to the design of Ion Mincu. In its fine concert hall Liszt once played during a visit to Bucharest. It is now a club for officials of the Ministry of Metalworking.

At Nᵒ. 125 is the **Academy of the Socialist Republic of Rumania,** a building in the classical style dating from the early 19th century. In the Park is the very important *Library* of the Academy, containing nearly 3 million volumes and 132,000 documents.

The **coin collection** was started in 1910 and has grown steadily until it now contains some 120,000 items. It possesses practically every coin used in the territory of Rumania, including a number of rare items (a dinar of Alexandru Lăpuşneanu, a 16th century coin of Despot Voda, etc.). It also includes a collection of medals, Rumanian banknotes, and a philatelic section containing 35,000 stamps.

At Nᵒ. 113 is the **Mihail Sadoveanu Writers' House,** in an old mansion built by a boyar in the 19th century and restored under the direction of Ion Mincu.

At Nᵒ. 152, in a handsome building designed by Duiliu Marcu, are the offices of the *Committee on the State Plan,* which is responsible for the national economic plan.

At Nᵒ. 111, in a large building erected in 1883 which formerly housed the Ministry of Finance, is the *Institute of Building Design and Materials.*

At Nᵒ. 107 is the **Museum of Folk Art,** which was established here in 1954. The building, erected in 1837 in the neoclassical style and restored in 1881, was formerly the residence of Prince Barbu Ştirbei (1849-56). The Museum contains a collection of over 25,000 items of folk art, and arranges special exhibitions on particular subjects.

The Museum was originally founded in 1906, but has been completely reorganised since 1954. It contains excellent collections in the field of ethnography and folk art, including in particular pottery, embroidery, peasant costumes and cottage furniture and furnishings from the different parts of Rumania, including the areas occupied by national minority groups (Saxons, Bulgarians, Magyars, etc.), carpets, objects carved in wood and bone, paintings on wood and glass in traditional style, etc.

At N°s. 69-63 is the *Ministry of the Foodstuffs Industry*, in a large building which has a famous *pâtisserie* and a number of shops at street level.

To the east of the Calea Victoriei, in the little square which forms the beginning of Str. Cosmonautilor, is the charming little *White Church* **(Biserica Alba),** with a fine iconostasis and wall paintings by Tattarescu.

Farther south, after a narrower stretch, the Calea Victoriei enters the **Piaţa Republicii.**

On the left-hand corner (east side, Str. Episcopiei) is the large *Hotel Athénée-Palace*, one of the oldest and best known in Bucharest. Beyond the gardens on the east side of the square can be seen the white façade of the **Rumanian Athenaeum,** a building characteristic of the old Bucharest.

The building was erected in 1886–88 to the design of Galleron, with money obtained by collections and donations, to provide a home for the *Society of the Rumanian Athenaeum*, founded in 1865 to spread culture among the people. It is an unusual and striking building, with a façade in the style of a Greek temple and a heavy baroque dome. In this hall concerts have been given by many musicians of world fame, including George Enescu, George Georgescu, Dinu Lipatti, Jasha Heifetz, David Oistrakh, Herbert von Karajan, Pablo Casals, Sir John Barbirolli, Artur Rubinstein and Yehudi Menuhin. It is now the headquarters of the George Enescu State Philharmonic Orchestra. Each week concerts are given in the main hall (800 seats), and recitals are also given in a smaller hall.

The **Palace of the Republic** occupies the west side of the square. It is a neo-classical building erected as a royal palace between 1930 and 1937 to the design of N. Nenciulescu, and is now the seat of the Council of State of the Socialist Republic of Rumania. The northern wing houses the **Art Museum** of the S. R. of Rumania, the largest museum of its kind in Rumania.

It contains altogether some 75,000 items, over 2,000 of which are permanently on show.

The Museum consists of three parts:

1. The National Gallery, which contains three sections. The first, the section of *feudal art*, shows Rumanian artistic creations dating from the 10th to 18th centuries (delicate embroidery, icons, objects in precious metal, manuscripts, carved furniture, stone sculpture), and an interesting collection of 16th century wall paintings.

The sections of *modern and contemporary art* give a complete picture of the development of Rumanian painting and sculpture from the beginning of the 10th century to the present day. The exhibits include works by the first secular painters and by the revolutionary painters of 1848 *(Negulici, Iscovescu, Rosenthal)*, the interesting historical pictures of *Theodor Aman*, the best works of *Nicolae Grigorescu*, the founder of the Rumanian school of painting, works by the fine colourist *Ştefan Luchian*, and many others.

There are also works by *Toniţa, Petraşcu, Pallady, Steriadi, Iser* and *Ressu*, and by the contemporary painters *Ghiaţă, Catargi, Baba* and *Ciucurencu*.

Rumanian sculpture is represented by *K. Storck, Georgescu* and *Ionescu-Valbudea*—the first Rumanian sculptors—and by *Paciurea, Jalea, Han, Medrea, Baraschi* and *Irimescu*. The work of *Constantin Brâncuşi* is represented by seven pieces belonging to different stages of his career.

2. The Gallery of World Art contains two sections. In the section of *European art* are paintings and sculpture ranging from the 15th to the 20th century and representing all the principal schools. The section also contains furniture, tapestries, and china and porcelain. The visitor can thus get a clear idea of the artistic styles of the various countries at different times. The 20 rooms in this section contain paintings by *Van Eyck*, the *Breughels, Memling, Rubens, Rembrandt, Lucas Cranach the Elder, Veronese, Titian, Murillo, El Greco, Delacroix, Monet, Sisley, Repin, Serov* and *Aivazovsky*, and sculpture by *Rodin, Bourdelle, Antokolsky, Mukhina* and others.

The section of *Eastern and Far Eastern art* contains, among other things, Chinese bronze mirrors, stone and marble statues from South-East Asia, China and Japan, kakemonos and drawings by Chinese and Japanese artists, jade statuettes, etc.

3. The Print Room contains a rich collection of prints and drawings, including 15,000 by Rumanian artists. There are also works by foreign masters such as *Rembrandt, Dürer, Goya, Daumier* and *Delacroix*.

To the west, behind the Palace of the Republic and attached to it, is a **large hall** in the contemporary style of architecture, built in 1959.

It has seating for 3,200, a stage 100 feet wide, and excellent acoustics which offer the best possible conditions for concerts and recitals. In this **"Palace Hall"** large congresses are held, and it is frequently used for theatrical performances and cinema shows.

The building forms the centre of an architectural scheme of ten blocks of flats with shops on the ground floor. The open space between the blocks of flats and the Palace Hall has been laid out as a public garden with large areas of grass, flower-beds and decorative shrubs.

Returning eastward after walking round the Palace, we pass the **Krețulescu Church** (N°. 47), an interesting example of old Rumanian architecture.

It was built about the year 1722 by Iordache Krețulescu, a son in law of Prince Brîncoveanu and a high dignitary, on a site which was then on the northern outskirts of the town. The building, with architectural features characteristic of the "Brîncoveanu style", was restored about 1935.

We now return to the *Piața Republicii*, through which the Calea Victoriei runs from north to south. Facing us on the east side are two buildings:

On the left, the *Central University Library*, projecting into the square. It was built in stages between 1890 and 1914 to the plans of P. Gottereau. It also contains a lecture hall.

On the right, the *offices of the Central Committee of the Rumanian Communist Party*, a monumental building in the neo-classical style. Opposite it, on the front of N°ˢ. 35–37, Str. Academiei, is a marble plaque recording that in this building, in May 1921, the meetings were held at which the Rumanian Communist Party was founded.

The shop, *Muzica*, at Nᵒˢ. 41-43, Calea Victoriei, is one of the most modern in Bucharest. It sells music, instruments and records, and has a section for rare and second-hand articles and a hall for recitals. On the other side of the street is the group of shops under the name *Romarta* (drapery, fancy goods, clothing, shoes).

The *plaque* with the date *"13th December 1918"* in the little square formerly occupied by the National Theatre (destroyed by German aircraft in August 1944) commemorates the death of 102 workers killed in the course of a great demonstration by the printers of Bucharest.

The *Palace of Telephones* (Nᵒ. 37), built in 1933 to the design of L. Weeks and W. Froy, contains the telephone exchange, offices and, on the ground floor, public telephones for local, trunk and international calls.

The *Comedia Theatre*, at Nᵒˢ. 42–44, is one of the two theatres used by the National Theatre since the destruction of its former building.

The **Central House of the Army**, formerly the *Military Club*, between Str. C. Mille and Bd Gh. Gheorghiu-Dej, is a massive building with a neo-classical façade. It was built in 1912 (architect D. Maimarolu), and is used for various meetings and cultural activities by service men and their families. It contains a fine marble hall, lecture rooms, rooms for exhibitions, a cinema and a restaurant.

The *Hotel Victoria* (Nᵒ. 15) was built on the site of the former Hotel de France, the first hotel in Bucharest (1860).

The *Savings and Deposit Bank* (No. 13) was built between 1896 and 1900, on the site of a church dating from the time of Constantin Brîncoveanu (1712). The Bank (architect P. Gottereau) has an imposing façade with a semicircular pediment supported by columns over the doorway; inside is a large hall lighted by a glass cupola.

The *Museum of the History of the Socialist Republic of Rumania* (Nᵒ. 12), opened in 1972, is built on the site of a famous 18th century inn and incorporates the old Post Office, a monumental building (architect

A. Săvulescu) in neo-classical style with a portico
supported on ten columns. Its sixty rooms display
material illustrating the history of Rumanian society.

We now turn into the *Str. Stavropoleos*, beside the Post
Office, to see two interesting buildings.

Behind the Post Office is the *Stavropoleos Church*, built
between 1724 and 1730 and carefully restored at the beginning
of this century by the architect Ion Mincu. Small but of graceful
proportions, it is a fine example of the Brîncoveanu style in
architecture. It is notable particularly for its portico, with
columns carved by the craftsmen of the period in a delicate
tracery of stone.

Also in Str. Stavropoleos, on the side opposite the church,
is a building in neo-Gothic style with arched vaulting which
provides an appropriate décor for the famous Bucharest brasserie *Carul cu Bere* (the "Beer Cart"). In a neighbouring street is
an old theatre recently modernised, the *Comedy Theatre*.

D. THE SOUTHERN DISTRICTS

Itinerary: Piața Splaiului, Piața Unirii, Dealul Mitropoliei –
Park of Liberty – Calea Șerban-Vodă.

We now return to the Calea Victoriei and continue
down towards the Piața Splaiului.

From this point the River Dîmbovița is covered by a concrete
conduit. In the square is the *Operetta Theatre*, a tower block
of 17 stories, and opposite it is the main bus station of Bucharest.

From here we continue east along the Splaiul
Independenței. To the south we see the *Courts of
Justice*, a monumental building in the French Renaissance style erected between 1890 and 1895 (architect
A. Ballu). The main front, which is approached by
a wide staircase, is decorated with six allegorical
statues.

Beyond the Courts of Justice is the *Domnița Bălașa Church*,
in the neo-Rumanian style, built between 1881 and 1888 on the

site of an older church dating from 1751. The church was founded by Princess Băleaşa, daughter of C. Brîncoveanu. Farther on are the Brîncoveanu Park and the Brîncoveanu Hospital, founded in 1834 by Safta Brîncoveanu, a descendant of the Prince. The Institute of Balneology and Physiotherapy is housed in the same building.

One of the largest food markets in Bucharest is held on the north side of the Splaiul Independenţei.

Farther east, we reach the largest square in Bucharest, the **Piaţa Unirii** (Square of Union). Beyond this is the gently sloping **Dealul Mitropoliei** (Hill of the Patriarchate), on top of which is the Patriarchate.

This hill was the scene of some important historical events. One of these is commemorated by a *stone cross* erected in 1713 in place of a wooden one marking the spot where Prince Constantin Brîncoveanu's father was killed in 1655, along with other boyars, by the "seimeni" (court bodyguard) and "dorobanţi" (foot-soldiers), who had risen against Prince C. Şerban-Vodă and his boyars because they had tried to abolish the bodyguard and restrict the privileges of the "dorobanţi".

On 13 May 1765 the Dealul Mitropoliei saw the rising of the "rufet" (guilds), which united the craftsmen of the guilds and the poorer townsfolk against the excessive taxation levied by the Phanariot Prince Ştefan Racoviţă. The signal for the outbreak of the 1848 revolution in Wallachia was given by the bell on Dealul Mitropoliei; and here too, on 22, 23 and 24 January 1859, thousands of the inhabitants of Bucharest demonstrated in favour of the election of Prince Alexandru Ioan Cuza and the union of the Rumanian principalities.

Here too, on 6 March 1945, took place the large meeting of the people of Bucharest—overflowing on to the Piaţa Unirii—which led to the establishment of the government of Petru Groza.

The upper part of the hill forms a plateau from which there is a fine *view of the town*. Here there was at one time a monastery, at the entrance to which C. Brîncoveanu erected in 1698 a **gateway with a belfry** (restored 1960).

Beyond the gateway, on the left, is a building erected in 1907 (architect I. Maimarolu) on the site of the old Prince's Divan, now the seat of the *National Assembly*. The building, in the neo-classical style, has a façade 260 feet long preceded by an imposing peristyle with 6 Ionic columns; it contains a circular assembly hall with seats for 900.

Next to this is the **Church of the Patriarchate**, built between 1654 and 1658 by the Prince Regnant Constantin Şerban Basarab, though the paintings and some of the finishing work were carried out in the reigns of his successors Mihnea III and Radu Leon. It was during the reign of Radu Leon that the seat of the Metropolitan of Wallachia was moved from Tîrgovişte to Bucharest; and the church then became a metropolitan church. In 1925 it became the seat of the newly instituted Patriarchate.

The building retains many features of Byzantine architecture and shows a marked resemblance to the Episcopal Church at Curtea de Argeş (p. 136). It was altered several times, but a complete restoration in 1960 gave it back its original appearance. The restoration raised no particular technical difficulties, for the church was solidly built and well preserved. (In this connection it may be noted that it was the only church in Bucharest which kept all its towers, in spite of the earthquakes which several times devastated the town).

"The cornice on the portico has been restored to its original height; the shallow pitch of the original lead roof has been reproduced, leaving visible from the outside the domes of the portico and the apse; the masonry which covered the lower parts of the towers has been removed; and the modern neo-classical cornices have been replaced by corbelled brick cornices. Similarly, the decoration and the ornament on the façade have been restored with the help of a very thin coating of plaster and with ceramic ornament, on the pattern of the fragments of the original work which have been found. The tower of the chapel, too, has been rebuilt on the basis of the surviving remains of the original tower (destroyed in the second half of the 19th century).

"The restoration work has made it possible to obtain further information about the stages of development of the buildings on the Hill of the Patriarchate and the line of the walls as they existed until the 19th century" (P. Miclescu).

Near the church is the *Palace of the Patriarchate*, with two loggias, one of them dating from the 17th century.

By way of Bulevard Coșbuc and Str. 11 Iunie we reach the **Park of Liberty,** laid out between 1904 and 1916 on the slopes of Filaret Hill, formerly occupied by vineyards. (A street in this neighbourhood still bears the name of Avenue of Vines).

In this park, which has an area of 90 acres, an imposing structure has recently been erected — the "Monument to the heroes of the struggle for the liberty of the people and the motherland, and for socialism".

Within the park also are an open-air theatre (the Theatre of Liberty, with 5,500 seats) and the *D. Leonida Museum* of *Technology*, illustrating the achievements of Rumania in various fields of technology. Near the south end of the park is the Bucharest *Observatory*, with sections concerned with astronomy and astrophysics.

Near the park, in Str. Dr C. Istrate, is the first railway station in Bucharest, opened in 1869 on the completion of the first railway line in Wallachia, between Giurgiu and Bucharest. It is now a car park.

Continuing south, we come to *Calea Șerban-Vodă*, formerly known as the "Bridge of the Bey" because it was used by envoys from the Sublime Porte on their way to Bucharest. The street soon forks to form the *Șos. Giurgiu* and the *Șos. Oltenița*, both lined with new blocks of flats.

Now return to the Piața Unirii by way of the Calea Șerban-Vodă. On the right of this street, at its intersection with Str. Cuza Vodă, is the little **Church of**

St Spiridion, built in 1747, with an unusual separate tower. Above the door in the picturesque porch is a *Turkish inscription* relating to an oath of loyalty to the Ottoman Sultan.

Turning right into the *Str. Radu Vodă*, we come to the church of the same name. This was built at the beginning of the 17th century by Radu Vodă, who is buried in the church (wall paintings). Not far away to the east is *Bucur's Church*, so named because of its legendary foundation by the shepherd Bucur. The present church dates from the time of Mircea the Old; the tower is shaped like a shepherd's cap.

Returning to the Piaţa Unirii, we can round off the tour of the southern districts of Bucharest with the **Church of St Antim,** a short distance to the west of the square. (Take Calea Rahovei, then turn right into Str. Antim.)

The Church of St Antim bears the name of the Metropolitan Antim Ivireano (1650–1717), a famous scholar who founded a renowned printing press. He was familiar with Georgian and Persian architecture, and the influence of these styles can be seen in the church. He himself is said to have done some of the decoration. Fine frescoes and iconostasis. Round the church are the buildings of the Holy Synod, with a fine tower at the entrance.

E. THE EAST-WEST LINE OF BOULEVARDS

A glance at the plan of Bucharest shows a succession of boulevards forming the axis of the city from east to west. At the eastern end of this axis the **Şos. Iancului** meets the Bulevard 23 August, one of the main approach roads to the *"23rd August"* Stadium (room for 80,000 spectators), a short distance to the south.

The Stadium is surrounded by a fine park, with an area of 130 acres, containing other sports facilities, a parachuting tower, an artificial skating rink and an open-air theatre with 4,300 seats. The Stadium was constructed in 1953, when the

Fourth World Youth Festival was held in Bucharest. Round the 23rd August Park are new housing areas (Vatra Luminoasă and Titan). This is also one of the city's industrial areas, with the 23rd August Engineering Works, a factory producing machine tools and equipment, the Republica tube-making plant, and the Bucureşti cement works.

At the western end of the Şos. Iancului is the *Şos. Mihai Bravul.*

In this street, at No. 281, is the *Institute of Inframicrobiology*, a large modern building of recent construction, like the many blocks of flats which line the street.

The line of boulevards continues with the **Bulevard Republicii.**

In this street are the *Building Institute* (N⁰. 80); the *Mihai Viteazul Middle School* (N⁰ˢ. 76–78), one of the oldest schools in the town; and the *Greek Church* at the end of the boulevard, built at the beginning of this century in the style of an Ionic temple.

Farther along the Bd Republicii are the *Armenian Church* (N⁰. 41), built in 1911; the *Ministry of Foreign Affairs* (N⁰. 33); a statue of *C. A. Rosetti*, the writer who was one of the promoters of the revolution of 1848; and the *Supreme Council on Agriculture* (N⁰. 24), in a building in the style of the French Renaissance erected in 1895 (architect Louis le Blanc).

We now come to the **Piaţa Universitaţii,** an important traffic junction and the point of intersection with the north-south axis of the city (p. 64).

On the north side is the *University of Bucharest*, built between 1856 and 1869 to the plans of A. Orăscu and Ghica-Budeşti. It is interesting to note that the area of the Piaţa Universităţii was occupied at the beginning of the 19th century by the *Sfíntu Sava Monastery*, which housed the first Academy of Bucharest, where teaching was given in the Greek language; later, from 1818, the first institute of higher education where teaching was given in the Rumanian language was established in the monastery. The University building contains the Institute of Foreign Languages (with a number of departments) and the departments of physics, mathematics, history, geography and geology. On the east side a new National Theatre is under construction.

On the opposite side of the square are two large buildings: the *Ministry of Forestry and Building Materials*, built in 1935 to the design of G. M. Cantacuzino, with the offices of Tarom, the Rumanian air line, on the ground floor; and the *Ministry of External Trade*, built in 1906 to the design of O. Maugsch, forming the arc of a circle which is cut by Str. Colonadelor.

In the square are four **statues.** Going from east to west, the first is a statue of *Ion Eliade Radulescu* (1802–72), one of the first Rumanian journalists and the founder of the Philharmonic Society, who took part in the revolution of 1848; it is in marble, and is the work of the Italian sculptor E. Ferrari, who also produced the statue of Lincoln in New York and two statues of Ovid, one at Constanța in Rumania and the other at Sulmona in Italy. The second statue is of *Michael the Brave*, Prince Regnant from 1593 to 1601, who fought victoriously against the Turks and in 1600 achieved a short-lived union of the three Rumanian principalities, Wallachia, Transylvania and Moldavia; the statue, in bronze, was executed in 1876 by Carrier-Belleuse. The third is of *Gheorghe Lazăr* (1779–1823), who in 1818 opened the first institute of higher education in the Rumanian language; the statue, in marble, is by I. Georgescu, one of the first Rumanian sculptors. The fourth is of *Spiru Haret* (1851–1912), Minister of Education, who did much to foster Rumanian culture; the statue, in marble, is by I. Jalea.

After the intersection with the Calea Victoriei we enter the **Bulevard Gh. Gheorghiu-Dej.**

In the first part of the boulevard are eight cinemas, including an open-air cinema, a variety of shops, including the Academy Bookshop, two elegant snack bars, etc. At Nᵒ. 27 is the *People's Council of Bucharest*, a building dating from 1910 (architect P. Antonescu) in which features of the traditional Rumanian architecture are used to excellent effect.

On the other side of the boulevard are the **Cişmigiu Gardens,** the oldest and finest public gardens in the city, laid out from 1851 onwards.

In one corner of the gardens is a small zoo, with pelicans and small water animals. The abundance of flowers and the lake, with white swans gliding about among the boats, give the Cişmigiu Gardens a particular charm. In the south-west corner of the gardens is the *Gheorghe Lazăr Middle School*, opened in 1860. The present building (architect Montereanu) was erected in 1890 and extended in 1932.

Farther along the Bd Gh. Gheorghiu-Dej are the *Club of the Teachers' Trade Unions*, built at the beginning of this century in the neo-Rumanian style (architect C. Iotzu); a statue of *Mihail Kogălniceanu* (1817–1891), historian and statesman, who was Prime Minister in the reign of Prince Alexandru Ioan Cuza; the *Faculties of Law and Philosophy*, in an elegant building in the neo-classical style erected in 1935 (architect P. Antonescu); and to the right of this a modern hall of residence for 1,000 students. Beyond this again is the *Theatre of Opera and Ballet*, built in 1953 (architect O. Doicescu), with seats for 1,200 and a stage 80 feet wide, 65 feet deep and 100 feet high. In front of the Opera is a statue of the great musician George Enescu.

Beyond the Piaţa Operă begins the avenue now named the **Bulevard Dr Petru Groza.** It was laid out in 1894 through the woods which at that time covered this part of the city, then known as the Cotroceni district. At the beginning of the boulevard is the *Monument to the Heroes of the Health Services* (sculptor Raffaello Romanelli), erected in 1932 to the memory of medical personnel who fell in the first world war.

About half way along its length the Bd Petru Groza cuts across the *Bulevard Eroilor* (Boulevard of Heroes), which runs past the *Military Academy* — in front of which is the *Monument to the Heroes of the Motherland*, by a group of sculptors led by M. Butunoiu — towards one of the large new districts on the outskirts of the town, Drumul Taberei.

Returning to the Bd Petru Groza, we soon come to the *Faculty of General Medicine* of the *Institute of Medicine and Pharmacy*. The Faculty was founded in 1856 by Carol Davilla, whose statue by Carol Storck stands in front of the building, erected in

1903 in the neo-classical style (architect Louis le Blanc).

The Bd Petru Groza ends at the park in which stands the **Pioneers' Palace.**

This is a former royal summer residence, built in 1893 to the design of G. Cerchez, with typical Rumanian architectural features. Over 10,000 pioneers belonging to the 47 clubs organised in the Palace are able to devote themselves to a variety of activities—model making, music, chemistry, carving, etc.

To the north-west of the Palace, beyond the Şos. Cotroceni, are the **Botanic Gardens,** established in 1860 and transferred to this site in 1886. They cover an area of 43 acres and contain over 10,000 species of plants from all over the world, some of them in special hothouses.

Farther along the Şos. Cotroceni, to the west of the town, is the **Bulevard Armata Poporului,** on which is the massive building of the Bucureşti clothing and knitwear factory, the first large industrial building erected in Bucharest after the second world war.

In the neighbouring *Militari* district a number of new factories have recently been built, including a factory producing metal equipment, a milk processing plant and a number of modern woodworking establishments.

F. THE CALEA GRIVIŢEI

The Calea Griviţei is one of the older streets of Bucharest, and one of the longest (over 3 miles). Until 1878 it was called the "Tîrgovişte Road", since it led to the town of Tîrgovişte. After the War of Independence (1877–78) the street received its present name in memory of the victory of Rumanian forces over the Turkish army at Griviţa to the south of the Danube.

The Calea Griviţei leaves the Calea Victoriei near the Museum of Folk Art, and is one of the approaches to the largest railway station in Bucharest, the Northern Station. Before reaching the station it passes the modern building of the Nord Hotel and the former *Gheorghiu-Dej Polytechnic Institute*, a building of ornamental brick with decorative features in ceramics. Beyond this is the modernised part of the Calea Griviței.

The old **Northern Station** was built in 1870; it has been extended on several occasions since then, and was restored after 1944. Round the station is a large square surrounded by modern blocks of flats with shops on the ground floor. On the part of the square nearest the Calea Griviței is a statue by C. Medrea and I. Jalea in memory of the railwaymen who fell in the first world war.

On the opposite side is another square which provides a fine view of the massive marble-faced building containing the *offices of the Rumanian Railways* (architects Duiliu Marcu and S. Călugăreanu). On the east and west sides of this square are new blocks of flats.

Beyond the Station the north side of the Calea Griviței is lined with a succession of new buildings, in a variety of styles and in warm bright colourings, which have replaced older houses, of poor quality and often insanitary.

Beyond the Station on the south side (N°. 193B) is the *Railway Museum*, with a rich collection of material on the development of transport in Rumania, from the cart to the diesel train. In the courtyard of the Museum is the first railway engine built in Rumania (in 1873 at Reșița).

A little farther along the south side of the street is a metal bridge, the Grant Bridge, providing easy access to the *Giulești* and *Cringași* districts, on the far side of the network of railway lines leaving the Northern Station.

Over the bridge, in the Șos. Giulești, are the *Giulești Theatre* and the *Giulești Stadium* of the Railwaymen's Sports Association. Beyond these can be seen the lines of modern buildings which run along both sides of the Șos. Giulești.

Continuing along the Calea Griviței, we soon see on the left, after the Grant Bridge, the "Grivița Roșie" workers' club and the Griviţa Roşie Works, which are associated with the struggle of the railwaymen culminating in the great strike of 16 February 1933.

A marble plaque on the outside wall and a monument in the courtyard of the works commemorate the railwaymen who lost their lives in these tragic events.

The old railway repair workshops have recently been replaced by a modern factory producing equipment for the chemical and oil industries.

On the other side of the Calea Griviţei are blocks of flats, modern shops, schools, and gardens with flower beds and lawns.

Near the bridge carrying the Bucharest-Constanţa railway line the Calea Griviţei ends at a group of new buildings, among which are a fine tower block and a modern cinema.

Beyond the bridge are more blocks of flats, with a large cinema and the Nicolae Bălcescu Park, in which can be seen the columns of an open-air theatre.

Continuing in this direction, the visitor would come to the commune of Mogoşoaia, in which is the fine mansion built by Prince Constantin Brîncoveanu (p. 91).

G. OTHER FEATURES OF INTEREST

Bucharest possesses other monuments of its past, museums, buildings and places of interest which can be seen by the visitor who has sufficient time on his hands. Some of these are listed below.

The hill of *Dealul Mihai Vodă*, on the right bank of the Dîmboviţa near the Izvor Bridge, is dominated by the building occupied by the **State Archives.** These were originally kept in the cells of a monastery built on this hill in 1598 by Prince Michael the Brave. Nothing is left of the original building but the monastery church (one of the oldest buildings in Bucharest) and the belfry.

The *Palace of Radio and Television*, at 60, Str. Nuferilor, is a new building containing offices and studios, together with a fine concert hall with seats for 1,000.

The *Circus*, a graceful circular building with an unusual dome, is equipped with the most up-to-date facilities and has accommodation for 2,500 spectators. It stands in a park of some 40 acres, recently laid out and ringed by modern blocks of flats.

The **Storck Museum**, at 16, Str. V. Alecsandri, contains works by the artists belonging to this family, particularly the sculptor Karl Storck (1826–87), the first professor of sculpture at the School of Fine Arts of Bucharest, and his younger son Fritz (1854–1926).

The **Medrea Museum**, at 16, Str. Budişteanu, contains works by the contemporary sculptor Cornel Medrea (born 1888).

The **Dona Collection**, at 12, Str. Dr Dona, contains works of art (mainly paintings) collected by Dr Dona (1875–1956). Works by Grigorescu, Luchian, Toniţa, Petraşcu, Pallady, Ressu, Ciucurencu, Aman, Andreescu, etc.

The **Oprescu Collection**, at 16, Str. Dr Clunet, contains a great variety of objects bequeathed by their owner in 1960 to the Library of the Academy: carpets, old furniture, pottery, Greek and mediaeval statuettes, paintings by Rumanian and foreign artists, incunabula and rare books.

The **Weinberg Collection**, at 36, Str. Al. Sahia, contains works by Rumanian artists, particularly I. Iser.

The **Minulescu Collection**, at 19, Bd Gh. Marinescu, contains a variety of works of art collected by the poet Ion Minulescu, who died in 1944.

The **Karadja Collection**, at 31, Str. Gr. Mora, belonged to the historian Constantin Karadja (1889–1950): various works of art and craftmanship.

The **Museum of Rumanian Literature**, at 4, Str. Fundaţiei, contains manuscripts, early editions and other material on the life and work of great Rumanian writers.

The **Severeanu Collection**, at 26, Str. I. C. Frimu, consists mainly of coins collected by Dr Severeanu (died 1939).

The **Tattarescu Museum**, at 7, Str. Domniţa Anastasia, near the Bd. Gheorghiu-Dej, is in an early 19th century house which belonged to the painter G. Tattarescu (1820–94), one of the founders of art teaching in Rumania. The museum contains works by Tattarescu, his studio, and a variety of material on his period.

The **Theodor Aman Museum**, at 8, Str. C. A. Rosetti, just off the Piața Republicii, was built to the design of the painter Theodor Aman (1831–91), and contains works by him, objects associated with him, and other material.

The *Central Military Museum*, at 137, Str. Izvor, near the Stadium of the Republic, illustrates the development of the Army and the art of war on the territory of Rumania, with exhibits of weapons of all periods, flags, coats of arms and other material.

Practical information on Bucharest: see at the end
of this volume, page 368.

2. SURROUNDINGS OF BUCHAREST

The countryside round Bucharest is attractive and unspoiled. The capital is surrounded by an extensive area of forest, lakes and rivers which offer scope for a variety of pleasant excursions.

A. MOGOŞOAIA

Mogoşoaia, a commune situated on D.N. 1A, to the north-west of Bucharest (15 km—10 miles—from the centre of the town), is much frequented, particularly during the warm weather. At this point the River Colentina forms a lake—Lake Mogoşoaia—surrounded by a forest, which on the north of the lake is laid out as a park. The park and the beach on the lakeside are very popular with the people of Bucharest. The main attraction of Mogoşoaia, however, is the *Museum of Art of the Period of Constantin Brîncoveanu* in the palace built by Prince Constantin Brîncoveanu in 1702.

The palace is surrounded by a courtyard with walls on three sides, the fourth side being formed by Lake Mogoşaia. It is built on a rectangular plan, with a basement, a ground floor and an upper floor, and is one of the most typical examples of the civil architecture of the Brîncoveanu period. It combines native architectural features (the loggia with eight columns on the east side, for example) with certain Venetian influences (the elegant loggia facing the lake). Inside the palace are displayed interesting objects from the feudal period (articles in precious metals, paintings, embroidery, old books, period costumes, a portrait of Brîncoveanu). The basement contains a lapidarium.

Outside the courtyard, near the entrance with its tower, is a small church dating from 1688; it contains a votive picture representing Brîncoveanu with his wife and his eleven children.

A building attached to the palace is a "Writers' House" where the occupants can devote themselves to creative work.

B. BUFTEA

Buftea is a commune in the same general area, also on D.N. 1A, 21 km (13 miles) from Bucharest. It lies close to an ancient forest, the remains of the old Vlăsia Forest. The River Colentina forms another lake here.

Attracted by the picturesqueness of the area, Prince Barbu Ştirbei built a palace in neo-Gothic style on the shores of the lake in the middle of the 19th century. On a causeway which extends into the lake for a considerable distance is the Kreţulescu Church (built in 1779).

To the right of the lake the visitor's eye is caught by the modern buildings of the *Centre of Cinematographic Production*, with sets covering an area of 75 acres.

C. BĂNEASA

The *Băneasa Wood*, situated near D.N. 1 (Bucharest-Ploieşti) some 10 km (6 miles) from the town and covering an area of 150 acres, is a pleasant place of recreation for the people of Bucharest. In the wood are two restaurants—one of them in the style of a typical Rumanian "wine cellar"—a zoo, a deer park, and a shooting range which was used in 1955 for the European shooting championships.

D. SNAGOV

At km 35 (22 miles) on D.N. 1 a road branches off on the right into the forest which surrounds one of the largest lakes in the countryside round Bucharest: Lake Snagov, with an area of rather more than 2 square miles, and with facilities for boating and other water sports.

A third of the area of the lake is designated as a nature reserve on account of the rare water plants which it contains. The large natural park formed by the forest round the lake contains two reserves for plants and animals. Round the shores of the lake are a number of beaches, landing stages and restaurants.

On an island in the northern part of the lake is a monastery dating from the 16th century, in which one of the first printing presses in Wallachia was established in the 17th century.

E. SOUTH OF BUCHAREST

The area to the east and south of Bucharest also contains much to interest the visitor. The woods of Pasărea, Pustnicul and Cernica (on the banks of the Argeş), to the south and south-west of the town, are much resorted to by the people of Bucharest at weekends.

Bucharest-Giurgiu (64 km—40 miles—by road; 95 km—60 miles— by rail).

D.N. 5 (which leaves Piaţa 1848 and continues by way of Piaţa Unirii and a series of main streets running south) connects Bucharest with the Danube. It is a modern road lined in the first part of its course by rows of new buildings and, after leaving Bucharest, by old trees.

Shortly before km 10 (6 miles) the modern buildings of the *Jilava Rubber Works* (brought into operation in 1957) are seen on the left. At km 19 (12 miles) the road crosses the River *Argeş*, with the Copăceni beach at an attractive bend in the river. The next bridge takes the road over the Neajlov, a tributary of the Argeş, and at each end of the bridge, on the parapet, are the bronze effigy and coat of arms of Michael the Brave, Prince Regnant of Wallachia (1593–1601). It was on and around this bridge, between the hills and the woods of Călugăreni, that

Michael the Brave on 13 August 1595 won a brilliant victory over a large Turkish army led by the Grand Vizier Sinan Pasha.

Beyond the bridge, on the high ground on which the commune of Crucea de Piatră stands, are two stone crosses; the one on the left was erected in 1682 by the Prince Regnant of the day, Şerban Cantacuzino.

Farther on the road descends into the Danube valley where, on a low terrace above the river, is the frontier town of **Giurgiu** (pop. 45,600).

Mentioned for the first time in a document of 23 September 1403, the town of Giurgiu had a troubled existence, undergoing Turkish occupation from the 15th century until 1829. After 1829 the town and the port began to develop. In 1869 Giurgiu was connected to Bucharest by the first railway in Wallachia, and today its port deals with more than a quarter of all the goods traffic on the Rumanian bank of the Danube.

The two Rumanian river steamers, the "Olteniţa" and the "Carpaţi", call regularly at Giurgiu during the summer. Plying between Vienna and Hîrşova (a port some 55 miles from Constanţa), they cater for the many people who enjoy a cruise on the Danube. From Giurgiu tourists are taken by bus to Bucharest, spending the day there and returning to the ship at night.

Downstream from the harbour can be seen the *Friendship Bridge*, opened in 1954. It is 2,400 yards long and has two levels, one (the upper) for road traffic, the other for the railway. The Friendship Bridge provides a direct connection with the Bulgarian town of Ruse and beyond this with the Balkan countries. See Nagel Guide *Bulgaria*.

3. TIMIŞOARA AND ITS SURROUNDINGS

Timişoara (in Hungarian *Temesvar*) is the capital of the Banat, a region of mixed population containing Rumanians, Magyars, Serbs, Swabians, etc. Part of the Banat, indeed, is in Yugoslavia. The town has 200,000 inhabitants, and has more than doubled in population since 1939.

Timişoara is reached from Yugoslavia by road N°. 59 (E 94) from Belgrade. (The distance from Belgrade to Timişoara is about 150 km—95 miles). This road is the main approach road to Rumania for motorists travelling by way of Yugoslavia. It crosses the frontier at *Moraviţa*. From the frontier to Timişoara is 60 km (38 miles) across the great plain of the Banat.

Timişoara: the Town

Timişoara is an important industrial and cultural centre. In recent years existing factories have been enlarged and modernised, and in addition a whole series of new ones have been built. Today 40% of the industrial production of the Banat comes from Timişoara—engineering (Technometal and other engineering works), electrical engineering, chemicals, foodstuffs and textiles.

Timişoara has a University, a Polytechnic Institute, an Institute of Medicine, etc., with over 13,000 students. Other cultural institutions are the Research Centre of the Rumanian Academy (which produced the first electronic calculating machine in Rumania), three theatres (including an opera house), a Philharmonic Orchestra, etc.

The parks lining the navigable Bega Canal which runs through the town and the many new buildings (housing areas, the University, the University City, the sports stadium, office blocks, etc.) give the town a most attractive appearance.

History

Mentioned for the first time in a document of 1212 under the name of Castrum Temesiensis (the *castrum* on the Timiş), the town grew up on an area of marshy ground crisscrossed by so many streams that it was impossible to say which of them flowed into the Timiş and which into the Bega. The site was in fact chosen because of the marshes, which made the fortress less accessible to enemies; but by the same token it is difficult to recognise traces of earlier periods in the marshy ground. In spite of this, however, the discovery of objects belonging to the Neolithic period and of the remains of Roman building proves that the site was occupied much earlier than the 13th century.

Destroyed in the 13th century by the Tatars, the citadel of Timişoara was rebuilt, and even became for a brief period at the beginning of the 14th century a royal residence. But it did not play a role of any importance until the 15th century, when it became a centre of resistance to the Ottoman expansion into Central Europe and the great military leader, Iancu of Hunedoara, decided to enlarge the citadel and rebuild the castle. Another well known figure of this period was Pavel Chinezul, Count of Timişoara, a giant of a man whose strength was legendary.

It was on the main square of the town that Gheorghe Doja, leader of the peasant rising of 1514, was executed along with his lieutenants. He was put to death with the most barbarous cruelty: he was made to sit on a throne of red-hot iron and an iron crown, also red-hot, was placed on his head, and his body was then torn to pieces and hun gon the city gates of Alba Iulia, Oradea and Buda in order to spread terror among the peasants. In 1552 Timişoara and its citadel were captured by the Turks, and the whole of the Banat became a "pashalik". In 1718 the citadel was rebuilt by the Austrians; a hundred and fifty years later it was bought by the town and demolished. Timişoara was restored to Rumania in 1918.

Sights of the Town

The *parks* along the Bega Canal, which made it possible to drain the marshes.

The **Historical Museum** in the Huniade Castle (built in the 14th century and enlarged in the 15th century by Iancu of Hunedoara): valuable collections of archaeological and ethnographical material, a section on the natural sciences, and an art gallery.

The *Iron House,* so called because a tree covered with a metal casing is built into one of its walls; the *Old Town Hall,* a Baroque edifice built in 1731–34; the *Turkish House,* a relic of the Ottoman occupation.

The **Catholic Cathedral,** a monumental structure (with a fine Baroque doorway) built between 1737 and 1773 by the famous Viennese architect Fischer von Erlach; the *Serbian Cathedral,* built in 1734 and enlarged in 1791; the *Franciscan Monastery,* built in 1733–36; the *Hospital and Church of the Brothers of Mercy,* two 18th century buildings situated near the ruins of the mediaeval cathedral.

The *Orthodox Cathedral,* a monumental building of the early 20th century; the *New University* and the *University City;* the *Green Forest,* a recreation area on the outskirts of the town, with a public swimming bath and a camping site; the *Bega Canal* (boating, trips in motor launches).

Tourist Office: 3, Str. Piatra Craiului (tel. 12.910).

Environs of Timişoara

1. *Buziaş* (35 km—22 miles—to the east), a thermal resort at an altitude of 433 feet. Recommended for heart disease, arteriosclerosis, gout, anaemia, rheumatism, diseases of the kidneys and bladder, etc.

TIMIŞOARA

1 Huniade Castle
2 House of Prince Eugene
3 Old Town Hall
4 Turkish house
5 Catholic Cathedral

6 Serbian Cathedral
7 Franciscan Monastery
8 Church of the Brothers of Mercy
9 Art Gallery
10 Tourist Office

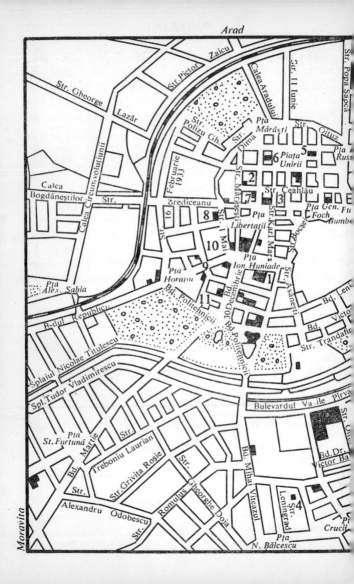

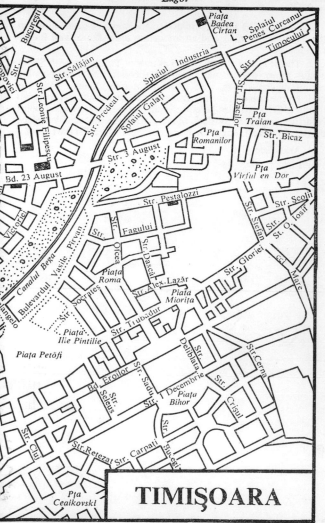

TIMIŞOARA

2. *Jimbolia* (39 km — 24 miles — to the west), a small town on the Yugoslav frontier and an important agricultural and industrial market.

3. The *Western Banat*. D.N.6 connects Timişoara with Sînnicolau Mare and Cenad, passing through the rich farming region of the Banat, with many attractive villages. *Cenad* is built on the site of a former Roman *castrum* near the Hungarian frontier. (The frontier here is closed: the nearest crossing point is farther north, at Nădlac). Sînnicolau Mare was the birthplace of the famous Hungarian musician Bela Bartok (1881–1945).

4. **Arad:** see p. 109.

4. FROM TIMIŞOARA
TO DROBETA-TURNU SEVERIN

D.N.6, asphalted, running parallel to the railway. One of the main approach roads to Bucharest. (The other is by Arad, Deva and Sibiu: see Itinerary 6.) 221 km (138 miles).

The road leaves Timişoara on the east. *Recaş* is noted for its red wines. *Chizătău* has a well known peasant choral society founded in 1857, a theatrical company and a folk orchestra. At km 60 (38 miles), **Lugoj.**

Lugoj grew up on the site of a Roman *castrum*, which in turn was built near a Dacian fortress of the 1st century B.C. In the Middle Ages there was a strong fortress here belonging to the Ban of Severin; this was demolished in 1701. In 1848 Lugoj played an important part in the nationalist movement in the Banat; in an area near the town, later called the "Field of Liberty", a number of popular demonstrations were held, including one at which over 10,000 peasants and townspeople were present.

Today Lugoj possesses a number of industries, including a silk spinning mill and a factory producing building materials. Here the famous singer Trajan Grozavescu was born and is buried. The town has a population of 33,400.

Among the buildings of interest are the *Franciscan Church* (18th century) and the *Greek-Catholic Church* (18th century).

D.N. 6 then passes through **Jupa**, which occupies the site of the Dacian settlement of Tibisis (after the name given to the River Timiş in ancient times). The long history of human settlement here is attested by the objects from the Bronze Age discovered on the site. In the Roman period a *castrum* was built nearby *(Tibiscum)*.

Caransebeş (103 km – 64 miles; altitude 690 feet) is the chief town of the district, a small industrial centre (mainly woodworking), and a junction point for road and rail communications.

It is situated at the foot of **Mount Mic** (the "small mountain", 5,925 feet), on the side of which is a plateau (5,052 feet), with facilities for tourists and many ski slopes. Mount Mic is approached by way of the village of *Borlova* (an old-established community going back to the Dacians). There is a road to the *Voinii Fountain* (4,012 feet), some 20 km (12 miles) from Caransebeş.

From Caransebeş D.N. 58 runs south-west to **Reşiţa** (41 km — 25 miles), an old Rumanian metalworking centre which has been much enlarged and modernised in recent years, and to *Văliug* (63 km — 39 miles — from Caransebeş), the starting point for the tourist centres of Crivaia (1,968 feet) and Semenic (4,626 feet). From Văliug there is a chair-lift to the resort of *Semenic* on the plateau.

There is a road from Reşiţa to *Anina*, 35 km (22 miles) to the south, a mining centre (iron and coal, worked since 1790). From here there is a road to *Bozovici*, 30 km (19 miles) to the south-east, in a beautiful valley.

25 km (16 miles) south west of Anina is *Oraviţa*, an ancient and important centre of Rumanian culture on the edge of the Banat. Gold, silver and iron mines worked by the Romans. Many excursions in the neighbourhood (to the south, the climatic resort of *Sasca Montană* and the vine-growing centre of *Moldova Nouă*, near the Danube; on the river itself is *Moldova Veche*, a river port on the site of the Roman *Mudava*).

An Excursion in Roman Dacia

From Caransebeş D.N. 68 crosses the mountains by the pass known as the "Poarta de Fier a Transilvaniei" (the Iron Gate of Transylvania, 2,293 feet), passes through the Haţeg depression, and runs into the Mureş valley. The asphalt ribbon of the modern road follows the line of the ancient road used by the Roman armies setting out to conquer the kingdom of Decebal. It was at the Iron Gate pass that the Dacians lay in wait for the Romans and fought the famous battle of Tapae. In spite of their heroic valour, however, Decebal's forces were defeated, and the way was open for the Roman advance to the Dacian capital in the mountains of Orăştie and the gold mines in the Apuseni Mountains.

The road now offers a pleasant run through the beautiful scenery of this "bridge" between the Southern and Western Carpathians, with many places of interest to be seen on the way, particularly the ruins of the capital of Roman Dacia, Sarmizegethusa.

After passing through *Oţelul Roşu* (18 km—11 miles), a metalworking centre, the road passes on the left a side road leading to the marble quarries of *Ruschiţa* (20 km—17 miles); then, after Zeicani (48 km—30 miles), where there is a monument commemorating the brilliant victory won in 1442 by Iancu of Hunedoara and his 15,000 men over a Turkish army of 80,000, it passes through the village (54 km—34 miles) which bears the name of the ancient capital of Dacia, **Sarmizegethusa.**

In fact the Dacian capital was not here, but farther east in the Orăştie Mountains (p. 116). The Romans, however, preferred the open plain in the Haţeg depression, where they founded, in the year 110, a town which was at first called *Colonia Ulpia Traiana.* Later they added the name of Decebal's capital, so that the new town became *Colonia Ulpia Traiana Augusta Dacia Sarmizegethusa.* In ordinary usage, however, this was abbreviated to "Colonia Sarmizegethusa". In the 2nd century the town was promoted to the rank of "metropolis" and was granted the privilege of *ius italicum,* exempting its inhabitants from the Roman land tax.

The centre of the **ancient town** (part of which, though not the most important part, has been excavated by the archaeologists) contained a citadel some 2,000 feet long by 1,750 feet wide, surrounded by many houses and an amphitheatre seating between 4,000 and 5,000 spectators. The visitor should see the *Local Museum* (inscriptions, statues, vases and other archaeological material from the Roman city); the *ancient city* with its main square or forum, the *Palace of the Augustales* (the most important college of priests in the town), part of the city wall, etc.; and the *amphitheatre,* an ellipse-shaped structure of stone and brick used for gladiatorial contests and theatrical performances.

10 km (6 miles) beyond Sarmizegethusa a country road branches off on the left to the village of **Densuş** (6 km—4 miles), where there is an *old church* built with material from the ruins

of Roman buildings; it was enlarged and partly rebuilt in the
13th century.

16 km (10 miles) from Sarmizegethusa is *Haţeg* (p. 114).

Beyond Caransebeş Ş.N. 6 runs southward along the
edge of the Cerna-Timiş depression and crosses the
pass known as the Eastern Gate (1,690 feet).

This route follows the line taken by the main body of Roman
troops setting out in conquest of Dacia. On this road the Romans
later built a number of strongly defended *castra*, on sites now
occupied by the villages of *Plugova*, *Mehadia* and *Teregova*.
The Roman road ran down the Timiş valley as far as the large
castrum of *Tibiscum* (now Jupa: see above, p. 101), and then
turned east towards Sarmizegethusa, the capital of Roman
Dacia.

Băile Herculane, one of the foremost health resorts
in Rumania, situated amid the magnificent scenery of
the beautiful Cerna valley, lies 5 km (3 miles) east of
D.N.6 (fork at km 175 – 109 miles – a short distance
south of Mehadia).

The Baths. Known since the Romans built their first *castra* in
Dacia, the therapeutic qualities of its mineral springs (sulphurous and radio-active), its mild—almost Mediterranean—climate,
and the beauty of its situation and surroundings have made
Băile Herculane a health resort of particular importance and
popularity. Its modern bathing establishments use water from 9
springs, at temperatures ranging between 45° and 55 °C. Some
are applied internally, others externally. The rheumatological
section treats chronic affections of the locomotor system such
as chronic rheumatism (arthrosis), arthritis and polyarthritis,
post-traumatic arthritis, osteitis, post-infectious periostitis,
slow-setting fractures, etc.

The neurology section treats—by means of baths—neuralgia,
infectious, traumatic or toxic neuritis and polyneuritis, and post-
traumatic sequelae in the peripheral nervous system. Similarly,
in virtue of the pharmacodynamic action of its mineral waters,
Băile Herculane is recommended for the treatment of a number
of other conditions found associated with those just mentioned:
e.g., affections of the digestive passages and associated glands,
and of the respiratory organs (bronchitis, pharyngitis, laryn-

gitis, chronic sinisutis, etc.), skin conditions, industrial diseases, gynaecological diseases, etc.

The waters of Băile Herculane are, however, contraindicated for people suffering from tubercular rheumatism (Poncet), high blood pressure (over 180 mm of mercury), bronchial asthma, nervous excitability, etc.

History. The existence of hot springs in the Cerna valley is recorded as early as the period of the wars between the Dacians and the Romans. Excavation has, however, brought to light flint implements dating from the Palaeolithic period, human habitations (in the Thieves' Cave) dating from the retreat of the ice, and objects from the Neolithic period, showing that this area was occupied by man from the most remote ages.

During the Roman period the Cerna valley was covered with temples, public baths, monuments of various types, and statues dedicated to Hercules, Aesculapius and Hygeia, giving rise to a settlement known as *Thermae Herculi* or *Ad Aquas Herculi Sacras*. This flourished, developing into a small town frequented by high dignitaries of the Roman province; it was in existence by 105–107 and continued for over 170 years. It was destroyed at the time of the barbarian invasions and disappeared from history; and it was not until the end of the 18th century, after 1789, when the Turks finally evacuated the Banat, that it began to rise from its ruins and achieve the reputation it enjoys today.

Excursions. The *Mount Domogled Nature Reserve*, on the mountain of that name (3,629 feet), which dominates the resort. This reserve—the first to be established in Rumania—covers an area of 2,200 acres and ensures the protection of many rare species from the flora of the Southern Balkan and Mediterranean areas. The fauna is abundant and varied; it includes a great range of butterflies and moths (317 species), a harmless snake which the Romans considered sacred *(Tropinopodus tesenatus)*, and the poisonous horned adder.

There are also easy and pleasant walks to the *Cave of Hercules* and the *Spring of Hygeia;* to the Cave of Vapours on Ciorici Hill (873 feet) and Coronini Hill (715 feet); to the "Seven Springs" and the Ghizela Cross. Motorists can drive up the valley to the Sources of the Cerna, a trip of rather more than 40 km (26 miles) through extremely picturesque scenery all the way.

At **Orşova** (196 km – 123 miles), a port and industrial town situated at the junction of the Cerna and the

Danube (on the site of the Dacian settlement'of Dierna and a Roman *castrum* bearing the samenam e), D.N.6 reaches the banks of the Danube.

The construction of the Iron Gates dam and hydro-electric station has led to the formation of a large lake, on the shores of which the new town of *Orşova* (pop. 11,000) is being built,replacing the old town which now lies under the waters of the lake.

A Dacian settlement, situated at the Tierna or Dierna springs, grew up round the Roman camp which defended the roads in the Danube valley. During the Middle Ages, when the town was also known as Ruşava, Orşova was the scene of frequent fighting, for whoever held it and the neighbouring island of Ada Kaleh (now also covered by the waters of the lake) controlled the Danube defile.

Trip to the Danube defile. Pending the completion of the road which is at present under construction, this trip is done by boat from Orşova or Drobeta-Turnu Severin. There are regular services and special trips between places in the Danube defile and Moldova Veche. 10 km (6 miles) from Orşova, on the Yugoslav side, can be seen a large Roman inscription, the *Tabula Traiana*, commemorating the construction of the road which the Romans hewed from the rock on the right bank of the Danube between the first and second Dacian wars. Other fortifications are to be seen on both banks, bearing witness to the region's troubled past. The road from Orşova skirts the lake for 12 km (7 ½ miles), offering splendid views.

The **island of Ada Kaleh** (Turkish, "island citadel") is now under the lake. Formerly known as Erythia, Ruşava and Continusa, it was fortified in the 15th century, in the time of Iancu of Hunedoara, Voivode of Transylvania, and remained a fortress until 1885, when it was declared an undefended garrison point. The last citadel (built from 1717 onwards on the initiative of Prince Eugene of Savoy, commander of the Austrian army) and the mosque have been partly rebuilt on the island of Simion, below Drobeta-Turnu Severin.

At the village of **Gura Văii** (213 km - 133 miles) is the Iron Gates dam, built jointly by Rumania and Yugoslavia between 1965 and 1971. This raised the level of the Danube by 110 feet and created a lake 95 miles long. At each end of the dam are a hydro-electric power station and a lock. A road runs across the Danube on top of the dam.

Drobeta-Turnu Severin (221 km—138 miles; 346 km – 216 miles from Bucharest; altitude 130 feet; 59,000 inhabitants). An important Danube port, Drobeta-Turnu Severin is also the principal town in western Oltenia. The "city of roses", as it is called, has developed considerably in the last ten years, becoming an industrial centre with a large engineering factory, a timber works, foodstuffs factories, etc. The beauty of its parks, its attractive appearance and its historical remains make it also a popular tourist centre.

History of the town. The town itself is relatively young, having been founded in the early part of the 19th century (in 1833). Its origin, however, goes back well before the Christian era, for it is mentioned by Ptolemy under the name of *Drobeta* or *Drubeta*. After the early wars between the Dacians and the Romans the latter built (between 103 and 105) a bridge over the Danube and established a strongly fortified *castrum* on the ruins of the old Dacian settlement. The town built beside the *castrum* flourished, becoming first a *municipium* and then a colony. Although several times destroyed during the great migrations, the ancient town survived and at the beginning of the feudal period became the centre of a small principality, the Banat of Severin. New buildings were erected, including a citadel mentioned in documents of the 13th century which was destroyed by the Turks in the 16th century and abandoned by its inhabitants.

Things to see: the *ruins* of the **Roman bridge,** built in the reign of the Emperor Trajan by Apollodorus of Damascus; the *ruins* of the **Roman castrum of Drubeta,** a large military camp established to guard the bridge used by the principal roads connecting Dacia with the Roman Empire; the *ruins* of the *Roman baths* and *palaestra;* the *ruins* of the *mediaeval church* (Romanesque, 13th century) and of the *citadel of Severin* (13th century); the **Museum of the Iron Gates,** with a large historical section containing, among other things, a model of the Roman bridge; the *Rose Park*, etc.

Tourist Office: 64, Str. Traian (tel. 103).

To Craiova and Bucharest: see p. 121.

5.   ARAD-DEVA-SEBEŞ
(The Mureş Valley)

From Nădlac (Hungarion frontier) *to Arad:* 25 miles of a monotonous road across the plain.

From Timişoara to Arad (52 km—33 miles). From Timişoara D.N. 69 runs north to Arad. From Arad roads lead to Oradea (D.N. 79; 164 km—103 miles) and to Bucharest (D.N. 7; 545 km—341 miles).

A. ARAD

Arad (altitude 360 feet; 141,000 inhabitants). Situated in the lower Mureş valley, Arad is one of the large industrial centres of Rumania (machinery, metalworking, textiles, chemicals, foodstuffs) and an important cultural centre (State Theatre, Philharmonic Orchestra, many schools, art institutes and technical schools).

History of the town. On the site of the town, which is built on an alluvial plain, remains from the Neolithic period have been discovered (in the Aradul Nou and Micălaca districts). On the banks of the Mureş, at Aradul Nou, the Romans built a small fortress to protect the western frontier of Dacia; like the fortresses at Bulci and Cenad, this was an outpost of the large *castrum* of Micia, near Deva. The existence of the mediaeval town is established from the 11th century; and it is mentioned in documents of the 12th century, when it became the centre of a small feudal state.

In 1552 the development of the town was interrupted by the arrival of the Turks, who with brief intervals (as in 1600, when Arad was liberated by Michael the Brave) occupied it until the 18th century. Between 1762 and 1783 a fortress was built here in the style of Vauban.

Things to See

The *Palace of Culture* is a 19th-century building with façades in different styles. The **Local Museum** contains a section on ancient history, an art gallery, and a section devoted to the revolution of 1848–49.

The *Serbian Orthodox Cathedral*, in the Baroque style, was built in 1698; the *Ion Slavici Middle School* was built in 1873; in the *Piața Mihai Viteazul* (the Square of Michael the Brave) is the municipal market.

In **Piața Plevna** is a post with a huge padlock attached to it, in which, according to tradition, every blacksmith's apprentice had to drive a nail when he was accepted as a master craftsman.

The *Town Park* is a magnificent stretch of greenery extending as far as the Mureș. The *Ceala Forest* and the *Island in the Mureș* are recreation areas (swimming pool, beach) some 4 miles from the town.

Tourist Office: 72, Str. Republicii (tel. 30.04).

B. FROM ARAD TO DEVA

On leaving Arad D.N.7 turns eastward up the gently sloping valley of the Mureș. At *Păuliș*, where there was fierce fighting in September 1944 with the Germans who were trying to penetrate in force into central Transylvania, the road enters the Arad wine-growing area.

Lipova (27 km—17 miles; altitude 450 feet), the chief town of the district, has developed from the fusion of three older settlements—Radna and Soimoș on the right bank of the Mureș, and Lipova on the left bank.

The town is mentioned in documents of the 13th century. In the Middle Ages it was the centre of a feudal domain which was several times attacked by rebellious peasants. In the 16th century mineral springs were discovered on the left bank of the Mureș, and these have been used since the beginning of this century by a local health resort.

Things to see: the *Local Museum*, a historical museum containing remains from the Roman period discovered in the town; the *Orthodox Church*, a 14th century building (converted into a mosque during the Turkish occupation, 1552–1718) which still preserves a few old frescoes and contains a small museum, recently established; the *Franciscan Monastery of Radna* (16th century); the *ruins of the citadel of Soimoş*, built in the 13th century and enlarged in the 15th by Iancu of Hunedoara.

Beyond Lipova D.N.7 enters the Mureş defile, which runs between the Zărand Mountains and the Metalliferous Mountains (outliers of the Western Carpathians) in the north and the mountains of Poiana Ruscăi to the south. In the narrowest part of the defile, at km 86 (54 miles), is the small village of *Săvîrşin*, with a 15th century castle. To the west of Săvîrşin is a nature reserve designed for the protection of the game which is so abundant in this large forest-covered area.

Beyond *Zam*, formerly a halting place for the rafts on which salt was transported along the Mureş, the valley begins to grow wider. At *Gurasada* (km 124— 78 miles), which is mentioned in a document of 1292 under the name of Zad, are a plantation of bamboos and a curious church built about the year 1300.

Beyond Ilia D.N.7 crosses to the southern bank of the Mureş, passes through Mintia (km 147—92 miles) and then reaches a flat terrace on which the ruins of the Roman *castrum* of *Micia* have been excavated.

This was the strongest Roman fortress in the lower Mureş valley. Round it a sizeable town grew up, as is shown by the remains of temples, baths and other public buildings discovered here.

C. DEVA

Deva (154 km—96 miles; altitude 590 feet; 44,000 inhabitants). Shortly after being joined on the left by D.N.76 from Oradea (189 km—118 miles) by way of Brad, Vaşcău and Beiuş, the road enters Deva, the chief town of the Hunedoara region. Picturesquely situated on the banks of the Mureş, the town is dominated by the Citadel Hill (1,217 feet), in the shape of a truncated cone. Deva, which has developed considerably in the past ten years, is an administrative, economic and cultural centre. There are a number of foodstuff factories; nearby are copper and andesite mines.

History of the town. Remains of the original settlement have been found both within the area of Deva and on the Citadel Hill. This outlier of the mountains on the banks of the Mureş, dominating the whole valley, was fortified both by the Dacians and the Romans. In the 13th century a citadel was built on top of the hill; it was enlarged in the 18th century and in the 19th, having lost all military significance, was sold to the highest bidder. In the 13th century, too, Deva gradually extended round the foot of the hill, and in the 14th century became the centre of a Wallachian military district; later it came into the hands of Iancu of Hunedoara.

In 1784 the citadel was attacked by peasants who had risen under the leadership of Horia, Cloşca and Crişan; and here, under the walls of the citadel, the rebels met with their first defeat. Between 1933 and 1944 Deva was the headquarters of the Farm Workers' Front under the chairmanship of Petru Groza.

Things to See

The *Town Park* (at the foot of the Citadel Hill), at the entrance to which is a statue of Decebal, last king of Dacia.

The **Regional Museum** is housed in the "Magna Curia", a fine building dating from 1621.

It contains a valuable archaeological collection consisting almost entirely of material from the Dacian and Roman cities of which there are so many in the Hunedoara region. There is also an interesting section on present-day developments in the region.

The main sight of Deva, however, is its **Citadel.** From the ramparts there is a magnificent view over the Mureş valley and the surrounding mountains. There are a number of paths (signposted) leading from the centre of the town, near the museum, to the summit of the hill, ringed with its triple circuit of ramparts. The luxuriant vegetation (with over 1300 species of plants) adds to the attractiveness of the climb.

Tourist Office: 1, Piaţa Unirii (tel. 20.26).

Excursion to Hunedoara (20 km — 13 miles — from Deva; 78,000 inhabitants). Beyond Deva D.N. 7 passes through the village of *Sîntuhalu,* from which a road branches off on the right to the town of Hunedoara, the main centre of the Rumanian steel industry. The town has developed considerably under the popular democratic regime. In addition to the steel works, much enlarged and modernised, a number of other industries have developed: chemicals (distillation of tars and desulphurisation of coke gas), building materials, foodstuffs. A new residential district (houses, shops, schools, sports facilities) has been built at the foot of Chizid Hill, facing the industrial area.

Hunedoara is a very ancient city. It is mentioned in documents of the 13th century; in the 14th century it became the centre of the fief granted by King Sigismund of Hungary to Voicu as a reward for his military achievements, and then belonged to his son Iancu of Hunedoara. Formerly renowned for the skill of its tanners, furriers and skinners, Hunedoara became in the second half of the 19th century an industrial centre equipped with blast furnaces for the smelting of iron ore from the mines of Ghelar and Teliuc, which were already being worked in the Roman period (2nd–3rd centuries). Today two of the new open-hearth furnaces alone produce 20 times as much steel as was produced by the whole of the works in 1938.

Hunedoara Castle is a most interesting and striking building. The first fortress was built in the 14th century. In the 15th and

16th centuries the descendants of the Rumanian *knez* Voicu, Iancu of Hunedoara and Matei Corvin (Matthias Corvinus), gradually transformed the fortress into a castle; and an additional wing was built on in the 17th century. The castle was partly destroyed by a fire in 1854, but restoration work begun in 1956 has reproduced its original appearance. As it stands today it offers a remarkable synthesis of the different architectural styles which have succeeded one another throughout the centuries, and is thus of great interest in the history of feudal art in Rumania.

D. SIMERIA

218 km—136 miles; altitude 656 feet. D.N.7, continuing up the Mureş valley, passes through **Simeria,** a small industrial centre and railway junction.

To the north of the town, on the banks of the Mureş, is an *arboretum* of 200 acres, established 250 years ago, when large numbers of trees and shrubs from different parts of the world were planted in the wooded country along the river. The mild damp climate which prevails here has made it possible to acclimatise species which grow nowhere else in Rumania. Today the arboretum contains some 500 species of trees and shrubs, mostly exotic (from China, Japan, North America), including in particular 9 species of magnolia, various species of bamboo, rare conifers from the Far East, eucalyptuses, etc. A series of new glasshouses has recently been installed. The park also contains a small zoo and an experimental station of the Institute of Silvicultural Research.

To Haţeg (the Streiu valley). D.N. 66 turns south from Simeria and runs up the Streiu valley, a depression with many old villages scattered here and there. Some remains from the Roman period can also be seen, for the main road to the heart of the province passed this way.

Călau, a steel-working town and health resort, is the most considerable place in the Streiu valley. Its hot springs, for external application only, are recommended for the treatment of affections of the locomotor system, gynaecological and rheumatic conditions, debility and anaemia. In the park is a basin hewn from the solid rock containing a hot spring. This was already in use in Roman times, and there was a Roman settlement here.

In the commune of *Strei* is a church built about the year 1300, with 15th century frescoes in an eclectic style (a mingling of Byzantine and Western).

Hațeg (31 km—19 miles) is the chief town of the district which includes the depression of the same name, and is mentioned in documents of the 14th century. 4 km (2½ miles) from Hațeg, in the Silvaș Forest, is a reserve containing colonies of aurochs and deer.

The National Park of the Retezat Mountains. South of Hațeg, D.N. 66 comes in 4 km (2½ miles) to the village of *Sîntămăria Orlea*. Here there is a church built at the end of the 13th century by the Rumanian *knezes* of the district, decorated with wall paintings which are the oldest surviving examples in Transylvania. The architecture of the church is an adaptation to the traditional local style of the Romanesque style which had just reached Transylvania.

From Sîntamăria Orlea a path runs up the valley of Rîul Mare (the "large stream") to the village of Rîu de Mori (16 km—10 miles) and then climbs up to the huts of Gura Zlata (36 km—23 miles; 2,543 feet) and Gura Apei (45 km—28 miles; 3,274 feet), on the edge of the Retezat National Park.

The *Retezat Mountains*, a range over 6,000 feet high with their highest point in Peleaga (8,232 feet), have the characteristic pattern of relief produced by ice action, with large numbers of Alpine lakes (over 80), deeply carved valleys and considerable areas of fallen boulders and scree.

In view of the many species of plants and animals found in these mountains (some of them designated as "natural monuments") and the striking glaciated features they display, the area has been made a nature reserve—the National Park of the Retezat Mountains—covering some 40 square miles. In order to protect certain rare animals (chamois and various species of eagles) and local species of plants, a special scientific reserve has been designated, to which admission is prohibited except with a permit issued by the Commission on Natural Monuments. The rest of the National Park is freely open to tourists. It contains many signposted paths and five tourist huts.

From the *Gura Apei* hut (which can be reached by car) it is 3 to 4 hours' walk to Lake Bucura (6,690 feet), the largest in the Carpathians (125, 000 square yards,) in the centre of the mountains, at the top of the valley of the same name, which was occupied during the glaciation of the Quaternary period by a glacier some 6 miles long. Three hours' walking farther on is the *Pietrele* hut (4,860 feet), approached through a valley lined by tall conifers of a type going back to the Ice Age *(Pinus cembra)*, now scheduled as "natural monuments".

After Haţeg D.N. 66 enters Oltenia (Tîrgu Jiu, p. 123), passing through the Carpathians by way of the *Petroşeni basin*. Magnificent scenery, with caves and picturesque limestone formations produced by weathering. The Petroşeni coalfield is in active operation. In this area are the industrial centres of Vulcan, Lupeni and Livezeni. D.N. 66 descends the Oltenian slope of the mountains through a beautiful defile between Mount Parîng (8,262 feet) to the east and Mount Straja (6,138 feet) to the west, in which heavy fighting took place in 1916.

E. ORĂŞTIE: THE DACIAN CITADELS

Beyond Simeria D.N.7 passes near the village of *Turdaş*, a well known archaeological site.

Near the village, on the banks of the Mureş, three ancient cultures have been found superimposed on one another. The earliest of these dates from the Middle Neolithic (3500–2600 B.C.) and is characterised by an abundance of pottery decorated with bands of incised ornament and sometimes with painting. The stratum discovered at Turdaş has given its name to the culture of this period (the Turdaş Culture).

Farther on the road passes through the town of **Orăştie,** the chief town of the district. Known since the 12th century, it is now a small centre of the timber industry.

The Dacian citadels. From Orăştie a country road runs south into the Orăştie Mountains, the last outliers of the Surian Mountains which form part of the Parîng range (8,262 feet).

The road ends at *Costeşti* (18 km—11 miles), where a citadel has been discovered, one of the complex of fortresses and settlements forming the nucleus of the Dacian state (which reached the peak of its prosperity between the 2nd century B.C. and the first century A.D.).

A forest railway makes it possible to go on to *Grădiştea Muncelului* (31 km—19 miles). The additional distance is well worth while, for it was in this area, 3 miles from Grădiştea Muncelului, that the ruins of the **royal Dacian city of Sarmizegethusa** were discovered. Situated at a height of 4,000 feet, the citadel contained a large number of military, religious and civil buildings erected on a series of terraces. In the centre was a large fortress (nearly 7½ acres) enclosed in stone ramparts of a style peculiar to the Dacians *(opus dacicum)*. On the neighbouring terraces were discovered blacksmiths', joiners' and potters' workshops, a water storage tank and a number of sanctuaries (four rectangular in shape and two circular).

Round the Grădiştea citadel were a number of others—*Vîrful lui Hulpe*, *Luncani* and *Piatra Roşie*. These, along with two others situated at a lower level—*Blidaru* and *Costeşti*—make up a unique archaeological ensemble and bear witness to the high technical and artistic level achieved by the Dacians in the final stages of their development.

Investigations are continuing in the mountainous region south of Orăştie, where Dacian sites both military and civil are scattered over an area of some 60 square miles, and in other places where the archaeologists have discovered the remains of ancient Dacian cities. We may thus hope to increase our knowledge of the civilisation of this people, who so heroically resisted the Roman conquest of their country.

F. TO SEBEŞ

5 km (3 miles) from Orăştie a country road branches off D.N.7 on the left to the health resort of **Geoagiu** (10 km—6 miles; altitude 1,150–1,300 feet).

The road passes through the commune of Geoagiu, on the right bank of the Mureş. Here in ancient times was *Germisara* (which means in Geto-Dacian "hot spring"), mentioned by Pliny as a large Dacian city. The Romans, who had built a *castrum* close to Germisara, used the hot springs a little higher up the Geoagiu valley, and founded a village which they called *Thermae Didonae*.

A number of inscriptions and small basins dating from Roman times can still be seen. The 7 hot springs (29–31 °C.) supply the Baths, and 3 others feed the fountain basins in the small squares which make Geoagiu Băi such an attractive place for those who want to spend a restful holiday in pleasant surroundings. The mineral waters (bicarbonated, calcium-magnesium) are recommended for internal use in the treatment of affections of the alimentary canal (chronic gastritis), chronic liver conditions, and diseases of the bile ducts and urinary passages. Applied externally, they give good results in the treatment of affections of the locomotor system and peripheral nervous system.

Thanks to the forests which surround it, the resort enjoys a very pleasant climate.

Beyond the road to Geoagiu D.N.7 passes through the only plain of any size in this mountainous region. This plain is the granary of the surrounding areas and has therefore been given the name of the *"Plain of Bread"*.

A great battle was fought here in 1479, when the forces of the Voivode of Transylvania (one of whose lieutenants was the valiant Count of Timişoara, Pavel Chinezul) inflicted a heavy defeat on a Turkish army greatly superior in numbers. In the middle of the "Plain of Bread" is the commune of *Aurel Vlaicu* (formerly Binţinţi), so called because it was the birthplace of Aurel Vlaicu, one of the pioneers of flying at the beginning of this century. There is a museum in the house in which he was born.

Still running along the Mureş valley, D.N.7 passes near the commune of *Tărtăria*, an important archaeological site on which remains of several successive cultures have been discovered, ranging from the Neolithic to the 10th century.

In the stratum belonging to a culture of Turdaş type (2600 B.C.) the excavators found 26 terracotta idols and three terracotta tablets on which a series of signs had been inscribed with a pointed instrument in a number of separate panels. The tablets have certain analogies with the tablets inscribed with ideograms found in the Indus Valley, in Pakistan. They represent the oldest form of writing so far discovered on Rumanian territory.

In the outskirts of the town of Sebeş D.N.7 joins up with D.N.1 coming from the north, by way of Cluj (110 km—69 miles), and the two roads follow the same line as far as Sibiu (see p. 169). Thereafter they separate again, D.N.1 reaching Bucharest by way of Braşov and the Predeal pass (3,389 feet), while D.N.7 follows the Olt defile through the mountains and reaches Bucharest by way of Rîmnicu Vîlcea and Piteşti (p. 137).

(Sebeş-Braşov-Bucharest 370 km—231 miles; Sebeş-Rîmnicu Vîlcea–Piteşti-Bucharest 328 km—205 miles).

To Alba Iulia and Cluj: see p. 185.

6. FROM DROBETA-TURNU SEVERIN TO BUCHAREST

After Drobeta-Turnu Severin (p. 107) D.N.6 enters the rich plain of Oltenia. 40 km (25 miles) from Drobeta-Turnu Severin is the town of **Strehaia,** the centre of a district specialising in vine and fruit growing.

It contains a church surrounded by walls, which has the unusual feature of having the sanctuary to the south-east rather than to the east as is the normal practice. The legend has it that the church was founded when Michael the Brave spent the night here between two battles, and that in his haste the founder gave it the wrong orientation. In reality, however, the church is much earlier (about the year 1500); it was altered by Matei Basarab in 1645. The reason for its incorrect orientation is that the surrounding walls took in a residence of the Bans of Oltenia, to which the church was connected by a corridor.

P. S. Năsturel interprets the evidence of the buildings as indicating the existence of an earlier fortified establishment belonging to boyars or more probably to the Bans (governors) of Oltenia, or perhaps to the Voivodes. This earlier building, dating perhaps from the 15th century, was converted about 1645 into a monastery in order to avoid the destruction of the fortress ordered by the Turks (just as the Moldavian fortress of Neamţ was transformed into a monastery at the same period). Only archaeological investigation can put the matter beyond doubt.

D.N.6 now runs down the Motru valley. At the junction of the Motru and the Jiu (2 miles to the right of the road) can be seen the **fortified monastery of Gura Motrului.**

The monastery was built about 1500 by an ancestor of the Brîncoveanu family of boyars, rebuilt about the middle of the 17th century by Preda Brîncoveanu, and decorated with painting in 1705 by Voivode Constantin Brîncoveanu. It was occupied for a short time by Tudor Vladimirescu, leader of the 1821 rising. Later it became a cultural centre. To Gura Motrului retired Eufrosin Poteca (one of Gheorghe Lazăr's disciples), formerly professor of philosophy at St Sava's School in Bucharest, the first institution of higher education in the country at which teaching was given in Rumanian.

The monastery is situated at the foot of the hills which stand above the right bank of the Motru at its junction with the Jiu. Its principal architectural feature is a church in trilobate form with three towers, standing in the middle of a rectangular courtyard protected by high walls, at the entrance to which is a massive two-storied belfry.

Various alterations were carried out in the 19th century: the walls and towers of the church were raised, the original saw-tooth cornices were removed, the external surfaces were covered with a thick coat of plaster, and the belfry heightened and deprived of its cornice. In addition the buildings suffered from a series of earthquakes and from neglect, so that by 1960 they were in very poor condition, with many large cracks in the walls.

Restoration work has been directed to restoring the features of the original buildings which were altered or destroyed during the 19th century. The walls and towers of the church have been brought down to their original height by the removal of the additions, the original saw-tooth cornices have been restored, and the plaster covering the original outside walls has been removed. The external painting—which was badly damaged during the preparation of the walls for the plaster coating applied in the 19th century—had to be completely repainted, apart from two panels which were left untouched as examples of the original work. The necessary work of consolidation has also been carried out: the cracks in the walls have been repaired, a girdle of reinforced concrete has been put round the church and the towers, the upper surface of the vaulting has been concreted, metal cramps have been fitted at the springing of the interior arches, and the belfry has been restored to its original form and strengthened.

Filiaşi (76 km—48 miles). At Filiaşi, a small timber-working centre and railway junction, D.N.6 is joined on the left by D.N.66, which runs up the Jiu valley to Tîrgu Jiu, passes through the mountains at the picturesque Jiu defile, and comes to the Petroşeni coalfield (see p. 116).

This road serves **Tîrgu Jiu** (67 km — 42 miles — from Filiaşi), which has become within the last ten years a rapidly developing industrial centre (timber, building materials, light industry, etc.).

This settlement on the banks of the Jiu has a long history. The Romans established a posting station at the point where the river emerges from the mountains. The existence of a small town here is mentioned for the first time in documents of the beginning of the 15th century. Later Tîrgu Jiu became the chief town of a district which was at first called Jales, and later Gorj. The town — until the 19th century the property of boyars — was frequently ravaged by war and pillage.

Things to see: the *Local Museum; works by Constantin Brâncuşi.* The great Rumanian sculptor was born in the village of Hobiţa, in the commune of Peştişani, 22 km (14 miles) west of Tîrgu Jiu. There is a fine display of his works in a park on the banks of the Jiu. This is conceived as a monument to the heroes of Rumania: of the seven pieces originally planned, however, only six were completed, five of them by Brâncuşi himself. These are the *Family Table,* also known as the "Table of Silence"; the *Avenue of Seats;* the *Gateway of the Kiss,* also called the "Gateway of Heroes"; the *Endless Column,* or *"Heroes' Monument";* and the *Feast.*

Tourist Office: 26, Calea Victoriei (tel. 13-45); 6 St. Eroilor.

35 km (22 miles) west of Tîrgu Jiu is the **Tismana Monastery,** in a very beautiful setting. Founded in the 14th century, it dates in its present form from the middle of the 16th. It was a meeting place of the rebels of the 1821 rising led by Tudor Vladimirescu.

Between Filiaşi and Craiova D.N.6 runs for 35 km (22 miles) along the valley of the Jiu. A road ran along this valley, protected by the *castrum* of Răcari, in Roman times; but the area was inhabited at a still earlier period, as is shown by the remains of settlements belonging to the transitional period before the Bronze Age (1900–1700 B.C.) and by the pottery with incised decoration characteristic of this culture—called the *Coţofeni Culture* after the village where the remains were discovered.

CRAIOVA

Craiova (altitude 440 feet), chief town of the region of Oltenia, is an important industrial and cultural centre which has developed considerably during the last 20 years, with the building of large new engineering works (the "Electroputere" and "7 Noiembrie" factories) and foodstuffs plants (the "Oltenia" vegetable oil and sugar plant). In addition the town contains textile mills, timber works, a large chemical plant and an electric power station. The main cultural institutions of Craiova are a National Theatre over a century old, a puppet theatre, a Philharmonic Orchestra, a university, an agricultural college and a teachers' training institute. The appearance of the town has changed considerably in recent years, with the construction of large new housing areas and many office buildings. The population is almost 175,000.

History of the town. The history of Craiova goes back a long way. Remains of the Neolithic period and of the Iron Age (a Thraco-Dacian tomb of the 4th century B.C. and a hoard of valuables) have been discovered in the town. The Romans built a *castrum* here—*Pelendava*—on the line of a mighty earthwork which ran across Oltenia from west to east ("Trajan's Rampart" or "Novac's Furrow"). The remains of this rampart are still visible in the neighbourhood of the town.

The settlement which existed here in feudal times is not recorded until the 15th century, when the Bans (governors) of Oltenia transferred their residence from Strehaia to Craiova. Later Craiova became a trading centre of steadily increasing importance.

Things to See

The **Art Museum** contains some fine works.

The Gallery of Foreign Art has works of the Flemish, Dutch and Italian schools (16th and 17th centuries), works of the French school (18th and 19th centuries), furniture, pottery and tapestries. The Gallery of Rumanian Art contains 5 works by the great sculptor *Constantin Brâncuşi*, 19 paintings by *Nicolae Grigorescu*, 9 by *Ştefan Luchian*, and a large number of works by the painter *Theodor Aman*, who was born in the town.

The *Historical Museum of Oltenia* contains an excellent historical section.

See also the *Museum of the Trial of the Railwaymen and Oil Workers* (June–July 1934); the **Bans' House**, the residence of the Bans of Oltenia, in the old Rumanian style to which Constantin Brîncoveanu gave a new lease of life at the end of the 17th century; the *Church of St Dumitru*, erected in the 17th century by Matei Basarab on the site of an older church and restored at the end of the 19th century by the French architect Lecomte du Nouy (the last building in the Byzantine style erected in Rumania); and the *People's Park*, formerly belonging to Prince Bibesco, with a beautiful lake and a small zoo.

In **Bucovăţ Church** (4 km – 2½ miles – west of the town), of uncertain date (15th century?), is a painting on the wall of the naos illustrating the chronicles of Wallachia.

Tourist Office: 9, Str. Ioan Cuza (tel. 1.51.46).

88 km (55 miles) south-west of Craiova, on D.N. 56, is *Calafat*, a small port on the Danube, founded in the 14th century opposite the Bulgarian port of Vidin. There is a striking contrast between the two banks, the Bulgarian bank being high, the Rumanian one low and marshy. The same difference is found at *Bechetu*, 67 km (42 miles) south of Craiova by D.N. 55, at *Corabia*, farther to the east, and at *Turnu Măgurele*, a former Roman *castrum* (grain trade, chemical plant producing fertilisers).

CRAIOVA

1 Hanul Hurez (17th century)
2 Bans' House (Casa Băniei)
3 Madona Dudu
4 Church of the Trinity
5 Maiorescu Monument
6 Vladimirescu Monument
7 Ion Cuza Monument
8 National Theatre
9 Dumba House (18th century)
10 Regional Art Museum
11 Museum of Oltenia
12 Museum of the Oil Workers' Trial (1934)
13 Traian Demetrescu Museum
14 Hotel Minerva
15 Hotel Palace
16 Tourist Office

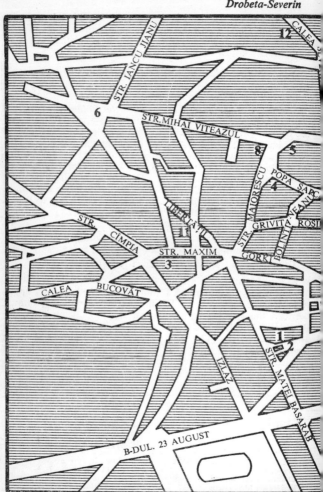

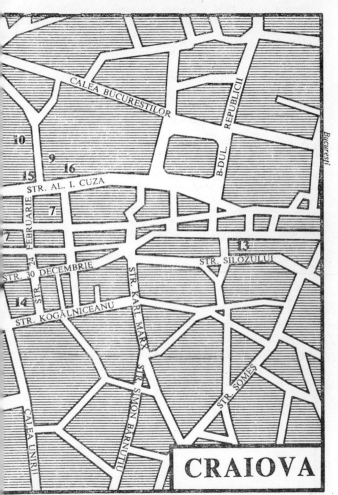

Calafat

From Craiova D.N. 6 reaches Bucharest by way of Caracal, Roşiorii de Vede and Alexandria (total distance 227 km — 142 miles). There is, however, a better and much more interesting route by way of Piteşti. This is the route described here, following D.N. 65 to Piteşti and then D.N. 7.

East of Craiova D.N.65 runs across the rich plain of Oltenia, passing through *Balş, Piatra Olt* and **Slatina.** This last place, 51 km (32 miles) from Craiova, is just after the crossing of the Olt.

Now an industrial centre with a recently built aluminium plant, Slatina is an old-established settlement which grew up near a ford on the Olt. Its existence is recorded for the first time in the 14th century. In the *Local Museum* are displayed tools of the "prund" culture (ordinary river pebbles shaped at one end) dating from the first period of the age of chipped stone (Lower Palaeolithic, 600,000 to 150,000 years before our era). These tools of the "monkey men", rarely found in Europe, were discovered in the Dîrjov Valley to the south of Slatina.

D.N.65 now crosses the Getic Plateau to Piteşti, passing through fields of arable land and orchards.

To the north is *Drăgăşani,* celebrated for its wines (p. 138).

Piteşti (122 km—78 miles—from Craiova). See description, p. 130.

From Piteşti to Bucharest, see below, p. 129 (in the reverse direction).

7. FROM BUCHAREST TO PITEȘTI AND SIBIU

This itinerary takes in a whole series of major tourist attractions, including scenery of extreme picturesqueness, a number of health resorts, and historical monuments of great interest. There is a motorway from Sibiu to Pitești, but the old road has much to offer the tourist.

A. FROM BUCHAREST TO PITEȘTI
(114 km—71 miles)

Leaving Bucharest (Piața Victoriei), D.N.7 follows the Bulevard 1 Mai, and then the road to Chitila, heading north-west. Beyond Chitila it passes through *Rîioasa Forest*.

This forest of young oak trees is all that remains of the great Vlăsia Forest which centuries ago covered much of the plain between the Subcarpathian hills and the Danube, providing shelter for the bands of heyducks who took refuge there.

10 km (6 miles) farther on, at Tartășești, D.N.71 branches off on the right to **Tîrgoviște** (82 km—51 miles—from Bucharest; 36,000 inhabitants), the former capital of Wallachia (from the 14th to the 17th century), now a centre of the oil industry, with many new buildings.

In 1944 a *Museum* was opened in Tîrgoviște, containing material discovered in the town and objects illustrating the development of society through the centuries. In the town and surrounding area a number of ancient monuments are still to be seen, including a 16th century *watch tower* (the Chindia Tower), near the ruins of the Prince's Palace of the same period; the **Prince's Church** (16th century), in the Byzantine style then in favour in Wallachia, with fine 17th and 18th century frescoes remarkable for their gilding and glowing colours; and the **Dealul Monastery** (1496–1508), which is said to have housed Macarie's printing press at the beginning of the 16th century, and to which Michael the Brave's head was brought back after his murder in Transylvania in 1601. The monastery church is a characteristic 16th century building, notable in particular for the slenderness of its lines compared with buildings in the Byzantine style. Finally there is the *Stelea Church* (17th century), founded by Vasile Lupu, Voivode of Moldavia, marking the appearance in Wallachian architecture of certain Moldavian features.

After passing through a succession of typical plain villages, followed by the small towns of *Titu* (54 km—34 miles) and *Găiești* (73 km—46 miles), D.N.7 enters the Subcarpathian hills and passes through a new oil-producing area opened up within the last few years.

The hills are covered with vineyards and orchards, and there are many villages strung out along the road. One of the largest of these, *Topoloveni*, contains a craft cooperative, "The Woman Worker", making carpets, articles of clothing (skirts, blouses, head veils) and wood carvings in the local tradition of folk art.

A mile or so off the road at km 105 (66 miles) is the former **manor of the Golescus**, a family of nobles with democratic ideas who took part in the 1848 revolution.

The manor, a fine example of old Rumanian architecture, was built in 1640 and enlarged at the end of the 17th century. Since 1958 it has been a museum, with a section on the Golescu family, a section on the rising of 1821 and the revolution of 1848, a section on the early days of nationally organised education in Wallachia, and a section on the ethnography and folk art of the Argeș region, which includes a number of areas famous for the beauty of their traditional costume and their pottery. In the courtyard is a hammam (Turkish bath), and opposite it is a church built in 1646, in which the influence of the Moldavian style can be seen.

Pitești (114 km—71 miles; altitude 1,000–1,150 feet; 84,000 inhabitants), chief town of the Argeș region, is situated in the Argeș valley surrounded by trees. It has developed considerably in the last ten years, becoming an important industrial centre (a large woodworking plant, oil and chemical plants, light industry) and a cultural centre (teachers' training institute, State Theatre, School of Folk Art, Doina Orchestra of the Argeș, etc.).

Within the town excavation has revealed tools and ornaments of the Neolithic period and Dacian and Roman coins. Its existence is first recorded in the 16th century, when it was a small town at the junction of important trade routes, retaining its function as a market town in which the inhabitants of the plain exchanged their products with the people from the mountains.

See the *Historical Museum;* the **Art Museum,** with the first gallery of *Rumanian naive art* (opened 1971); the *Trivale Park*, a natural park with an area of 67 acres; the new Park of Culture and Rest on the banks of the Argeș; the *Prince's Church* (1656); and the *tree nursery* in the Găvana district.

Tourist Office: 2, Str. Plevnei (tel. 14.998).

B. FROM PITEȘTI TO CÎMPULUNG
(51 km—32 miles)
AND BRAȘOV (135 km—84 miles)

From Pitești D.N. 73 runs north-east, passing through the Carpathians at the Bran-Giuvala pass (4,068 feet) en route for Brașov. This route was already in use during the Roman occupation of Dacia, and it was a busy trade route throughout the Middle Ages. It is now popular with tourists on account of the magnificent scenery through which it passes.

Mihăești Park (30 km—19 miles). Running along the foot of the Subcarpathian hills, D.N. 73 skirts a beautiful forest which is in fact an arboretum with an area of 150 acres containing over 120 species of trees, including many exotic species—a huge laboratory attached to the forestry experimental station of Mihăești. Adjoining this is the Cîlceasa Forest, containing a large reserve for roe-deer (30,000 acres).

Beyond Mihăești the road passes through a coal basin (lignite) and then enters a small depression dominated to the north by Mount Mateiaş (4,068 feet) and to the south by Mount Măţău (3,337 feet). In this area is the town of **Cîmpulung,** the first capital of the feudal state of Wallachia and now an industrial centre (metalworks, woodworking, building materials) with a population of 27,000. Altitude 1900 feet.

History of the town. The origins of Cîmpulung go back to a remote past—probably earlier than the period at which the Romans built the *castrum* of Jidava, 4 km (2½ miles) southeast of the town. The feudal town developed in the 14th century, when it become the capital of the independent Voivodate of Wallachia. Even after the capital was transferred to Curtea de Argeş, Cîmpulung remained an important town on the road to Braşov, with guilds of craftsmen and carriers who transported goods as far afield as the ports on the Danube.

Things to see: the **Negru Voda Monastery,** built in 1215, according to tradition, by Voivode Radu Negru, the legendary founder of Wallachia. Reconstructed at the beginning of the 14th century by Basarab the Great and completed by his son Alexandru Basarab, the monastery was twice destroyed by earthquakes (in 1628 and 1819), after which it was restored on the original plan; the *Prince's House*, built by Matei Basarab in 1635; the *Bărăţiei Tower* (the tower of the Catholic church), built in the Gothic style in the 14th century; the *Cross of the Oath* in the town square, on which are inscribed the privileges granted to the citizens by Prince Duca in 1674, and in front of which the dignitaries of the town took the oath after their election; the *Subeşti Church* (16th century); the *Prince's Church* (16th century); and the *Local Museum* (with sections devoted to history, natural history and art).

Excursions in the neighbourhood: to the thermal resort of *Bughea de Sus* (3½ km—2 miles; altitude 1,940 feet); to the ruins of the Roman *castrum* of *Jidava* (4 km—2½ miles), a fortified camp built in the 2nd century, and the nearby *salt mines of Apa Sărată,* worked from Roman times until the 12th century; the limestone quarries of *Albeşti,* 2 miles from Bughea, now a fossil reserve designated as a "natural monument"; to the hut at *Voina-Păpuşa* (18 km—11 miles; altitude 3,120 feet), at the foot of the Iezer-Păpuşa massif (8,075 feet), on which there are many signposted footpaths.

Immediately after Cîmpulung the road passes close to the village of *Nămăeşti*, on the outskirts of which is a church entirely hewn from the sandstone of the mountain (16th century).

Only the tower and a corner of the pronaos are in masonry. Near this unusual hermitage are a number of cells, also hewn from the rock by the hermits. In the village is the house (now a museum) of the poet G. Topîrceanu (1886–1937).

After crossing the crest of Mount Mateiaş, where there was fierce fighting during the first world war (there is a mausoleum for the Rumanian soldiers who fell here), D.N.73 descends into the **Dîmboviţa valley.**

This narrow and thickly wooded valley is dominated by Mounts Leaota (7,002 feet), Roşu (5,069 feet) and Vîrtoapele (4,715 feet). Along the river are scattered the houses of the commune of **Dragoslavele** (most of them in wood, in the style characteristic of the folk art of this area). The handsome traditional costumes of the local people, mainly worn on feast days, are also renowned throughout Rumania. In addition to being a small health resort, Dragoslavele also has a woodworking plant and quarries of building stone.

6 km (4 miles) upstream, at km 74 (46 miles), the road passes through *Rucăr*, a timber working centre and health resort renowned for the beauty of the local traditional costumes and the architecture of its wooden houses.

Above Rucăr the Dîmboviţa passes through a defile so narrow that the road is compelled to climb to the crest of the ridge before descending again into the depression of **Podul Dîmboviţei,** the centre of an area of karstic landscape with scenery of striking beauty.

Flowing southward, the Dîmboviţa and its tributary the Dîmbovicioara have carved their way through a massif of limestone. Paths now run through the gorges cut by the two rivers, so that the visitor has easy access to this wildly beautiful district. In the Dîmboviţa gorges there is a small cave, *Peştera Urşilor*, and immediately beyond the Dîmbovicioara gorges is the Dîmbovicioara Cave. To the south of Podul Dîmboviţei the river is engulfed in the *Ghimbav Gorges*, which are even narrower and more impressive than the others.

Approaching the **Giuvala Pass** (93 km—58 miles; height 4,068 feet), the road climbs in hairpin bends, passing the ruins of a small 13th century *citadel* built to watch over the old trade route, which was farther to the east than the present road. At the top of the pass is the village of *Fundata*, one of the highest permanent settlements in Rumania, with its houses climbing up to over 4,200 feet.

The road runs into Transylvania down a mountainside from which there is a magnificent *view* over the whole of the Bran depression and the mountains which surround it: to the left Piatra Craiului (7,346 feet), to the right the Bucegi Mountains (8,225 feet).

Piatra Craiului is a narrow limestone ridge, some 12 miles long, running in a south-westerly and north-easterly direction. Its east face, overlooking the small town of Bran, falls in a regular slope at an angle which rarely exceeds 60°. The west face, on the other hand, is a steep and irregularly shaped cliff which is a climber's paradise. Its interest for the tourist is increased by a great variety of karst features—arches, swallow-holes, caves, etc. Its abundance of animal life (chamois, Carpathian bear, lynx, etc.) and its rich and varied flora (including a species of pink, *Dianthus callizonus*, which grows nowhere else) has led to the establishment of a nature reserve on the north-east face of Piatra Craiului.

The *Bucegi Mountains* extend as far as the Prahova valley. On this side we see their north-west face, a sheer cliff which has less attraction for tourists, and their highest peak, Mount Omul, with its hut, the highest in Rumania (8,225 feet). (See *Sinaia*, p. 153.)

Bran Castle (107 km—67 miles). Immediately we emerge from the mountains we see the silhouette of Bran Castle, a mediaeval fortification built in 1377 by the city of Braşov to watch over the defile. The castle was built on top of a crag, replacing a small wooden fortress built 150 years earlier. Altitude 2,460 feet.

Many features of the original Gothic construction are still visible. The castle now contains a museum of mediaeval art. In the park is a small open-air museum—peasant houses and equipment, several centuries old, from villages in the surrounding area, the inhabitants of which are renowned for their skill as shepherds.

Bran is a health resort, and the ten villages scattered about the depression have retained their old traditional costumes and characteristic wooden cottages.

Two tourist huts, *Bran Poarta* (2,490 feet) and *Bran Castel* (2,530 feet), are convenient for visitors who want to spend a holiday in this area or to climb the Bucegi range by the sign-posted paths which leave Bran just at the castle. (It is roughly 8 hours' walking to the Omul hut.)

Near Bran Castle, on the left, a country road branches off to *Zărneşti* (7 km—4½ miles), an industrial centre (paper and cellulose factory) and the starting point of the many signposted paths on Piatra Craiului. Three tourist huts (Gura Rîului, 2,460 feet; Plaiu Foii, 2,790 feet; Curmătura, 4,820 feet) provide accommodation for visitors exploring this range.

Reaching the Bîrsa plain, D.N.73 passes through **Rîşnov,** a new industrial centre (tool factory, chemical works) which has achieved the status of a town within the last few years.

On the hill above Rîşnov can be seen the ruins of a *peasant citadel* built in the 15th century and enlarged in the 17th. (It is a quarter of an hour's walk away).

In a cave in the neighbourhood were discovered traces of man in the Palaeolithic period. The ruins of a *castrum—Cumidava—* built by the Romans in the 2nd century were found in the plain on the banks of the Bîrsa.

At Rîşnov D.N. 73A branches off to *Predeal* (3,720 feet), passing through the small health resort of Pîrîul Rece (3,150 feet). There are two huts on this road—the Cheişoara hut (2,625 feet), 7 km (4½ miles) from Rîşnov, and the Pîrîul Rece hut (3,150 feet), 18 km (11 miles) from Rîşnov.

Beyond *Cristian*, a small town with a church surrounded by the walls of a citadel built in the 15th century, D.N.73 comes into the outskirts of **Braşov** where it joins D.N.1 (see p. 161).

C. CURTEA DE ARGEŞ

Leaving Piteşti on the north, D.N. 7 meets a country road which runs up the valley of the Argeş to Curtea de Argeş, 35 km (22 miles) away (altitude 1,480 feet). A health resort situated in a hilly area and a small industrial centre (woodworking, textiles, foodstuffs), Curtea de Argeş is one of the oldest settlements in Rumania.

Recorded as a small town from the end of the 13th century, Curtea de Argeş became in the 14th century the capital of Wallachia and the seat of the Metropolitan of Wallachia, who was recognised in 1359 by the Patriarch of Constantinople.

Things to see: the *ruins of the Prince's residence*, built about 1370 with large river boulders; the ruins of the *Church of Sîn Nicoară*, in the Byzantine style of the end of the 13th or beginning of the 14th century; the **Church of St Nicholas** (14th century), in the Byzantine style, on the plan of Greek churches, with fine 14th century and 17th century frescoes; the **Episcopal Church,** a 14th century building enlarged and decorated at the beginning of the 16th century by the Voivode Neagoe Basarab, and restored at the end of last century by the French architect Lecomte du Nouy. Its special feature is the wealth of ornament on its exterior, consisting of stone sculpture in the Oriental style (considerable fragments of the 16th century wall paintings are now in the Art Museum in Bucharest); and the **Olari Church,** a small but picturesque building on an asymmetric plan (date uncertain). This church receives its name from the fact that it is situated in the district of the "olari" (potters), one of the oldest pottery-producing centres in Rumania, notable in particular for its fireproof pots and its large jars decorated with a dark green glaze and with patterns of plants and animals. Good external frescoes.

Beyond Curtea de Argeş the road continues up the Argeş valley towards the *Gheorghiu-Dej Hydro-electric Station*.

The dam being built across the gorges of the Argeş will form a reservoir 9 miles long; and this new lake, in its beautiful natural setting, has become a considerable tourist attraction. From here several footpaths lead up to the main ridge of the Făgăraş Mountains, which contain the highest peaks in the Rumanian Carpathians (Moldoveanu, 8,344 feet; Negoiul, 8,317 feet). There is a road round the lake.

D. RÎMNICU VÎLCEA
AND ITS SURROUNDINGS

Leaving Piteşti, D.N. 7 bears north-west to run through an area of hills covered with fruit trees; then, in 60 km (38 miles), enters the Olt valley.

Rîmnicu Vîlcea (altitude 750-820 feet; 22,536 inhabitants), the chief town of the Vîlcea district, is well known for the beauty of its folk art (wooden buildings, costumes, pottery). The town is laid out on successive levels of a river terrace above the west bank of the Olt. During the last ten years it has developed into an industrial centre (factory—at Govora—for sodium products, joinery works, leather and shoe factory, drilling plant, etc.), and its character has changed considerably. Another famous product of the town is plum brandy *(ţuica)*.

The history of Rîmnicu Vîlcea goes back a long way. As early as 1392 it is mentioned in the documents as a town; and throughout the Middle Ages it was an active market town, rising in the 16th century to the status of a princely residence.

Things to see: the *Local Museum* (sections on history and art); *Zăvoi Park;* the *house of the writer Anton Pann* (1797-1854), a typical example of the traditional local architecture; the *churches* of *St Parasceva* (16th century), of the *Annunciation* (16th century, rebuilt in the 18th) and *All Saints* (18th century); the *Bishop's Palace*, with a church decorated with paintings by G. Tattarescu in the 19th century and a chapel built and decorated with paintings in the 18th century; the *Citadel*, a small 15th century church, so named because it was formerly surrounded by walls.

Excursions in the surrounding area

1. Băile Olăneşti (20 km — 12 miles; altitude 1,480 feet). This resort lies north of Rîmnicu Vîlcea in a narrow, heavily wooded valley which is traversed by D.N. 64A. There is a modern bathing establishment using mineral water from 30 springs (sodium chloride and iodide; sodium chloride and ferruginous; alkaline, sulphurous and radioactive), renowned for their therapeutic effects in the treatment of diseases of the kidneys and stomach, affections of the gall bladder, diabetes, etc. The establishment is open all year.

2. The vineyards of Drăgăşani (52 km — 33 miles). The Drăgăşani vineyards, on the slopes above the Olt to the east and south of Rîmnicu Vîlcea, are said to go back to the time of the Dacians, and cover an area of some 25,000 acres. The name of Drăgăşani is recorded for the first time in the 16th century. Many indeed are the foreign visitors who have found their way to Drăgăşani since then and have expressed their appreciation of the light dry wines, of medium alcoholic content, which are produced from late grapes picked in October. The centre of this vine-growing area is the small town of Drăgăşani on the banks of the Olt.

As D.N. 64 descends the Olt valley towards Drăgăşani another road (D.N. 67) branches off on the right and bears west towards Tîrgu Jiu (114 km — 71 miles). From this road a number of country roads run north and south to various interesting features in the Subcarpathian depression of the Olt.

3. Ocnele Mari and **Ocniţa** (8 and 10 km — 5 and 6 miles — from Rîmnicu Vîlcea; altitude 1,020 feet), where there are salt mines which have been worked since Roman times. In these resorts there are small bathing establishments using the water (high in salt content) of the lakes formed in the hollows left by the old salt workings, and springs of mineral water (containing sodium chloride).

4. Govora Monastery (19 km — 12 miles), founded in the 15th century and rebuilt in the 17th by Matei Basarab, who installed a printing press here in 1640. The present church is the result of a restoration of 1707.

Băile Govora (21 km — 13 miles; altitude 1,180–1,540 feet), an important bathing resort (open all year) situated in an area of wooded hills. Its mineral waters (containing salts, iodides, sulphur) were discovered in the 19th century in the course of prospecting for oil. They are piped from depths of between 1,000 and 1,300 feet and distributed to the modern bathing establishments of the resort. Used by themselves or in combination with mineral mud, the waters of Govora are effective in the treatment of many affections of the locomotor system and peripheral nervous system, gynaecological conditions, chronic industrial diseases, skin diseases, and digestive and urinary conditions.

There is a fine park containing many species of trees and shrubs which flourish in the Mediterranean climate.

5. The monasteries of Bistriţa, Arnota and Hurez

Bistriţa Monastery, founded at the end of the 15th century by the boyars of Craiova, was an important centre of Slavonic culture during the 16th century. It contains old manuscripts and works of feudal art.

Arnota Monastery was founded by Prince Matei Basarab in 1653. Its church still retains some of the original frescoes.

Hurez Monastery (45 km — 28 miles) is the largest complex of religious architecture of the Brîncoveanu period and the masterpiece of 17th century Wallachian art. In the centre of the monastery is the "Great Church", built 1691–93 and decorated internally with *frescoes* which are remarkable for the harmony of their colouring and their wealth of detail, including portraits of the founders (Constantin Brîncoveanu and his whole family) and the architects and master masons. Note also the fine *doors* in carved pear-wood, the *iconostasis* in carved and gilded lime, the furnishings, etc.

In the monastery itself, a single-storey building in the old Rumanian style, note particularly the *narthex of Dionisie* (1753) with its stone balustrade and columns covered with fine carving. The old *Prince's House* and *chapel* should also be seen.

Near the monastery is the *Hermitage of St Stephen*, a small but extremely graceful building dating from the beginning of the 18th century.

Hurez (43 km—27 miles), a small town situated in an area of fine orchards, is an ancient and famous pottery-producing centre. The pottery of Hurez (mainly plates and dishes) is notable for the quality of the paste and the beauty of the decoration, produced with old traditional tools.

6. The fortified manors of Măldăreşti (47 km—29 miles), 2½ miles south of Hurez. These fortified manors of stone and brick, built to provide protection from the bands of Turkish marauders who ravaged the countryside in the 18th and 19th centuries, have a lower floor raised above ground level, with narrow slits of windows. The first floor—and the second floor if there is one—have large windows or balconies with arcades supported by pillars. There are two manors of this type at Măldăreşti, one dating from 1790, the other from the 19th century. The older one now contains a small local museum.

7. Polovragi Monastery (67 km—42 miles), built in the 17th century, with fine *frescoes* inside the church. Half a mile north of the monastery are the *Olteţ Gorges*, with a forestry road cut from the rock some 60 feet above the river bed. In the east wall of the gorge is the *Polovragi Cave*, used by the heyducks as a hiding place.

8. The Muierii Cave (77 km—48 miles), in the little Galbenul defile, north of the commune of Baia de Fier. The cave, which is lit by electricity and well arranged for visitors, consists of two passages with a total length of 1,000 yards, and is designated as a "natural monument" on account of its fine stalagmites. In the lower passage was found a cemetery of cave bears containing 183 skeletons. These first occupants of the cave were hunted by the men of the Middle Palaeolithic period (*Homo primigenius*, 150,000 to 100,000 years before our era) who settled in this area. The archaeologists also discovered remains which prove that the cave was used as a shelter (mainly for women and children) in later periods.

After making these side trips it is possible, instead of returning to Rîmnicu Vîlcea, to continue towards Tîrgu Jiu (p. 123).

For all information, apply to the Tourist Office in Rîmnicu Vîlcea (30, Str. Argeş tel. 236) or to the local office in Olaneşti.

E. THE OLT DEFILE

After Rîmnicu Vîlcea D.N. 7 turns north along the west bank of the River Olt and then crosses the Subcarpathian depression of *Jiblea*. Near the mountains the road passes through the town of **Călimănești**, an important health resort open all year round.

Discovered in 1830, the mineral springs of Călimănești (containing sodium chloride, iodide, sulphur) are effective in the treatment of diseases of the liver and kidneys, diseases of the locomotor and cardiovascular systems, gynaecological and digestive conditions, etc. The resort of Călimănești also includes, for administrative purposes, the smaller resort of *Căciulata*, rather more than a mile to the north, with springs (containing sodium chloride and sulphur, sodium chloride and iodide, and bromide) recommended for the treatment of arteriosclerosis, asthma, chronic bronchitis, diseases of the digestive apparatus, rheumatism, urinary and nutritional conditions, allergic states, industrial diseases, etc. The Emperor Napoleon III, who suffered from a stone, sent for Călimănești water to treat it.

Just in front of the Baths of Călimănești, in the middle of the Olt, is a small island, the **Ostrov**, laid out as a Park of Culture and Rest. On the island is a small *church* belonging to an old hermitage for nuns founded in 1522.

3 km (2 miles) from Călimănești the road passes through the remarkable group of buildings of **Cozia Monastery.** On the right is the **Cozia Church,** surrounded on three sides by the other buildings of the monastery. The church is one of the oldest buildings in Wallachia preserved in its entirety.

The building of the church was begun by Radu I Basarab and completed in 1386 by Mircea the Old, who is buried here. The *portico* with stone columns was added by Constantin Brîncoveanu in 1707. This building marks the starting point of Byzantine architecture in the feudal state of Wallachia. Note the fine *decoration of the façades* (based on the alternating use of stone and brick) and the beauty of the stone carving. Note also in the naos some fine original *frescoes* (14th century) and in the pronaos some 18th century frescoes.

The surrounding buildings show typical features of the old Rumanian style of architecture. A small *museum of religious art* has been arranged in a belvedere, from which there is a magnificent view of the Olt valley and the mountains which dominate it.

On the left of the road is the small **Bolniţa Church**, gracefully proportioned, which served the mediaeval hospital attached to the monastery. This was built in 1543 by Voivode Petru, who entered the monastery under the name of Radu Paisie, and is one of the most characteristic examples of 16th century architecture. Inside the church are fine original *frescoes* (by the painters David and Raduslav, 1543).

Beyond the monastery, on the other bank of the Olt, are the remains of the Roman *castrum* of *Arutela* (2nd century), built close to hot springs which supplied the bathhouse of the camp.

This *castrum*, on the left bank of the Olt, was one of a series of fortifications built by the Romans along the river, from its junction with the Danube to beyond the defile which it has cut through the massive rampart of the Southern Carpathians. This fortified line, the *Limes Alutanus*, was for a time the eastern frontier of Roman Dacia. It included a road built by the Romans along the river as far as the entrance to the defile. Beyond this point the road bore round the east side of Mount Cozia and returned to the Olt in the Brezoi-Titeşti depression.

The more direct modern road passes through the defile, taking the visitor through 48 km (30 miles) of scenery of striking beauty. Here the Olt has cut through the Carpathians to their very base in an area where they are at their highest, forming a transverse valley which is equalled only by the Danube defile at the Iron Gates.

Soon after entering the defile we see on the other bank the towers of *Turnul Monastery* (17th century), in the courtyard of which are cells hewn from the living rock about 1590 by hermits from Cozia Monastery and occupied by them for 72 years. From Turnul Monastery a path leads to the summit of **Mount Cozia** (5,502 feet), which dominates the defile on the east. Being sheltered from the north-east winds by the main ridge of the Făgăraş Mountains, Mount Cozia enjoys a milder climate, so that walnuts, oaks and wild roses can be found growing on its slopes up to a height of 4,200 feet. The edelweiss *(Leontopodium alpinum)* and the white ivy *(Daphne blagayana)* are among the rare plants found here. From the summit of the mountain there is a magnificent view of the surrounding peaks.

In the middle of the defile the river and the road pass through a small depression of tectonic origin, the *Brezoi-Titeşti depression*. Here, where the defile is a little wider, a few small villages have grown up.

After passing the River Lotru, renowned for its abundance of trout and the picturesque scenery of its valley, running down from the Parîng massif (8,262 feet), we see on the right the **Hermitage of Cornet**, built in the 17th century and decorated with paintings at the beginning of the 18th. In the characteristic style of the period, the external surfaces are ornamented with glazed ceramic, tiles and studs.

The Brezoi-Titeşti depression, formerly known as the "Lovişte Country" (meaning the "hunting country") ends at **Cîineni.** This is an ancient settlement, where the remains of a Roman *castrum* known as "Pons Vetus" were discovered—indicating that there was a bridge here before the Romans came. During the Middle Ages Cîineni belonged to the voivodate of Seneslau, the existence of which is recorded at the beginning of the 13th century. There are two 18th century *churches* in Cîineni.

Beyond Cîineni the road re-enters the narrow defile. At its far end, on the left, is a small tourist hut and restaurant called "Valea Oltului" ("The Olt Valley"). Higher up, between the road and the river, is a defensive *tower* which is mentioned in documents of the 14th century and was partly destroyed in 1533 when the river rose in spate.

D.N. 7 emerges from the defile at *Turnul Roşu* (the Red Tower), a fortress built in the 13th century to protect the northern entrance to the defile.

After the village of *Boiţa*, where the Romans had a *castrum (Caput Stenarum)*, the road passes a hill on which are the ruins of a fortress of the 16th century, and then descends to *Tălmaciu*. It then crosses the plain of the Cibin depression to Sibiu. Before reaching this important tourist centre it is joined on the right by D.N. 1 coming from Braşov (see p. 171).

8. BUCHAREST - PLOIEŞTI
(60 km – 38 miles) -
BRAŞOV (172 km – 108 miles)

D.N. 1 connects Bucharest with the principal towns in central and north-western Rumania and with the frontier station of Borş-Oradea, and thus with the great capitals of central and western Europe (Budapest, Vienna, Paris, etc.)—for D.N. 1 is the continuation in Rumanian territory of the international road E 15. It is accompanied by a railway line, which is used by the great European expresses, the *Balt-Orient-Express* (Bucharest-Budapest-Prague-Berlin) and the *Nord-Orient-Express* (Constanţa-Bucharest-Budapest-Warsaw). The *Orient Express*, which provides a direct link between Bucharest and Paris, also passes through Braşov.

The road cuts across the centre of Rumania, linking important towns like Ploieşti, Braşov, Sibiu, Alba Iulia, Cluj and Oradea, and passing through districts renowned for their scenery (the Prahova valley, the Braşov, Făgăraş and Cibin depressions, the middle Mureş valley and the Criş Repede defile). For all these reasons D.N. 1 is the main tourist route in Rumania and is fully entitled to its designation as the *main central artery of Rumania*. At Braşov, Sibiu and Cluj other highways branch off D.N. 1, leading to the main beauty spots and places of interest in Transylvania. Most of these roads pass through the defiles in the Carpathians, renowned for the beauty of their scenery, and provide links between the most important towns on either side of the mountains.

The road leaves Bucharest by the Şoseaua Kiseleff and Băneasa. After skirting the airport and *Băneasa Forest*, it crosses the *Vlăsia plain*, in the middle of which are the park and lake of *Snagov* (see p. 92).

A. PLOIEŞTI

The first town of importance on D.N. 1 is Ploieşti (60 km — 38 miles; 170,000 inhabitants), the chief town of Ploieşti region, which includes the southern slopes of the Bucegi Mountains and Ciucaş, the Subcarpathian hills with their rich stores of oil, salt and coal, and part of the Rumanian Plain.

The town of Ploieşti is the capital of the Rumanian **oil** industry, and its prosperity has followed the fortunes of the industry. Largely destroyed by air bombardment during the second world war, Ploieşti made a rapid recovery and has continued to flourish, becoming one of the main centres of Rumanian industry.

Ploieşti is surrounded by many factories and refineries with the most modern equipment, including in particular the large petro-chemical complex of Brazi, where a refinery with a catalytic cracking plant with an annual throughput of a million tons and a distillation plant, both atmospheric and vacuum, with a capacity of several million tons annually, were brought into service in 1960. At the same time Ploieşti has acquired an important plant producing equipment for the oil industry, well known in many foreign countries for the high quality of its production: in 1964 its "3 DH" medium-depth drilling rig won a Gold Medal at the International Fair in Leipzig.

Within the last ten years the appearance of Ploieşti has changed considerably as a result of the building of new housing areas. With many cultural institutions (State Theatre, Symphony Orchestra, People's Art School, etc.) and schools, it is also a cultural centre.

History of the town. Ploieşti, situated in the area of contact between the plain and the Subcarpathian hills, is a town of considerable age. Within the town, near the Southern Station, excavation has revealed a large cemetery of Geto-Dacian burial urns bearing witness to human occupation of the site since the early Bronze Age. Near the town, at Tîrgşorul Vechi (12 km — 8 miles), have been found traces of still older human settlements showing evidence of occupation from the end of the Palaeolithic period to the Middle Ages.

PLOIEŞTI

1 Town hall
2 Historical Museum
3 Art Museum
4 Oil Museum
5 Caragiale Museum
6 Church of St George (1831)
7 Church of St Basil (1857)
8 Hotel Central
9 Hotel Prahova
10 Tourist Office
11 Main post office

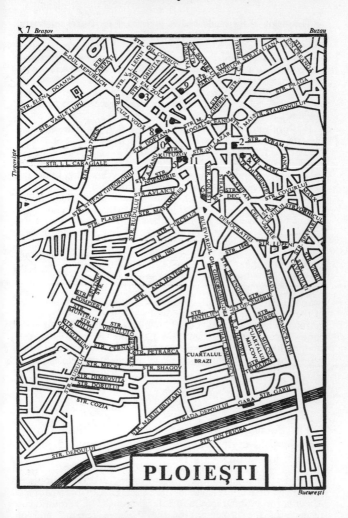

PLOIEȘTI

The origin of the mediaeval settlement of Ploieşti is uncertain. According to an old legend an aged man, Father Ploaie, had fled from Transylvania with his seven sons to escape persecution and settled here; and the seven sons thereupon cleared enough space to make a field in the vast oak forests which then covered the plain as far as the Danube, and founded a village of free peasants (for according to an old local custom any man who cleared a stretch of forest and made a field became the owner of the land).

It is not until 1503, however, that we find the first record of Ploieşti, the village inhabited by the descendants of Father Ploaie. In 1597 the village achieved the status of a town, granted by Michael the Brave when he established a camp here for the army with which he succeeded, two years later, in uniting under his own control the three provinces of Rumania—the Rumanian Land (Wallachia), Transylvania and Moldavia. The "free princely city" of Ploieşti lost its liberties at the end of the end of the 18th century, when it became the property of some boyars of Greek origin. The people of Ploieşti, however, fought tenaciously for their freedom, and so there developed in the town a revolutionary tradition which again came to the fore, in the form of the heroic struggles of the workers at the time when the oil industry was taking a great leap forward.

In 1856 one of the first oil refineries in the world was built near Ploieşti; fifty years later there were ten. The whole history of the town during the last hundred years is bound up with the petroleum industry, which until 1948 was in the hands of companies dependent on foreign capital. A long sequence of strikes, culminating in the great strike of oil workers in 1933, bears witness to the continuing struggle of the people of Ploieşti.

Things to See

The **Palace of Culture,** a monumental building in the neo-classical style, was built at the beginning of this century as the Law Courts.

In addition to a number of cultural and artistic institutions, the Palace of Culture contains three sections of the *Historical Museum* (on ethnography and folk art, on "The revolutionary struggle of the proletariat of the Prahova region" and on

"The building of socialism in the Prahova region") and the *Museum of Natural Science*.

Near the main square of the town is the *Caragiale Museum*, containing material on the life and works of the great Rumanian dramatist, who was educated at Ploieşti and spent several years of his life there. (The museum is in a house built in 1710, a fine example of old Rumanian architecture.)

The *National Oil Museum* (opened in 1960) gives a picture of the development of the Rumanian oil industry.

Other interesting museums are the *Museum of Art* at 1, Bd Gheorghiu-Dej and the Clock Museum at 1, Str. 6 Martie.

The *Hagi Prodan House*, another fine example of old Rumanian architecture (17th century), is furnished in the Brîncoveanu style.

See also the *Statue of Liberty* representing Minerva and the *commemorative plaque* at the place where the 2nd Congress of the Communist Party of Rumania was held in 1922. Near the Southern Station is the *Hunters' Monument* by the classical Rumanian sculptor I. Georgescu. Finally, near the square containing the Central Market, a large complex of commercial buildings, is the tower *of St John's Cathedral* (200 feet high).

Excursion in the District

Valea Călugărească (15-20 km–9-13 miles) is a village to the east of Ploieşti in a famous vine-growing area which is also a centre of the chemical industry.

The vineyards of the State farm of Valea Călugărească and the experimental station of the Research Institute of the Rumanian Academy have a considerable reputation, as have the cellars which tunnel to a great depth under the terraces of the surrounding hills. Valea Călugărească also has a wine-producing plant, a regular factory of excellent wines which are stored and left to age here.

Vălenii de Munte (27 km–17 miles; altitude 1,410 feet), north of Ploieşti in the Teleajen valley, is mentioned in official documents from the beginning of the 16th century.

Vălenii de Munte is a pleasant health resort, but also a renowned centre for the production of plum brandy. It contains a house built in the attractive traditional style of the area, now a museum in honour of the Rumanian historian *Nicolae Iorga*.

Slănic (39 km-24 miles; altitude 1,280-1,310 feet), north of Ploieşti, is a health resort with sodium chloride springs and an important salt mine which has been worked since the 17th century.

Near *Baia Baciului*, a lake with a high salt content used as a public swimming bath, is an open-cast *salt mountain* which is designated as a "natural monument". The external surface, furrowed by gulleys and runnels carved out by rainwater, is extremely picturesque. Inside the hill is a cave (the Bride's Cave), with a lake formed in the old salt workings.

Tourist Office: 34, Piaţa 16 Februarie (tel. 1.45.63).

B. CÎMPINA

D.N. 1 continues its northward course a cross the plain lying between the foothills of the Subcarpathians. After a secondary road which goes off on the right to *Băicoi*, an old and famous oil centre (some wells can be seen close to the road), the main road passes close to the monument to Aurel Vlaicu, the pioneer of flying who crashed here in 1913, and then enters **Cîmpina** (26,000 inhabitants), a centre of the engineering industry and of oil refining.

Cîmpina is now a rapidly developing town. A House of Culture, a number of workers' clubs, an open-air theatre and many sporting facilities are available for the benefit of the workers, who formerly had to put up with very hard conditions

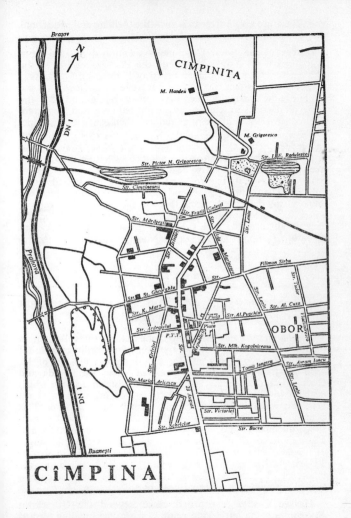

CÎMPINA

here. There are also a Research Institute (drilling and extraction) and several middle and technical schools.

History of the town. Cîmpina is mentioned in 1503 as a customs post on the road through the Prahova valley. In the 18th century we find the customs records referring for the first time to the oil which was to bring fortune to the town and the whole region in the 19th century. Between 1890 and 1895 the first 5 oil derricks in Rumania were erected here, and these were followed in 1897 by the largest refinery then existing in Europe.

The frantic rush to make the most of the Cîmpina oilfield, and indeed of all the oil resources of the Ploieşti region, and in particular the oil companies' practice of letting the oil gush freely, led—as might have been expected—to a rapid fall in production, and in the end the scale of working had to be reduced. Then came the second world war, during which the refinery was destroyed. After the war the refinery was rebuilt, enlarged, and equipped with modern plant for atmospheric and vacuum distillation, and the wells were brought back into operation in accordance with the most modern working methods.

Things to See

The **Nicolae Grigorescu Museum,** just to the right of the road beyond the northern outskirts of Cîmpina.

Nicolae Grigorescu (1838–1907), one of the greatest Rumanian painters of the 19th century, the son of an ordinary peasant family who showed his gift for painting from the age of 12, lived for many years in the Prahova valley (at Posada and Cîmpina), and spent the last years of his life in a house which he built in Cîmpina. Destroyed by fire during the first world war, this was rebuilt in 1957 and turned into a *museum*. This contains furniture, tapestries and a variety of personal possessions, documents and other material on Grigorescu's life, and a large number of pictures and sketches representing all stages of his development, including in particular the period of over 20 years which he devoted to painting the peasant life and the landscape of Rumania. The house containing the museum is a typical example of traditional peasant architecture.

Hasdeu Castle. A short distance beyond the Grigorescu Museum, on the left of the road, is a strange building erected

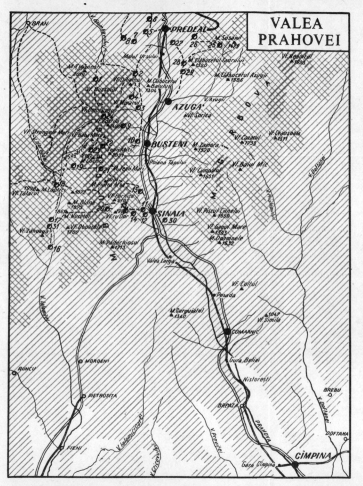

VALEA PRAHOVEI

1 Chalet Mălăiești	1 Mălăiești hut	1 Mălăiești-Hütte
2 Chalet Diham	2 Diham hut	2 Diham-Hütte
3 Chalet Poiana Dihamului	3 Poiana Dihamului hut	3 Poiana Dihamului-Hütte
3 Chalet Gura Dihamului	4 Piana Izvoarelor hut	4 Piana Izvoarelor-Hütte
4 Chalet Piana Izvoarelor	5 Trei Brazi hut	5 Trei Brazi-Hütte
5 Chalet Trei Brazi	6 Poiana Secilor hut	6 Poiana Secilor-Hütte
6 Chalet Poiana Secuilor	7 Pîrîul Rece hut	7 Pîrîul Rece-Hütte
7 Chalet Pîrîul Rece	8 Cerbul hut	8 Cerbul-Hütte
8 Chalet Cerbul	9 Coștila mountain hut	9 Coștila-Berghütte
9 Refuge Alpin Coștila		
10 Chalet Alpin	10 Alpin hut	10 Alpenhütte
11 Chalet Furnica	11 Furnica hut	11 Furnica-Hütte
12 Chalet Schiori	12 Schiori hut	12 Schiori-Hütte
13 Chalet Valea cu Brazi	13 Valea cu Brazi hut	13 Valea cu Brazi-Hütte
14 Hôtel et chalet «Cota 1400»	14 «Cota 14» Hotel and hut	14 «Cota 14», Hotel und Hütte
15 Chalet Poiana Stînii	15 Poiana Stînii hut	15 Poiana Stînii-Hütte
16 Chalet Scropoasa	16 Scropoasa hut	16 Scropoasa-Hütte
17 Chalet Bolboci	17 Bolboci hut	17 Bolboci-Hütte
18 Chalets Padina I et II	18 Padina huts 1 and 2	18 Padina-Hütten, 1 und 2
19 Complexe touristique de la grotte de Ialomița	19 Ialomita Cave tourist centre	19 Ialomița-Höhle, Touristenzentrum
20 Chalet Vîrful cu Dor	20 Vîrful cu Dor hut	20 Vîrful cu Dor-Hütte
21 Chalet Piatra Arsă	21 Piatra Arsă hut	21 Piatra Arsă-Hütte
22 Châlet Caraiman	22 Caraiman hut	22 Caraiman-Hütte
23 Chalet Babele	23 Babele hut	23 Babele-Hütte
24 Chalet Omul	24 Omul hut	24 Omul-Hütte
25 Chalet Susai	25 Susai hut	25 Susai-Hütte
26 Chalet Cioplea	26 Cioplea hut	26 Cioplea-Hütte
27 Chalet Clăbucet	27 Clăbucet hut	27 Clăbucet-Hütte
28 Chalet Clăbucetul Taurului	28 Clăbucetul Taurului hut	28 Clăbucetul Taurului-Hütte
29 Chalet Gîrbova	29 Gîrbova hut	29 Gîrbova-Hütte
30 Chalet Piscul Ciinelui	30 Piscul Ciinelui hut	30 Piscul Ciinelui-Hütte
31 Chalet Cheile Zănoagei	31 Cheile Zănoagei hut	31 Cheile Zănoagei-Hütte

CARTOGRAPHIE NAGEL

between 1893 and 1896 by Bogdan Petriceico Hasdeu (1838–1907), linguist, historian and writer, a prominent figure in 19th century Rumanian culture. The house is built in the shape of a cross, with battlements on the sides and buttresses on the north front.

Doftana. 4 km (2½ miles) from Cîmpina, on the opposite side of the Doftana valley, near the old salt mines of Telega (to which in former times were sent those who rebelled against oppression), is the old Doftana Prison. Built between 1894 and 1897, it contained 8 sections (with a total of 397 cells), of which only three were lit by natural light and one (the ill-famed "Section H") was in complete darkness. Here were imprisoned the peasants sentenced after the 1907 rebellion. Later Doftana became the place of detention of the leaders of the workers' movement, and at the same time a training school for the revolutionary struggle. Sometimes the prisoners were able to circulate handwritten newspapers ("Doftana", "The Antifascist in Chains", etc.). In the night of 9–10 November 1940 an earthquake destroyed part of the prison, and a large number of prisoners perished in the ruins.

The prison has now been partly rebuilt and turned into a *museum* containing material illustrating the harsh treatment of the prisoners and their constant struggle against the authorities.

Tourist Office: 93, Str. 23 August, Cîmpina (tel. 13.77).

C. SINAIA

After Cîmpina D.N. 1 descends to the Prahova, crosses it and climbs on to the terrace on the right bank on which is situated *Breaza*, a health resort mainly used by holiday homes for children.

The village, which is mentioned in documents from the 16th century onwards, contains many wooden cottages in the traditional peasant style. There is a cooperative ("Casnica") producing embroidery and carpets in accordance with the finest traditions of the area, which is renowned for the delicacy of its folk embroidery.

Beyond Breaza the road descends again to the Prahova and runs alongside the river to a point bet-

ween Comarnic and Sinaia where it has cut a narrow
passage through the mountains. Just before reaching
this defile the river passes through the town of *Comarnic*, a health resort and industrial centre (timber,
building materials).

Until last century Comarnic was the last place which the
traveller coming from Ploieşti encountered in the upper valley
of the Prahova. Beyond this point the road—or rather the
track, fit only for horses—passed through country frequented
only by shepherds, hermits and heyducks.

Occasionally, too, a merchant would pass through the
Prahova valley. The defile is mentioned in documents of the
15th century, but the first road worthy of the name was not
built until the end of the 18th century, purely for military purposes. It was not until the middle of last century (1846) that
a proper road was constructed, and this has been steadily
improved until it is now a pleasant and picturesque road which
is no longer in danger of being swept away by the river in
spate.

After **Posada** the road climbs up the side of the Baiul Mountains, the range which dominates the left bank of the Prahova.
At the entrance to Posada is a small country house, a residence
of Prince Bibesco, who gave directions for the building of
the present road but was driven from power by the 1848 revolution before it was completed. The house and a modern extension are now used as a holiday home.

On the far side of Posada is a motel, "Izvorul Rece",
occupying the position of an inn which stood here between
100 and 150 years ago, named "Fruntea lui Vasîi" after a
famous heyduck.

The road now returns to the left bank of the Prahova
and enters **Sinaia,** a famous health resort whose
beauty fully justifies the name "Pearl of the Carpathians" which is given to it. Sinaia—which also
contains a metalworks, a building materials factory and
a foodstuffs industry—is situated at the foot of
Mounts Vîrful cu Dor (6,582 feet), Furnica (6,897 feet)
and Piatra Arsă (6,585 feet) in the Bucegi massif. A

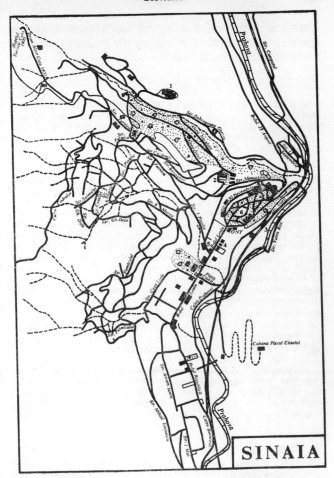

SINAIA

SINAIA
1 Peleş Castle
2 Monastery
3 Station

4 Post office
5 Police office
6 Central Park
7 Peleş Park

luxuriant forest of beech and larch surrounds the resort, which is busy throughout the year with tourists from Rumania and abroad.

The Baths use mineral springs similar to those of Căciulata-Călimăneşti in the Olt valley. Rich in bicarbonate, calcium, magnesium, sulphur and—to a lesser degree—iodine, bromine, lithium and iron, the waters of Sinaia promote the gastric secretions, the reduction of bile secretion and the flow of bile, and are indicated in the treatment of chronic gastritis and the diuretic cure of stones in the bladder.

Sinaia's main attractions, however, are its sub-Alpine climate, its ozone-rich air, and its nearness to the Bucegi Mountains, with all the facilities they afford for easy and interesting excursions in summer and for skiing in winter. There is also a modern casino, with a restaurant, a bar, and a hall for entertainments. The *Hotel Alpin* stands 4,600 feet high, on the edge of the forest, but is easy of access. Skiers have a wide choice: on the very outskirts of the town, at a height of 3,300 feet, are nursery slopes for beginners, with a ski-lift; for experienced skiers there is a cabin-lift from the Hotel Alpin to the summit of Mount Furnica (6,897 feet), the starting point for the fine ski slopes of Valea cu Brazi (the Valley of Firs); and high up on the Bucegi plateau are large areas of snow suitable even for beginners, which remain useable into the month of April. In summer the cabin-lift enables visitors for whom a climb to 6,900 feet would be too much to enjoy the splendid panorama of the Prahova valley and the surrounding mountains.

History of the town. A deposit of tools dating from the Bronze Age was found in Sinaia; but this does not mean that the area was inhabited at that period, for the tools seem to have been abandoned for some reason while being transported through the mountains. The first permanent building was not erected at Sinaia until 1640, when a heyduck from Breaza gifted a sum of money to some hermits who desired to build a wooden hermitage. In 1695 the *spătar* (noble) Mihail Cantacuzino replaced the hermitage by a monastery to which he gave the name of *Sinaia*, in memory of his visit to the monastery on Mount Sinai. It was not until a century later, however, that a few houses and an inn were built round the monastery. Sinaia began to develop into a health resort only after 1870, when it became a royal summer residence, and particularly after the opening of the railway (1879). In 1880 it achieved the status of a town. In 1912 a casino built on the model of the one at Monte Carlo appeared beside the large hotels and the luxurious villas.

Things to See

Peleş Castle (now a museum), a former royal summer residence, was built between 1875 and 1883 and underwent some alteration after 1896.

The castle, which has more than 160 rooms, is built mainly in the German Renaissance style, with Italian Renaissance, German Baroque and French Rococo elements. On each side are terraces in the Italian Renaissance style laid out in the shape of an amphitheatre and decorated with statues and fountains. The rooms (concert hall, guest suites, theatre, library, reception rooms, etc.) contain many valuable objects. The interior finish is also very fine—carved woodwork and stained glass (some from Switzerland, dating from the 16th and 17th centuries, others from Munich).

In the park, which is laid out in the English fashion, is *Pelişor Castle* ("Little Peleş"), also in the German Renaissance style, now a house for creative workers, and the *Foişor*, a belvedere in the Swiss style.

Another place of interest is the **Sinaia Monastery,** with its two *churches*, one in the Brîncoveanu style (end of 17th century), the other built in 1841 and restored in 1903, with fine decorations in the traditional Wallachian style.

Excursions by Car in the District

To *Poiana Stînii* (the Clearing of the Sheepfold, 5 km— 3 miles, 4,167 feet), a beautiful clearing on the slopes of Mount Piatra Arsă, above which is a nature reserve of mountain flowers.

To the *Hotel Alpin* (6 km—4 miles; 4,530 feet) and the cabin lift to the top of Mount Furnica (6,897 feet).

To the *Ialomiţa valley* (34 km—21 miles; 5,282 feet). This is reached by a road which branches off the main road from Sinaia to Moroeni and Tîrgovişte and runs into the heart of the Bucegi range, the karst area of the Ialomiţa Gorges and the Ialomiţa Cave (lit by electricity).

There are many signposted footpaths from Sinaia to the huts in the Bucegi Mountains (2–3 hours' walking).

The Bucegi Mountains

The road from Sinaia to Predeal passes under the majestic escarpments of the Bucegi Mountains, a wall of rock rising nearly 5,000 feet above the valley. The great geographer G. Vîlsan, writing about the Bucegi, said: "They have not the wild and dizzy grandeur of the Alps, nor the brilliance and ermine whiteness of their perpetual snows, nor the fascinating colouring of the Pyrenees, nor the finely etched sculpture and theatrical beauty of the Ligurian coast; but they have the simple and graceful lines of our old monasteries, their massive forms are characteristic and unmistakeable, and their ever-changing pattern of light and shade has the restrained and yet warm colouring, the good taste and the delicate gradations found in our traditional peasant costumes."

The Bucegi Mountains, a massive pile of conglomerates and limestones, occupy an area of some 120 square miles between the valleys of the Prahova and the Dîmboviţa. The Ialomiţa, which rises under their highest peak, Omul (8,225 feet), cuts a passage through the mountains to the south, carving out in the process a series of five defiles of remarkable beauty. Towards the Prahova valley, the Braşov depression and the Bran corridor the Bucegi present steep rock faces with impressive walls of cliff. In contrast, the summit consists of a rolling plateau on which there is easy walking in every direction and on which shepherds have tended their flocks since the remotest times.

The Bucegi are mentioned in the documents from the 16th century, but it is certain that they had been known for much longer than that. In the 19th century they became a happy hunting ground for tourists and climbers, and they now attract thousands of "Bucegi fans". A considerable network of signposted footpaths runs through the range from end to end. Even the mountain faces in the Prahova valley, which seem impassable when seen from below, can be climbed without great difficulty. A number of nature reserves have been established to protect the rich and varied flora of the mountains.

More than twenty tourist huts provide facilities for a pleasant stay in the most attractive parts of the mountains. Most of them are at heights of between 4,600 and 5,250 feet, in the forest area, but some are higher and may expose the visitor to the winds—sometimes biting—of the Alpine zone (the Omul hut at 8,225 feet and the Babele hut at 7,218 feet). In winter the Bucegi Mountains are a paradise for skiers, with snow until the end of April. In certain valleys, like the Valea Albă (White Valley), skiing is possible until June, though the slopes are so steep that they are suitable only for the most expert skiers.

Tourist Office: 19, Bd Carpaţi (tel. 15.15).

D. PREDEAL

After passing through Poiana Tapului, a small health resort, the road enters **Buşteni,** situated at the foot of the imposing escarpments of Mounts Jepii Mici (7,031 feet), Caraiman (7,628 feet) and Coştila (8,766 feet).

A health resort and industrial centre (paper and cellulose factory), Buşteni is a relatively young town, the first houses having been built here from 1830 onwards. The steep rock faces above the town have made the area a happy hunting ground for climbers. A great variety of routes, from the easiest to the most difficult (grade VI, upper limit) give rock climbers every possible scope for practising their skill. In addition signposted footpaths, suitable for all climbers and hill walkers, lead from Buşteni to the summits of the Bucegi range.

Predeal (altitude 3,389 feet). Beyond *Azuga* is *Predeal*, the last of the series of health resorts in the Prahova valley and the highest town in Rumania.

The discovery of a deposit of bronze axes here shows that the Predeal pass and the Prahova valley served as a route for communication and trade between Transylvania and Wallachia from the remote times of the Bronze Age. Passage along this route was extremely difficult until last century, so that the area was little frequented until quite recent times: Predeal itself, as we have already noted, did not begin to develop until after 1830. Before then there was nothing there but a few inns, to which was added in 1771 a hermitage founded by monks who settled here.

A favourite holiday place for the middle classes until 1937, Predeal began thereafter to vie with Sinaia as a popular holiday resort. In the last few years Predeal has changed considerably, and is now in the process of becoming one of Rumania's most flourishing mountain resorts, favoured as it is by its sunny and sheltered position in the midst of huge pine forests. The town is surrounded by beautiful scenery, and the neighbouring "clăbucete" (hills with bare tops) offer excellent walking. But Predeal is also a much frequented resort for winter sports, particularly skiing. Since it is only 2½ hours by train from Bucharest, Predeal—like Buşteni and Sinaia—is much visited at weekends by the inhabitants of the capital.

Tourist Office: 14, Str. Panduri (tel. 13.75).

After Predeal D.N.1 enters the **Timiş valley** — a young valley, geologically speaking — which is dominated on the west by Mount Postăvarul (5,912 feet) and on the east by Mount Piatra Mare (6,067 feet), between which the Timiş has carved out a narrow passage.

The whole of the valley is lined with groups of houses—most of them holiday homes to which school children come in summer to enjoy the very mild climate of the district. Beyond *Timişu de Jos*, on the right of the road, is a tourist hotel ("Dîmbul Morii", 163 km—102 miles). From Dîmbul Morii a number of sign-posted footpaths lead up to the hotel and to the summit of Mount Piatra Mare (3 to 4 hours' walking). An hour's walk from Dîmbul Morii is a picturesque natural feature, the water-falls of Scări.

Before entering the Braşov depression D.N.1 skirts *Săcele*, a new township formed by the amalgamation of the "seven Sacelian villages". Formerly the Sacelians were renowned transhumant shepherds. Their town is now an industrial centre (electrical goods, building materials, foodstuffs). In the *Tithe House*, a 16th century building referred to in the documents as *"domus dominorum"*, a *Museum of the Seven Villages* was opened in 1963.

9. BRAŞOV
AND ITS SURROUNDINGS

Braşov, 168 km (108 miles) from Bucharest, at an altitude of 2,000-2,300 feet, is a large city with some 189,000 inhabitants.

Character of the Town

Braşov lies in the centre of Rumania, at the foot of the mountains, and at the entrance to the passages through the mountains which have been used as trade routes from mediaeval times. The old town nestles between the slopes of Mount Postăvarul (5,912 feet) and Mount Tîmpa (3,150 feet); the new town has developed in the open plain of the large Braşov depression. Braşov is today one of the leading cultural and economic centres of Rumania.

The economy of the town depends mainly on the engineering and metal-processing industries, but it also contains other industries of first-rate importance (textiles, foodstuffs, building materials, timber, chemicals). The main factories (producing tractors, lorries and ball-bearings) have been built since 1947. Braşov also possesses a variety of institutions which make it a considerable cultural centre: the Polytechnic Institute, the State Philharmonic Orchestra, the State Theatre, the Operetta Theatre, the Puppet Theatre, technical schools, etc. Finally Braşov's situation near Mounts Postăvarul and Piatra Mare, the Bucegi Mountains and Piatra Craiului makes it also an important tourist centre. It is not surprising, therefore, that the population of Braşov—in which many new housing areas have been built—should have doubled between 1945 and 1967.

History

Archaeologists have discovered in the town many traces of human settlement dating from the Neolithic period, followed by settlements of the Bronze Age. In the Iron Age the Geto-Dacians established townships of some size in the valleys now occupied by the suburbs of the town; and remains dating from the period of Roman occupation have been discovered on the hill of Sprenghiul.

The existence of Braşov is mentioned in documents of the 13th century, when Saxon settlers established themselves alongside the native population. Having gained the status of a free city, with the right of holding markets, Braşov soon achieved considerable prosperity, thanks to the reputation of its craftsmen and to its thriving trade with Wallachia and Moldavia. Thus in 1368 the Voivode Vlaicu, Prince Regnant of Wallachia, granted trade privileges to the merchants of Braşov; and similar privileges were granted by Alexander the Good, Prince Regnant of Moldavia, in the first decade of the 15th century.

At the end of the 14th century Braşov decided to build a citadel; but having failed to complete it by the time of the Turks' first incursion into Transylvania (1421), the town was captured. The Turks returned to the attack in 1434, but by this time the town had been surrounded by massive walls and a moat, and the attack was repelled. Within the shelter of its walls Braşov continued to prosper and became a centre of culture. In 1539 the Protestant humanist Honterus established a printing press here. Between 1557 and 1581 Coresie, a printer from Tîrgovişte, produced at Braşov some of the first works printed in Rumanian.

In 1689 Braşov, fighting to defend its rights as a free city, was set on fire by the Austrians. In the 19th century the first newspapers printed in Transylvania in the Rumanian language, including in particular the famous "Gazette of Transylvania", were published here.

In 1916 the Rumanian army entered Braşov, but had soon to withdraw in face of the German counter-offensive. It was not until 1918 that the town finally returned to Rumania. There are still Saxon and Magyar communities in Braşov, with their own churches and cultural institutions. The German name of the town is *Kronstadt*, the Hungarian *Brasso*.

Tour of the Town

The wide **Bulevard Gheorghiu-Dej,** with its banks of flowers, runs between the citadel hill (Cetăţuia) and the commercial district. On the boulevard are the Tourist Office, the large Carpaţi Hotel (Nº. 9) and the Museum of Art (Nº 21).

The *Citadel*, lying to the north, is a group of fortifications in brick built towards the end of the 16th century, replacing an older fortress in wood. On the wooded slopes of the hill are many fine villas.

At the western end of the Bd Gheorghiu-Dej is a crossing with traffic lights. To the right is **Str. Lungă** ("the long street"), which runs north to Sighişoara, Sibiu and Bran-Cîmpulung.

At the end of this street is the **Church of St Bartholomew,** a 13th century Saxon church in the Romanesque-Gothic style. Behind the church to the west is the hill on which remains of the Stone Age were discovered. On the other side of the street, to the east, before the level crossing, are a number of graves, recalling the heroic sacrifice in 1916 of a handful of Rumanian soldiers in face of the German forces.

Now return to the traffic lights. Straight ahead, running uphill, is the road to Poiana Braşov (below, p. 167). On the left, between the Carpaţi Hotel and the Prefecture, is a street leading to the main square of Braşov, the **Piaţa 23 August.**

In the middle of the square is the **Casa Sfatului** *("Council House"),* the former town hall, built in the 15th century. The *Trumpeters' Tower* was built beside it in the 16th century.

The Council House contains a historical museum

Nearby, on the south-east side of the square, is the **Merchants' Hall** *(Podul Bătuşilor),* built in the 16th century and recently restored. It now contains a restaurant called "The Carpathian Stag" (Cerbul Carpaţin), with a cellar in the mediaeval style, a bar, and a wine bar.

The old Merchants' Hall of Braşov (also known as the Hirscher House) was built between 1539 and 1545 in the style of the Transylvanian High Renaissance. It was the centre of the trading activities of the various guilds, and its internal layout, on three floors, indicates the multiplicity of purposes which it served: wine cellar in the basement, warehouses and shops on the ground floor, sale-rooms on the first floor. The building is laid out round two inner courtyards 12 feet wide, bounded by three vaulted passages on the ground floor which support the upper storey. It was altered several times in the course of the centuries, to a large extent losing its original character. After being damaged by fire in 1957 it was rebuilt in 1960–61 in the style of the original building by the Directorate of Historical Monuments.

The present-day use of the building continues its ancient commercial tradition. There are restaurants on the first floor and the east side of the ground floor; the rooms opening on to the portico have been turned into shops selling craft goods; and the wine cellar, with a wine bar in the northern wing, still serves its original purpose.

On the south of the square is the **Black Church** *(Biserica Neagră)*, a hall church in late Gothic style, which took almost a century to build (1385-1477).

In the interior are a fine collection of **Oriental carpets** of the 16th and 17th centuries and a large **organ** (4000 pipes) built in 1839. (Organ recitals are given weekly.)

The church is dedicated to the Virgin. It acquired its name after a fire in 1689 which left nothing standing but the blackened walls. It was restored in 1711–15 and is one of the finest examples of Gothic art in Rumania. It is also the largest church in Rumania, 290 feet long and 75 feet wide. It has a nave with side aisles.

Opposite the south front of the church is a local museum.

To the south is the **Şchei district,** formerly the quarter occupied by the Rumanians, who were allowed

---

BRAŞOV

1 Black Church
2 Ecaterina Gate
3 State Theatre
4 Cetăţuia
5 Carpaţi Hotel

6 Hotel Postăvarul
7 "Carpathian Stag"
8 Bureau de change
9 Arte Populară
10 Tourist Office
11 Church of St Bartholomew
12 Regional Museum

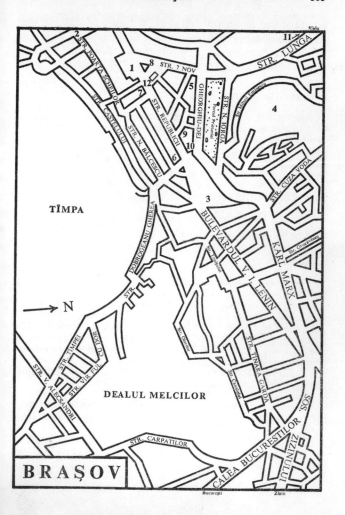

to enter the town only at certain times of day. It was dominated by a **fortress,** the well preserved remains of which can be seen at the foot of Mount Tîmpa (14th, 15th and 16th centuries). The paths which run round the remains are a favourite place of recreation for the people of Braşov.

Among the most interesting remains are *Catherine's Tower* (1559), still bearing the coat of arms of the citadel; the *Blacksmiths' Bastion* (containing the town archives), with some remains of the fortress walls; and the *White Tower* and the *Black Tower*, outposts of the citadel on the Warthe hill. The very well preserved **Weavers' Bastion** (15th century) contains a section of the Historical Museum devoted to the fortress of Braşov and the fortifications of the Bîrsa district.

Also in the Şchei district is the Orthodox **Church of St Nicholas,** which was for long the centre of Rumanian resistance to Habsburg attempts to impose Catholicism.

There was a wooden church here in the 14th century; its position is now marked by a stone cross. The building of a stone church was begun at the end of the 15th century and continued throughout the whole of the 16th century, being largely financed by the Voivodes of Wallachia and Moldavia. The *clock tower* dates from 1751 and was built with the support of the Empress Elizabeth of Russia, who protected the Orthodox Rumanians of the Şchei district against the encroachments of the Austrian court. In the interior are 19th century wall paintings.

The visitor may also wish to visit the industrial parts of the town, seeing in particular the modern building of the *New Station*.

Tourist Office: 9, Bd Carpaţi (tel. 13.831).

Surroundings of Braşov

1. Mount Tîmpa (3,150 feet, 1 hour's walking); from the summit there is a magnificent view of the town and its surroundings. Cabin-lift.

2. Poiana Braşov (10 km–6 miles; 3,350 feet) and *Mount Postăvarul* (5,912 feet). Poiana Braşov is one of the principal health resorts in Rumania and a winter sports centre where most of the Rumanian ski and skating races are held. It has several first-class hotels and large numbers of villas and huts scattered about in attractive clearings among the trees.

It is a restful place for a holiday, with many pleasant walks, and there are also a small lake (swimming, boating) and facilities for sports and games. The town is dominated by *Mount Postăvarul*, reached in 8 minutes by a cabin-lift which in winter serves many skiing slopes (some of them easy, others real competition runs). Close to the cabin-lift station is the Cristianul Mare hut (5,594 feet), from the terrace of which there is a wide-ranging view of the Bucegi Mountains and the Braşov depression. Both at Poiana Braşov and on Postăvarul there are many skiing slopes particularly suitable for beginners.

The pleasant climate of Poiana Braşov—sheltered as it is from high winds—and the excellent facilities it offers make it an ideal holiday place both in winter and in summer. Among its sporting facilities are its stadium (with a running track), the Valea Lupului ("Wolf's Valley") ski run (approved by the International Ski Federation for international competitions), the ski-jumping platform (for jumps of up to 85 metres) and an artificial skating rink. There is a good road from Braşov to Poiana Braşov.

3. Hărman, Prejmer, Sf. Gheorghe

Take D.N. 11, which runs intoMold avia. *Hărman* (8 km–5 miles), a village on the left of the road, has a 13th century church which was fortified in the 15th century. Carpets in the Persian style are woven here.

Prejmer (16 km—10 miles—from Braşov), a
village lying 3 km (2 miles) off the road on the right,
contains a magnificent *fortified settlement* dating from
the 13th to 15th centuries.

Within the enclosure is a 13th century **church,** showing the
full tide of Cistercian influence.

The first **defensive wall** was built round the church in the
15th century. It is 40 feet high, with a sentry walk round the
upper part. The wall is on a circular plan, with four semicircular
towers and another tower above the gate. Between the semicircular towers ran an inner wall of smaller size. In the 16th
century about 300 cells were built against the inner side of the
defensive wall; they were arranged in four tiers and were intended to provide shelter for the population of the village in
case of a siege.

A second fortified enclosure, known as the *"Courtyard of
the Town Hall"*, was built in the 16th and 17th centuries in front
of the entrance tower. The outside is decorated with arcatures
in the Renaissance style.

Finally, in the 18th century, a third enclosure—the *"Bakers'
Courtyard"*—was added, and an arcaded corridor in the baroque
style was built in front of the "Courtyard of the Town Hall".

The whole complex was restored in 1960–63 by the Directorate of Historical Monuments.

Prejmer contains a textile factory and a large
agricultural cooperative, as well as a trout hatchery.

The road to Sf. Gheorghe branches off the main
road to Moldavia at Chichiş, 21 km (13 miles)
from Braşov. This is D.N. 12, which goes off on
the left, heading north. **Sf. Gheorghe** contains a
fortified church and a small museum. Now an
industrial centre (textiles, timber), this town on the
banks of the Olt is the successor to an earlier Daco-
Roman settlement. In mediaeval times it was
occupied by Szekler settlers brought here to guard
the eastern frontier of Transylvania.

The town has a fine **Local Museum,** founded in 1875. The many remains of earlier civilisations which it contains include painted pottery found on the Neolithic site of Ariușd (on the banks of the Olt), a Dacian hoard of silver and—among material belonging to later periods—a master potter's workshop dating from 1649. The ethnographical section contains a peasant cottage from the commune of Armășeni and fine examples of Szekler doors of carved wood.

In the district there are a number of other villages with interesting *fortified churches: Arcuș* (which is also a small thermal resort), *Ghidfalău, Ilieni.*

4. Rîșnov and **Bran:** see pp. 134-35, itinerary from Cîmpulung to Brașov.

10.   FROM BRAŞOV TO SIBIU

From Braşov to Făgăraş (68 km — 43 miles) and Sibiu (142 km — 89 miles) the road runs across the high plateau, ringed by mountains, of Transylvania. The valleys of the great rivers are the gateways to this natural fortress, which was the heart of Decebal's Dacian kingdom and of Roman Dacia. A voivodate which in mediaeval times became subject to Hungarian, Ottoman or Habsburg control, Transylvania had a troubled history which in many places had left a mark still visible today. These remains of the past, including many fortifications, combine with the attractive towns and the beautiful scenery to draw tourists to Transylvania. Other attractions are the folk art and traditions of the district, which are of striking variety and interest. In the villages of Transylvania the peasants can still be seen wearing their beautiful traditional costumes on feast days; and there are many dance teams and choirs in the villages which perpetuate the traditional folk songs and folk dancing.

Immediately after leaving Braşov by Str. Lungă and the old part of the town, D.N. 1 heads across the Braşov plain towards the Perşani Mountains. At the foot of Mount Măgura Codlei (4,246 feet) it comes to **Codlea** (14 km–9 miles), an industrial centre with a number of factories (woodworking, chemicals, foodstuffs, etc.), which has in recent years developed from a village into a sizeable town.

Codlea's many glasshouses for the production of flowers and vegetables have earned it the name of the "Town of Flowers". It is of very ancient origin: indeed, traces of the primitive commune have been discovered here. In the Middle Ages the guilds of craftsmen built a *citadel*, the walls of which can be seen in the centre of the town. This citadel replaced an older fortress on Măgura Codlei which was pulled down in 1333 because it had become a centre of resistance to the Hungarian crown.

5 km (3 miles) from Codlea is the *Forest Bath*, a public swimming bath fed by thermal springs, situated in the middle of the forest which clothes the slopes of Măgura Codlei. Round it are a number of tourist huts.

After Codlea D.N. 1 passes through the Perşani Mountains and then descends into another of the depressions within the Carpathians, the Făgăraş depression, extending from the Făgăraş Mountains to the Tîrnave plateau.

At Sercaia (52 km—33 miles), where there is a large State farm, a country road branches off on the left to the village of **Vad** (4 km—2½ miles), which contains a 15th century *church* with many *icons on glass*, a branch of folk art much practised in this district. 4 km (2½ miles) from Vad is the *Daffodil Clearing*, a large clearing in an oak forest (Dumbrava Vadului) which is covered with daffodils in flower at the end of May and beginning of June. It is remarkable sight, particularly on account of the large area of flowers, and is designated as a "natural monument".

Făgăraş (68 km–43 miles; 23,000 inhabitants) takes its name from the Făgăraş depression, in which it is the largest town. Some 7 centuries old, it has developed considerably in the last ten years, becoming an important centre of the chemical industry.

In the centre of the town is **Făgăraş Castle,** the fortress round which the mediaeval town grew up. The castle was built in 1538 in place of an earlier fortress of earth and timber dating from the early 14th century, owned between 1366 and 1460 by the Voivodes of Wallachia.

The other tourist attractions of Făgăraş are its *Historical Museum* and the *Church of St Nicholas,* founded at the end of the 17th century by Constantin Brîncoveanu and containing frescoes of the period.

Tourist Office: 1, Str. Constantin Pop (tel. 272).

The Făgăraş Mountains

Beyond Făgăraş the road gradually draws closer to a long chain of mountains which bounds the plain to the south. These are the Făgăraş Mountains, which the French geographer Emmanuel de Martonne called "the Alps of Transylvania". The chain is part of the Southern Carpathians and contains the highest peaks in Rumania, Moldoveanul (8,348 feet) and Negoiul

(8,317 feet). It is not surprising, therefore, that there are places in the Făgăraș Mountains that are under snow for 8 or 9 months of the year. And for the tourist they offer a magnificent panorama which forms the background to his journey for some 45 miles.

Formed of crystalline schists with occasional outcrops of limestone, the Făgăraș Mountains consist of a series of pyramid-shaped peaks joined by narrow ridges. To the north they descend to a height of 2,300 feet in a series of parallel ridges extending over a distance of some 6 miles, the valleys in which show the mark of the glaciers of the Quaternary period. On these mountain terraces many lakes have been formed, and these "eyes of the sea", as they are called locally, give the landscape a peculiar attraction. The Făgăraș lakes, more than 70 in number, are scattered throughout the range, at heights of from 5,900 to 7,500 feet, the largest of them (Bîlea and Urlea) reaching an area of 6,000 square yards. The slopes of the mountains up to a height of 5,600–5,900 feet are covered with huge forests of coniferous and deciduous trees.

The mountains contain a rich and varied fauna, including deer and the large Carpathian bear. In the Alpine zone chamois are frequently seen, and in many valleys are under statutory protection. Also in this zone, particularly on the south-facing slopes, are large areas of pasturage used for stock rearing. Many signposted footpaths climb up through the most beautiful of the Făgăraș valleys to the path which runs along the crest, from Piatra Craiului in the east to the Olt defile in the west. This path provides one of the finest excursions in the Rumanian Carpathians, for it enables the climber to ascend or to skirt six peaks of over 8,200 feet and 30 of over 7,900. A series of huts —some at the foot of the mountains, others on the upper margin of the forest, others again close to the summits (Bîlealac, 6,700 feet; Podragul, 7,000 feet)—provide accommodation for tourists. Throughout the winter and into spring these are popular with skiers, who find in the area of the huts good skiing slopes and an abundance of snow lasting until the end of May.

From the villages scattered out along D.N. 1 there are country roads leading to the foot of the mountains, and from there signposted footpaths take the climber into the heart of the range.

At *Ucea de Jos* (90 km–56 miles) a country road branches off on the left, coming in 8 km (5 miles) to the town of *Victoria*.

This centre of the chemical industry is quite new, for it was only in 1949 that the first houses appeared among the scrub at the foot of the highest peaks of the Făgăraş Mountains. A footpath leads to the Arpaş hut (1,970 feet) and from there, by way of the Podragul valley, to the highest hut in the range (Podragul, 7,000 feet).

At *Arpaşu de Jos* (94 km–59 miles) a country road goes off on the left to the village of *Cîrţişoara*, the inhabitants of which, like those of Arpaşu de Jos and Arpaşu de Sus, are renowned for the painting of icons on glass.

From here a footpath climbs up the Bîlea valley to the *Bîlea-Cascada* hut (4,050 feet), one of the finest tourist centres in the Făgăraş Mountains. It then passes the Bîlea waterfall and comes to the *Bîlea-Lac* hut (6,700 feet), on a small peninsula in the largest glacial lake in the Făgăraş, in an Alpine setting of striking beauty.

Farther along the road a track goes off on the right to the village of *Cîrta*, rather more than a mile away, with the ruins of the oldest Gothic building in Rumania (a 13th century Cistercian monastery). Then, after passing through *Porumbacu de Jos*, the starting point for the *Negoiul hut* (5,070 feet), D.N. 1 enters the village of **Avrig** (115 km–72 miles).

Avrig was the birthplace of *Gheorghe Lazăr* (1779–1823), who founded in Bucharest in 1818 the first higher educational establishment in which the teaching was in Rumanian. The visitor should see the house in which he was born, his grave, and his bust by Cornel Medrea. Here also, in the middle of a beautiful park, are the former summer residence of the Governor of Transylvania, Brukenthal, and a 13th century church (Evangelical). On feast days the peasants wear the beautiful traditional costumes of Avrig and the other villages of the Făgăraş depression (Porumbacu de Jos, Sîmbăta, Drăguş, etc.).

After Avrig D.N. 1 leaves the Făgăraş depression and enters the Sibiu depression. Shortly before

Veştem (km 129–81 miles) it is joined by D.N. 7, coming from Bucharest by way of the Olt defile (see Itinerary N⁰ 7, p. 141).

The road passes *Selimbăr* and the plain on which Michael the Brave defeated the Governor of Transylvania, Andreas Bathory, in 1599.

142 km (89 miles): **Sibiu** (see next chapter).

11.   SIBIU

Sibiu (altitude 1,350-1,400 feet; 125,000 inhabitants). An important tourist centre, but also an industrial town (engineering, textiles, foodstuffs, etc.) and an old-established cultural centre (State Theatre, symphony orchestra, an important museum, etc.), Sibiu has developed considerably in the last few decades, its population having doubled since 1930.

History of the town. Men have lived here since the remotest times. In addition to Stone Age remains, the archaeologists have discovered on Guşteriţa Hill a bronze foundry of the Hallstatt period, pointing to the existence here of a settlement of craftsmen, and a Daco-Roman village which grew up round the *castrum* of *Cedonia,* built by the Romans to watch over the road which led from the Olt valley into the heart of Transylvania, to *Apulum* (Alba Iulia) and *Napoca* (Cluj).

In the early Middle Ages (12th century) Saxon settlers also made their appearance in the area of Sibiu, which they called *Hermannstadt.* In the 13th century they built a small citadel on the river terrace above the Cibin. This citadel was destroyed by the Tatars in 1241 and rebuilt on a larger scale in the 14th century.

In the 14th century, too, Sibiu obtained the right to hold fairs and became a free city. It then grew into a prosperous town, thanks to the efforts of its merchants and craftsmen and to its busy trade with Wallachia, the Voivodes of which granted it trading privileges. In the 15th century Sibiu surrounded itself

---

SIBIU

1 Town hall
2-3 Defensive towers
4 Council Tower
5 Haller Bastion
6 Soldasch Bastion

7 Guild of Furriers
8 Brukenthal Palace
9 Evangelical Church
10 Hotel Impăratul Romanilor
11 Tourist Office
12 Main post office

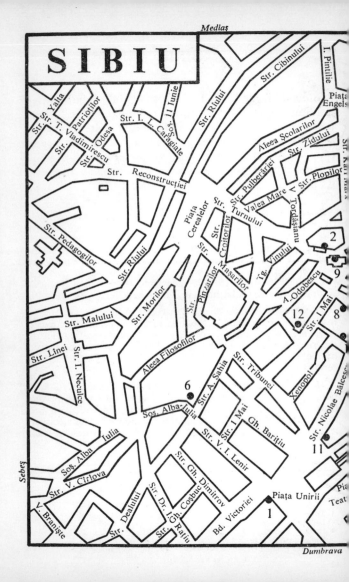

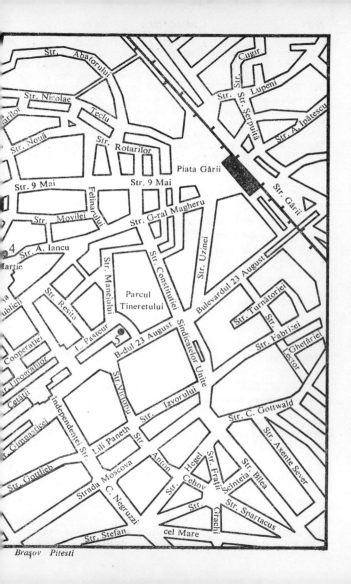

with new fortifications considerably larger than the previous ones, and this time built in brick so as to provide a better defence against firearms, which were now coming into general use. The walls of Sibiu must indeed have been substantial, for they withstood the most furious attacks by the Turks, encouraging the other towns of Transylvania to surround themselves with walls likewise. And it was the possession of a powerful citadel that enabled Sibiu to become the military capital of Transylvania and even, on two occasions (1703–91 and 1849–65) the capital of the Voivodate.

Things to See

The main attractions of Sibiu are its *Cetăţi* (fortifications), parts of which still survive, and the houses built within the walls, which give the centre of the town a typically mediaeval aspect in striking contrast with the new districts.

In the centre of the *Piaţa Griviţa*, which marks the approximate site of the first citadel (13th century), is the **Evangelical Church,** a massive structure which took almost two centuries to complete (14th and 15th centuries).

Originally built on the plan of a Romanesque basilica, it was later rebuilt as a hall church. In the interior, on the north wall of the choir, are *a secco* tempera paintings by Ioan of Rîşnov. In the crypt are a number of gravestones, including that of Mihnea the Bad (1508–09), Voivode of Wallachia, who was killed under the walls of the church by his political enemies.

In the **Piaţa 6 Martie** (the site of the 14th century citadel) is the *House of the Guild of Furriers and Skinners*, which was used as a theatre in the 18th century. (The coat of arms on the façade, bearing the date 1787, was put there in the course of restoration.) In the same square are a number of "*houses* *on legs*", as the local people called the old houses with porticoes in which the craft guilds sold their wares.

Between the Piaţa 6 Martie and the Piaţa Republicii —the main square of the town in the 15th century— is the **Council Tower,** a 14th century structure which now house the *Municipal Historical Museum.*

The **Piaţa Republicii** is surrounded by *houses*, now designated as historical monuments (Nos. 6, 8, 10, 13, 15 and 20), which have preserved their 16th and 17th century doorways. Here also is the house in the Austrian Baroque style built between 1777 and 1785 by the Governor of Transylvania, Brukenthal, partly for the purpose of housing his library and collection of works of art. This collection formed the nucleus of the **Brukenthal Museum,** which was opened to the public in 1817 and is one of the oldest museums in Europe.

Enlarged and reorganised since 1948, the Brukenthal Museum now contains a *section on folk art* illustrating the wealth and variety of the folk art of Transylvania; a *historical section* (history of Transylvania and in particular of Sibiu); a *library* (over 200,000 scientific works in various fields, plus a rich collection of incunabula, manuscripts, etc.); and a **picture gallery** renowned both for its foreign and for its Rumanian art. The foreign collection contains works of the 16th century Flemish and German schools and of the Dutch school, its finest pieces being pictures by *Titian, Rubens, Jordaens* and *Van Dyck.* The works of Transylvanian artists of the past are better represented here than anywhere else, with works by the Stranovius family, Franz Neuhauser, Theodor Glotz, Frederich Miess, Robert Welmann and others. The last rooms contains paintings by *T. Aman, S. Hentia, N. Grigorescu, I. Andreescu, Ş. Luchian, N. Toniţa, T. Pallady* and *A. Ciucurencu,* works of sculpture by *I. Jalea* and *C. Medrea,* and drawings by the Sibiu artist *H. Hermann.*

The Brukenthal Museum also contains, in a separate building, a *section on natural science;* and an open-air section, to be devoted to a display of peasant tools and equipment, is in process of being established in the Dumbrava forest.

Other things of interest in Sibiu include the *Passage of the Staircases*, a typically mediaeval corner formed by the walls of the lower town; the *Old Town Hall*, a building in the Gothic style erected in 1470 and bought by the town in 1548 to serve as town hall; the *Towers of the Guilds* (the carpenters, the potters and the crossbow makers) and the south-east wall of the citadel; the *Haller Bastion* (1551); and the *Orthodox Metropolitanate* (built in 1906; beautiful choral singing at Sunday morning services); the *Permanent Exhibition of Hunting Weapons and Trophies* at 4, Str. Şcoala de Înot; the *Museum of the History of Pharmacy* at 26 Piaţa 6 Martie; and the *Museum of Natural History* at 1 Str. Cetăţii.

Excursions in the Surrounding Area

1. To the *Dumbrava*, a forest on the outskirts of the town: lakes (boating), a small zoo, a section of the Brukenthal Museum (mentioned above), a restaurant and a camping site.

2. To *Răşinari* (12 km–8 miles), a commune with a long tradition of folk art and traditions. Ethnographical Museum. House of the poet Octavian Goga (d. 1938).

3. To *Păltiniş* (34 km—21 miles; altitude 4,760 feet), the highest health resort in Rumania, in the wooded region of the Cindrel Mountains (7,366 feet). From Păltiniş there are many footpaths leading to the *Cibin Gorges*, the *Cindrel Lakes*, the *Sad valley*, etc.

4. To *Cisnădie* (14 km—9 miles), with an interesting church built in the 13th century and fortified in the 15th. Rather more than a mile from Cisnădie is *Cisnădioara*, a village famed for its cherry orchards and its 12th century Romanesque church, which stands on top of a hillock in the centre of the commune, surrounded by its defensive walls.

5. To *Ocna Sibiului* (13 km—8 miles; altitude 1,340 feet), a resort known for its mineral springs (containing sodium chloride and bicarbonate) and its muds (containing sodium chloride, calcium, magnesium and ferrous sulphide) from the salt lakes formed in the abandoned salt workings. The water of Ocna Sibiului, used in the form of cold baths from the 16th century, is now also used for hot baths in a well equipped bathing establishment which is open throughout the year. Bathing in the warm lakes is recommended for the treatment of affections of the locomotor system, chronic gynaecological conditions, diseases of the peripheral nervous system and the after effects of thrombophlebitis.

Tourist Office: Sibiu, 53, Str. N. Bălcescu (tel. 1.25.99 and 1.11.88).

12. FROM SIBIU TO ALBA IULIA
(70 km – 44 miles)

AND CLUJ (171 km – 107 miles)

D.N. 1 now continues on its course through the most picturesque parts of central Transylvania. Leaving Sibiu by the *Turnişor* district (13th century church), the road skirts the town airport and passes through the commune of **Cristian,** in the centre of which are the massive towers of a fine *fortified church*. Built in the first half of the 14th century, the church was fortified in the 15th century and surrounded by a double line of walls.

At the end of the Cibin depression a road branches off on the left, leading in a mile or two to the villages of **Sălişte** and **Tilişca,** old established communities of Mărgineni shepherds well known for the beauty of their folk art and ancient traditions.

At **Sălişte** the tourist can see the *Ethnographical Museum* or hear the *peasant choir* (founded in 1883) singing in the community centre. The village also contains a *craft cooperative*, which produces *carpets* famed for their beauty and embroidered traditional costumes.

The neighbouring village of *Tilişca* (3 km—2 miles; altitude 2,070 feet), is also remarkable for the quality of its folk art, both in the style of building and interior decoration and in the costumes worn on feast days. Tilişca is mentioned in documents of the 14th century, but seems to be much older than this; for there has recently been discovered, on *Cătinaş* Hill, a fortified Dacian settlement which was occupied from the first Iron Age (Hallstatt) until the Roman conquest. A citadel was also built on this hill in the 14th century, but of this nothing is left but a few shapeless ruins.

After passing through *Apoldu de Sus*, D.N. 1 enters (km 35–22 miles) the commune of **Miercurea.**

The name Miercurea comes from the word *miercuri* or Wednesday, the day on which the market used to be held. In the middle of the commune is a church, small but well preserved, built in the 13th century and fortified in the 15th. Under the sentry walk which runs round the defensive walls are storehouses in which until the 19th century the inhabitants stored their food. Some 5 km (3 miles) away is a small local health resort (Băile Miercurea), with a camping site.

A. SEBEŞ

Near the River Mureş is the town of Sebeş, a considerable industrial centre (woodworking, textiles, leathers and skins). Distance from Sibiu 55 km (34 miles).

History of the town. The town of Sebeş occupies the site of an old Daco-Roman settlement (2nd and 3rd centuries). To the south of the town, at Petreşti and Căpîlna, remains dating from the end of the Neolithic period (2800–1900 B.C.) have also been discovered. The mediaeval town was established in the 12th century, when Saxon settlers were sent here. The town was devastated by the Tatars in 1241, but soon recovered. It is mentioned in documents of the 14th century as being the chief town in the Apold depression, and in 1387 it was granted the right to build fortifications. Throughout the 14th century the town flourished, thanks to its close trade relations with Wallachia, where the leather of Sebeş in particular was much in demand. During the whole mediaeval period the town played an important part in the history of Transylvania, and the Diet of the Voivodate met here several times.

Things to See

The **Evangelical Church** is a monumental structure built at a number of different periods.

Begun in the 13th century in the style of a Romanesque basilica (as can be seen from the west front), it was continued at the end of the same century under the influence of the early Gothic style. In the 14th century the east end was demolished and a *Gothic choir* (completed in 1383) was built. Finally, in the 15th century, the church took on its present aspect with the demolition of the walls of the lateral aisles of the Romanesque basilica and the building of new walls linked with the Gothic choir, producing a building remarkable for its rich carved decoration and its harmony of line. The church also contains a fine reredos of large size (43 feet high by 16 feet wide) decorated in the late Gothic style and dating from 1518–26. The *Chapel of St James*, close to the church on the north side, was built in 1383 in the Gothic style.

The **House of the Voivodes** (15th century), where the Diet of Transylvania met several times and where the Voivode Ioan Zapolya died in 1540, now contains an interesting *District Museum* containing material on the history of the town and district.

The *Roman Catholic Church* was built in the 14th century and restored in the 18th. Of the *Citadel of Sebeş* there remain only a few towers and some pieces of wall.

An interesting story is told about the *Tailors' Tower*. In 1438 the Turkish armies of Sultan Murad II arrived under the walls of Sebeş. The Voivode of Wallachia, Vlad the Devil, who was with the Turks, held a parley with the principal citizens of the town, and persuaded them to abandon the struggle and open their gates to the invaders. Some of the inhabitants, however, mistrusted the Turkish promises, barricaded themselves in the tower and continued to resist. The Turks then set fire to the tower and captured it; and the only survivor, a young man of 16 who was studying at Sebeş, was taken prisoner and sold as a slave at Adrianople. After five unsuccessful attempts to escape and twenty years of captivity the student managed to flee to Italy and then to Germany. There he wrote in Latin a work entitled *Of the Religion, the Manners and the Infamies of the Turks*, which was published in 1458, its author being described merely as "the Nameless One of Sebeş". Since this was one of the first works about a people who were feared but little known in central and western Europe, the book achieved enormous success and went throughout 25 editions up to the end of the 16th century. In memory of the student of Sebeş, therefore, the people of Sebeş have given the old Tailors' Tower the name of the *"Student's Tower"*.

Rîpa Roşie (the Red Ravine), 3 km (2 miles) north of the town.

Here, on the *Secaşe plateau*, erosion has exposed red rocks in fantastic shapes carved out of the marine sediments which built up the plateau some 60 million years ago. Rîpa Roşie is designated as a "natural monument".

A mountain road (very difficult) runs through beautiful scenery in the Parîng range to *Novaci* and *Bengeşti*, on the road from Tîrgu Jiu to Rîmnicu Vîlcea (p. 137). Distance 110 km (69 miles).

Beyond Sebeş D.N. 1 and D.N. 7, which joined before Sibiu and have since been following the same line, separate again, D.N. 7 running westward to Deva (65 km–41 miles) and Arad (see Itinerary 4, Arad-Deva-Sebeş), D.N. 1 heading north to Alba Iulia and Cluj.

B. ALBA IULIA

Alba Iulia (30,000 inhabitants) lies in the Mureş valley, in the heart of Transylvania, and stands high among Rumanian towns for its wealth of historical associations and its rich heritage from the past. It is the chief town of the district and also an industrial town (foodstuffs, leather, boots and shoes, building materials). Distance from Sebeş 20 km (13 miles).

History of the town. Alba Iulia is a very ancient town, for the site has been continuously occupied from the 5th millen-

---

ALBA IULIA

1 Hotel l Mai
2 Post office
3 Tourist Office
4 Historical Museum
5 Batthyanaeum
6-8 Gates of citadel

7 Maieri Church (18th century)
9 Monument to Horia, Cloşca and Crişan
10 Orthodox Cathedral
11 Bastion
12 Prince's Palace
13 Catholic Cathedral
14 Catholic Bishop's Palace

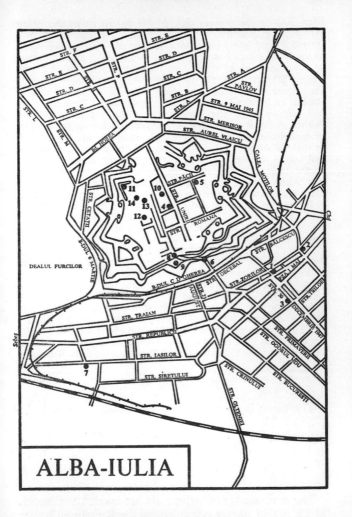

ALBA-IULIA

nium B.C. to the present day. In the district called the "New World", for example, the remains of a Neolithic settlement (fireplaces and huts) have been discovered; material belonging to the Bronze Age has been found in the town; and at Teleac, on the other bank of the Mureş, the largest citadel of earth and timber belonging to the first Iron Age. And quite recently there have been discovered near Alba Iulia the remains of *Apulon*, an important Dacian city mentioned by Ptolemy in the 2nd century B.C. The importance of the site increased still further in the Roman period, when beside the strong fortress of *Apulum* there grew up the Roman town of the same name which at the end of the 2nd century became the political, economic and administrative centre of the province of *Dacia Apulensis*. In the 10th and 11th centuries, under the name of *Bălgrad* (the White Town), the town came under Slav and Rumanian control, and then became the chief town of the comitat of Alba.

In the 16th and 17th centuries Alba Iulia became the capital of the principality of Transylvania. In 1599 Michael the Brave entered the town as a conqueror and had himself proclaimed Prince of Wallachia and Transylvania; then, adding to this the title of "Prince of all Moldavia", achieved for the first time the union of the three great provinces of Rumania. In the 17th century Alba Iulia was an important printing centre, producing books in the Rumanian language. After the quelling of the peasant rising of 1784 its leaders Horia, Cloşca and Crişan were imprisoned here. Crişan committed suicide in his cell, and Horia and Cloşca were broken on the wheel, on 28 February 1785, on the plateau which is still called Horia's Field. Finally it was at Alba Iulia that a great popular assembly proclaimed on 1st December 1918 the union of Transylvania with Rumania.

Tour of the Town

The town is in two parts—the *lower town* and the *Citadel*. The road which climbs up to the Citadel passes through a complex pattern of fortifications in the style of Vauban. From the entrance, in front of which there is a monument to the rebels of 1784, there is a fine view.

The main sights of Alba Iulia are inside the **Citadel,** which is still partly occupied by the Rumanian army.

The 18th century Citadel was the last great fortress to be built in Rumania, and 20,000 serfs were employed for 24 years (1715-38) on its building. It was designed by the Italian architect Giovanni Morando Visconti, and was built under the direction of Prince Eugene of Savoy. It is in the shape of a star and consists of a central fort flanked by 7 bastions and surrounded by an outer wall with 4 bastions and a double line of ditches in front of each wall. Inside is a network of casemates, tunnels and passages, some of which are now used as cellars by the wine and spirits enterprise *Vinalcool*.

Apart from the massive *brick walls*, the main features are the fine **entrance gates,** decorated with a profusion of carving and stone statues in the purest Baroque style. Above the main gate is the cell in which it is said that Horia was imprisoned before his execution.

The Citadel occupies the end of the terrace above the Mureş on which the four fortresses which preceded it were built: the stone-built Roman *castrum* belonging to the XIIIth legion (Gemina), the most powerful of all the Roman fortresses built in Dacia; the palisaded earth citadel of the local voivodate (9th-10th centuries); the citadel of the comitat of Alba (13th century), consisting of a stone rampart round the Catholic Cathedral, the Bishop's Palace and their precincts; and the citadel built at the beginning of the 16th century and strengthened in the following century, in which Michael the Brave resided. The remains of the walls of this last citadel are still to be seen behind the Bishop's Palace.

Entering the Citadel, we see on the right the *Historical Museum*. The Museum offices occupy the house in which, on 1 December 1918, the act of union restoring Transylvania to Rumania was signed.

The Museum itself, which contains a considerable collection of material on the history of Transylvania and the district round Alba Iulia, is near the Orthodox Cathedral. The exhibits include a large number of statues, inscriptions, sarcophagi, etc., from the ruins of the Roman city. There is also a section devoted to the history of the peasant rising of 1784.

A short distance beyond the Museum, on the right, is the (Orthodox) *Cathedral of Reunification*, built in

1921–22 on the model of the Prince's Church at Tîrgo-viște. The interior contains some fine neo-Byzantine frescoes. In the pronaos are portraits of Voivode Michael the Brave and his wife Princess Stanca.

King Ferdinand and Queen Marie were crowned here in 1922.

To the south, a few yards away on the other side of the central avenue, is the **Catholic Cathedral,** an interesting combination of the Romanesque, Gothic, Renaissance and Baroque styles and one of the finest buildings in Rumania.

The building was begun in the 13th century on the site of a 12th century Romanesque church destroyed by the Tatars in 1242. The work was carried out under the direction of a French architect, who followed the plan of the Romanesque three-aisled basilicas. Completed in the year 1300 with the construction of its cross vaulting in the style characteristic of early Gothic, the cathedral has undergone much later repair and alteration. Thus in 1512 the North Chapel, in the Renaissance style, was added; in the 17th century the south tower was completed by Italian craftsmen who gave it the aspect of a campanile; and in the 18th century the west doorway was rebuilt and embellished with a triangular pediment with four statues in the Baroque style.

In the interior, note the bas-relief in the main apse (13th century), and the pillared south apse with traces of 14th and 16th century frescoes. In this apse also are a number of sarcophagi: on the right those of Iancu of Hunedoara, Voivode of Transylvania, his brother and his son, in the Gothic style with some Renaissance features; on the left those of Queen Isabelle and her son John Sigismund, Prince of Transylvania, with delicate Renaissance carving.

In front of the entrance to the Catholic Cathedral is the *Bishop's Palace*, much altered at different periods. Its present aspect dates from the 18th century. The park round the Palace, on one of the bastions of the Citadel, contains a number of Roman inscriptions.

Other sights of interest in Alba Iulia include:

The **Batthyanaeum Documentary Library,** in a building
dating from 1719, a former church converted after 1784 into a
library and astronomical observatory by Bishop Ignatiu Bat-
thyani. The observatory and the instruments of the period have
been preserved, along with the library, which contains a large
number of old and valuable manuscripts and over 500 incunabula. Among the manuscripts is a "Codex Aureus" of the
9th century, written on parchment in letters of gold. Among
other old Rumanian books are a *Palia of Orăştie* (the oldest
Rumanian translation of the Bible, published at Orăştie in
1582) and the "Bălgrad New Testament" (1648).

The *Prince's Palace*, the former residence of the Voivode
of Transylvania. The main building, dating from the 14th
century and destroyed in 1662 during a Turkish and Tatar
invasion, was later converted into a barracks.

The *Plateau of the Romans*, to the south-west of the Citadel,
with the remains of the Roman *castrum* of *Apulum*, and also
of the feudal town which was demolished to make room for
the latest fortress.

Tourist Office: 3, Str Republicii (tel. 2.38).

C. THE WINE COUNTRY. AIUD

North of Alba Iulia D.N.1 continues up the Mureş
valley, with views on the left of the last summits of the
Apuseni Mountains (the Western Carpathians), dominated by the pyramid-shaped peaks of Piatra Craivii
(3553 feet) and Piatra Cetei (4,049 feet). Stretching up
to the foot of the mountains is an area of hills and
large vineyards, with many old established villages and
towns, which is known as the **Wine Country.**

The ancient road—the *Via Magna* of the Romans—was not
on the line of the present road, but ran through the villages
at the foot of Piatra Craivii, on the summit of which was discovered the large Dacian city of *Apulon*. It is certain that in those
days the hills on which the villages of Sard, Ighiu, Telna,
Bucerdea-Vinoasă, Cricău, etc., now stand were already covered
with vines. At Telna can be seen a cellar 500 feet long, dug
deep underground by serf labour. The wines stored in the cellars
of the State farm (white Fetească—the commonest type in the

area—Italian Riesling, Pinot Gris and Ottonel Muscat) are of high quality, with a high alcohol content (a minimum of 13°), and have won many gold medals in international competitions.

After passing through *Teiuş*, a small industrial town with a church built by Iancu of Hunedoara in the 15th century, D.N.1 enters the town of **Aiud**, famed for its high quality wines.

History of the town. Aiud is a very ancient town. Remains of a Celtic settlement of the 3rd century B.C. have been discovered here. During the Roman occupation there was a rural settlement with the name of *Brucla*. In the feudal period there grew up a township of craftsmen and vine-growers, and at the beginning of the 14th century they built a small citadel. The large citadel which dominates the present-day town dates from the 15th century. Each of its 9 towers was built by a different guild (on the tower to the left of the entrance can be seen the insignia of one of these guilds). After 1662 Aiud also became a cultural centre, following the foundation of a college at which many men of letters and scientists—such as the mathematician Farkas Bolyai—were students.

The visitor to Aiud should see the *Citadel*, in the centre of which is a *church*, also dating from the 15th century; the *Historical Museum*, in a 15th century house near the walls of the Citadel; and the *Documentary Library* of the college, founded in 1662, now a branch of Cluj University Library. It contains over 66,000 works (books and manuscripts).

An excursion can be made to the *Sloboda hut* (1,800 feet), in an attractive forest 12 km (8 miles) west of Aiud.

After the monument at Mirăslău commemorating the battle fought here in 1601 by Michael the Brave, and the cemetery with the graves of the soldiers who fell here in 1944 in the struggle against Nazism, the road passes through the village of *Decea*, an important archaeological site.

Here, on the banks of the Mureş, was discovered a Neolithic settlement which has given its name to the Decea Mureşului Culture. This dates from the late Neolithic period and is characterised by large numbers of flint knives, the frequent use of copper axes, and the first occurrence of gold ornaments in this part of Europe (the gold being found in the sand of the rivers rising in the Apuseni Mountains).

D. TURDA

After Unirea D.N.1 leaves the Mureş valley, crosses a series of hills, and comes to the town of **Turda** in the valley of the Arieş.

An important industrial centre (chemicals, building materials, timber products, foodstuffs), the town has developed considerably in recent years. Several new housing areas have been built between the old centre of the town and the industrial areas. The population is 52,000.

Near Turda, on the "Plateau of the Romans", is the thermal resort of *Turda* (altitude 1,150 feet), using water from the salt lakes formed in salt workings dating from ancient times and from mineral springs (sodium chloride).

History of the town. On the site occupied by the present town there was an important Dacian city called Potaissa. Near it, on the plateau east of the present town, the Romans built the *castrum* of *Potaissa*, round which there grew up a town with the same name, at first a *municipium* and later a colony. It was at this period that the salt mines on the plateau were first worked. In the Middle Ages Turda was the centre of a large feudal domain, and for some centuries was the meeting place of the Diet of Transylvania.

Things to see: the *Princes' House*, a 16th century building used for the accommodation of those attending the Diet of Transylvania, now the *Local Museum*, with a valuable collection of historical material; the *Evangelical Church*, a 15th century Gothic building, largely constructed with stone from the ruins of Roman buildings; and the *old salt workings* and the 15 salt lakes on the "Plateau of the Romans", used by the local bathing establishment.

Excursions in the district: to the *Turda Gorges*, a picturesque and impressive feature of karstic geology some 7 km (4 miles) west of the town. The gorges are hewn from the limestone plateau, forming a series of steep rock faces pierced here and there by caves which once provided hiding places for the heyducks. On account of their rich and varied vegetation, and particularly because at a height of 1,500 feet species of mountain plants are found side by side with the flora of the plain, the Turda Gorges are designated as a "natural monument". At the entrance to the gorges is a tourist hut, and a signposted footpath runs through them.

Tourist Office: 34, Piaţa Republicii (tel. 15.54).

The Arieş Valley. D.N. 75 runs west from Turda up the valley of the Arieş to *Cîmpeni* (83 km–52 miles) and *Abrud* (95 km–59 miles). This road is one of the principal means of access to the *Apuseni Mountains*, a very large massif which, with its variety and beauty of scenery, offers great attractions to tourists who like mountain country. Some 30 km (19 miles) from Turda the road passes through a defile which the Arieş (the *Aurarum* of the Roman period, so called because of its gold-bearing sand) has cut between Mount Bedeleu (4,029 feet) and Mount Scărişoara-Belioara (4,439 feet). These two great masses of limestone have weathered into a complex pattern of caves and gorges, steep escarpments and ravines. These geological features and the rich and varied flora have led to the establishment of a number of nature reserves. *Lupşa* (70 km–44 miles), a village which in 1325 was the residence of a Rumanian *knez*, contains two 15th century churches and an interesting village ethnographical museum. From *Cîmpeni* (83 km–52 miles) a side road leads to the village of *Gîrda de Sus* (30 km–19 miles), from which there is a signposted footpath to a hut at an altitude of 3,635 feet and from there to the *Scărişoara Glacier* (3,940 feet), an interesting natural feature (2 hours' walking from Gîrda de Sus).

Beyond Turda D.N.1 crosses the hill of Feleac (2,395 feet) and then descends to **Cluj,** one of the largest towns in Rumania (p. 215). Distance from Sibiu 171 km (107 miles).

13. SIGHIŞOARA
AND ITS SURROUNDINGS

A. FROM BRAŞOV TO SIGHIŞOARA
(118 km—74 miles)

From Braşov D.N.13 runs north-west towards Sighişoara.

Passing through a region of varied and picturesque scenery, the road also allows the visitor to see a number of the **peasant fortresses** built round churches in the 15th century, when the Turks and the Tatars made frequent incursions into Transylvania. The fortified churches of the Tîrnave plateau are a characteristic feature of the region. Unlike other fortified churches which are merely surrounded by a wall, the churches on the Tîrnave plateau are regular fortresses with sentry walks, bastions, battlements, etc., built on to the church. They are structures in a style quite different from that of a church and based on an entirely different architectural conception. Many of them are perfectly preserved and are now features of outstanding interest to tourists.

The commune of **Feldioara** lies at the end of the Braşov plain, at the entrance to the second defile in the Olt valley.

It is of very ancient origin, for there was a *castrum* here in the period of Roman occupation. In the early Middle Ages the Teutonic Knights, who had established themselves in the Braşov depression between 1211 and 1225, built a citadel, the ruins of which can still be seen. The commune also contains a 13th century *church*, with features in the early Romanesque style.

Near here in 1529 the Moldavian army of Voivode Petru Rareş, who was supporting the Voivode of Transylvania, Ioan Zapolya, in his claim to the throne of Hungary, won a victory over the armies of the towns in Saxony who were supporting the claims of Ferdinand I of Habsburg. As a result of this victory the Voivode of Moldavia gained control of large domains in Transylvania.

After passing through *Rotbav* and *Măeruş*, two villages on the banks of the Olt with old fortified churches, the road crosses one of the wooded summits of the Perşani Mountains and rejoins the Olt as it emerges from the defile at *Hoghiz*.

From here there is a country road to *Homorod*, *Caţa* and *Drăuşeni*, where there are also fortress churches. The one at **Homorod,** built at various times from 1270 onwards and completely restored in 1657, is one of the largest and strongest of the peasant fortresses. It is only 2 km (1¼ miles) from the main road.

Rupea (66 km—41 miles; altitude 1,480 feet) owes its position as a thermal resort to the springs of sulphurous and salt water at the foot of the volcanic hill which dominates the town.

It is of very ancient origin. Remains have been found here dating from the late Neolithic period (5500-3500 B.C.). The settlement of the 8th, 9th, and 10th centuries was succeeded by a feudal town which in the 12th century built a citadel on the summit of the basalt hill. On this hill there are now the remains of **three fortresses,** for in the 15th century a second wall was built round the first, and in the 17th century a third wall was built at the foot of the hill.

After Rupea the road passes through *Saschiz*, where there is a fortified church dating from the 15th and 16th centuries and, on the neighbouring hill, a citadel built in the 14th century.

In the valley of the *Tîrnava Mare* D.N.13 passes through **Albeşti,** where in 1849 was fought the battle between the Hungarian revolutionary forces and the armies of the Habsburg Empire in which the Hungarian poet *A. Petöfi* was killed. Petöfi was buried here, and there is a *museum* commemorating his career. Albeşti now contains one of the largest undertakings belonging to the town of Sighişoara, the glass and china factory. Soon after Albeşti the road enters *Sighişoara* (p. 202).

B. FROM SIBIU TO MEDIAŞ (54 km—34 miles) AND SIGHIŞOARA (93 km—58 miles)

From Sibiu D.N.14 runs north towards the heart of the Tîrnava plateau and Transylvania to Mediaş and Sighişoara.

After *Şura Mare*, a commune established on the site of a Daco-Roman village, where there is a church built in the 13th century and fortified in 1523, D.N.14 passes through the commune of **Slimnic,** dominated by the walls of a *citadel* built in the 15th century on a neighbouring hill. Within the citadel is a squat little church dating from the same period.

After passing through a number of other villages the road comes to **Axente Sever,** so called because it was the birthplace of Axente Sever, one of the leaders of the 1848 revolution.

In the commune is a *church* built in the 13th century and considerably modified in the 15th, with the addition of a massive tower with a wooden platform for the defenders. It is surrounded by a wall, on the inside of which are numbers of cells which served for the storage of food supplies; there are no towers.

The road now enters the Tîrnava valley and passes through **Copşa Mică,** a centre of the chemical industry (lamp-black and fertilisers produced from methane) and of zinc processing.

The existence of Copşa Mică is recorded in 1700, but its fame dates from the discovery of the rich reserves of natural gas in the region. Here, in 1936, lamp-black was produced from methane for the first time in Rumania. The size of the town and the scale of its production have considerably increased in the last ten years.

At Copşa Mică a country road goes off on the right to the commune of *Valea Viilor* (4 km–2½ miles), where there is a well preserved fortified church built in 1525.

Beyond Copşa Mică, on the other bank of the Tîrnava, can be seen the commune of **Tîrnava** (Prostea Mare), near which there was a stone fortress in the Daco-Roman period. Here also there is a fortified church; and there is another at *Ighişu Nou*, 4 km (2½ miles) to the right of the road.

The road now enters the largest town in the Tîrnava Mare valley, **Mediaş,** which is chiefly dependent for its prosperity on vines and methane. In the last twenty or thirty years the population of Mediaş, has doubled. It is now an important industrial centre (chemicals, metalworking, leather and skins, foodstuffs) with a population of 47,000.

History of the town. The origins of Mediaş go back to a remote antiquity. In the Iron Age there was a Geto-Dacian village here, defended by a stone rampart. In the Roman period a larger settlement flourished at Mediaş, which was an important road junction. The existence of the mediaeval town is recorded in 1263, and by 1522 it had a population of 2,400. From its earliest days this town possessed a small citadel built round a Romanesque church, of which only one of the aisles is left. A larger citadel was built in the 16th century. After 1918, when the first gas pipeline was constructed, Mediaş began to develop into an industrial town.

Things to see: the *Evangelical Church*, built in the 14th and 15th centuries, with a belfry 250 feet high, leaning slightly as a result of a landslide. The church contains a fine triptych painted in 1747-79 and many Oriental carpets. See also the *ruins of the walls and towers of the citadel* (16th century) and the *Historical Museum* of the town.

Excursion in the district: to the vineyards of Hula Blăjelului (2 km – 1¼ miles); to *Buzd, Atel* and *Moşna*, villages to the south of Mediaş with fortified churches of the 15th and 16th centuries.

Tourist Office, Mediaş (tel. 385).

From Mediaş to Tîrnăveni

From Mediaş D.N. 14A runs north to Tîrnăveni and then joins D.N. 15 at Iernut in the Mureş valley (see p. 207).

At Blăjel, famed for the large vineyards which surround it, a road branches off on the left to **Bazna,** a thermal resort situated in a beautiful district rich in vineyards and deposits of natural gas. The existence of mineral waters (which, in addition to salt, contain iodine and sulphuretted hydrogen in higher proportion than in any similar springs in Rumania, and indeed in many famous springs elsewhere in Europe) was discovered by shepherds who had by accident set fire to the gas from one of the springs. The "inextinguishable fire" which followed attracted the attention of scientists, and in 1749 the water of Bazna became famous. No one, however, took any interest in the natural gas which had led to the discovery of the springs until the beginning of the 20th century, when it was rediscovered. The bathing establishment at Bazna dates from 1843, but it was not until a century later that the therapeutic qualities of the springs and the mud of Bazna were put to full use by modern facilities which are available throughout the year. The waters of Bazna are recommended for the treatment of chronic affections of the locomotor system (chronic arthritis, spondylitis, traumatic arthritis, painful calluses, etc.), chronic gynaecological conditions, diseases of the peripheral nervous system, and skin conditions. They have also a favourable effect in the treatment of asthenia, infantile physical debility, scrofula and rickets. After concentration in a special plant they also produce the "Bazna salt" which can be used in the bath at home.

Tîrnăveni (75 km–47 miles) is a centre of the chemical industry (chemicals produced from natural gas). In 1936 there was built here the first plant in Europe for the production of synthetic ammonia from hydrogen extracted from methane and from the nitrogen in air.

From Tîrnăveni D.N.14A continues northward and at *Iernut* (93 km–58 miles) joins Ş.N.15 (see Itinerary 14, p. 207), running to *Tîrgu Mureş* (28 km–18 miles) and *Turda* (47 km–29 miles).

East of Mediaş D.N.14 runs through *Brateiu* (fortified church) and then passes close to **Dumbrăveni.**

Many Armenians were settled in this area by Prince Apaffy. An *Armenian Church* was built here in 1780. Prince Apaffy's palace dates from the 16th century.

9 km (6 miles) south is **Biertan**, where there is a fine 16th century *fortress church*, with a beautiful carved altar and pulpit. There is a triple ring of walls round the church. The Evangelical bishops of Transylvania resided at Biertan from 1572 to 1867: see their tombs.

39 km (24 miles) from Mediaş, the road enters *Sighişoara*.

C. SIGHIŞOARA

Sighişoara (Hungarian *Segesvar*) is renowned for the beauty of its situation and its mediaeval aspect, still preserving the appearance of a cluster of houses huddled round the citadel perched on the summit of the hill. It has a population of 30,000.

History of the town. The origins of Sighişoara go back to a distant past, as is shown by the Bronze Age objects discovered on *Dealul Turcului* (Turk's Hill), near the town, the remains of a 1st century settlement, and the cinerary urns of the Daco-Roman period which prove the existence of a *castrum* on the site of Sighişoara which continued to be occupied even after the Roman administration had left Dacia. In the pre-feudal period the settlement — hitherto no more than a village at the crossing of busy trade routes — became a town of merchants and craftsmen, referred to in 13th century documents as *Castrum sex*.

In the 14th century Sighişoara became a free city and enlarged the small citadel which had stood here since the 12th century, each of the craft guilds contributing to the building of one of the towers and part of the walls. From now on the town prospered,

---

SIGHIŞOARA

1 Hotel Central
2 Tourist Office
3 Covered staircase

4 Goldsmiths' Bastion
5 Ropemakers' Tower
6 Church on the Hill
7 Clock Tower and Museum
8 Monastery Church
9 School

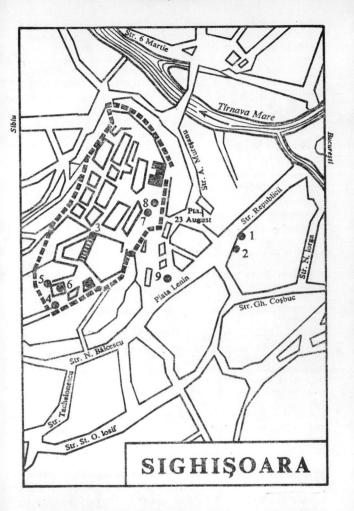

SIGHIȘOARA

particularly from the second half of the 16th century, when it
intensified its trade with Moldavia and Wallachia. To this period
belong most of the buildings of interest in the town. The houses
which crowd together at the foot of the citadel are more recent,
for in 1668 the town was ravaged by an earthquake, and this was
followed in 1676 by a terrible fire; nevertheless they are of respec-
table age, being nearly 300 years old.

Things to See

The **Clock Tower** (14th century), 200 feet high, at the
entrance to the citadel. In 1648 a local craftsman installed an ingenious mechanism, and every night, at
midnight, a figure over 3 feet tall emerges, symboli-
cally representing the day of the week. See the very
interesting *Municipal Museum* in the Clock Tower.
From the tower there is a splendid view of the town.

The *mediaeval citadel* still retains three rings of walls and
9 towers, out of the 14 existing at the beginning of the 15th century. The Church on the Hill, "de pe munte" (14th–15th centuries), in the late Gothic style, contains some fine 15th century
paintings and a beautiful lectern of yew-wood. The church is
approached by a covered wooden stair-case of 175 steps. (17th
century).

The *Monastery Church* (the original building dates from the
13th century) contains a painted altar and an organ dating from
1680; many Oriental carpets.

D. TO SOVATA

From Sighişoara D.N.13 turns north, passing through
the villages of *Măgherus* (fortified church) and *Ţig-
mandru* (famous vineyards), and reaches the valley of
the Tîrnava Mică at Bălăuşeri. From here D.N.13 continues to Tîrgu Mureş (23 km—14 miles: see Itinerary
14, Turda–Tîrgu Mureş–Borsec). To the right D.N.13A
runs to Sovata (40 km—25 miles) by way of Sîngiorgiu
de Pădure.

Sovata (188 km—118 miles; altitude 1,610 feet), a thermal resort, lies in wooded country at the foot of Mount Sacca (5,830 feet), in an area containing the largest deposits of salt in Rumania. Open throughout the year, it owes its reputation to its sun-warmed salt lakes.

The lakes of Sovata occupy the cavities left by the salt workings. They have a surface layer of fresh water which enables the heat of the sun to be stored up in the lower layers of salt water. In consequence the temperature is 19–20 °C. at the surface, 30–40° at a depth of 1 metre and 40–60° at 1½ metres, a significant difference for therapeutic purposes. The largest of the lakes is Lake Ursu (altitude 1,610 feet), which has an area of 54,000 square yards. In immediate proximity are several smaller lakes (Aluniş, Negru, Roşu, Sarpelui) with the same properties. In addition Lake Negru (1,710 feet) contains a mud rich in inorganic substances, particularly chlorides.

Also important from the therapeutic point of view is the Ghera Spring, the water of which has a high salt content. The most recent analyses have shown that its water contains appreciable quantities of substances with hormonal qualities. There are a number of other springs with water of high salt content.

There are five sanatoria (3 gynaecological, 2 rheumatological) for the proper use of the warm lakes in the treatment of chronic gynaecological conditions and glandular (particularly ovarian) deficiencies, and of the other mineral springs and muds in the treatment of chronic rheumatism.

The surrounding mountains and forests afford magnificent walking and fishing (trout). There are also interesting excursions to the *Praid salt mine* (6 km—4 miles), the aragonite quarries in the *Corund valley* (15 km—9 miles) and *Tîrgu Mureş* (63 km—39 miles).

14. THE UPPER MUREŞ REGION

FROM TURDA TO TÎRGU MUREŞ
(75 km—47 miles)
TOPLIŢA (177 km—111 miles)
AND BORSEC (203 km—127 miles)

From Turda (p. 195) this itinerary runs eastward by D.N.15 to Tîrgu Mureş, Reghin, Topliţa and Borsec. From there it is possible to cross the Eastern Carpathians and descend to the Bicaz reservoir in the valley of the Bistriţa (p. 259). The route through the upper Mureş valley passes through pleasant and, in the mountains, strikingly beautiful scenery.

The road first passes through *Cîmpia Turzii* (9 km— 6 miles), a centre of the metalworking industry. In the town park is a small calvary commemorating the treacherous murder of Michael the Brave here in 1601.

After passing through a number of villages—including *Luncani* (19 km—12 miles), where there was a settlement in the 4th and 3rd centuries B.C. and where the Romans built a *castrum*—the road enters *Ludus* (30 km—19 miles), a new industrial centre with a large electric power station and a sugar refinery built about 1960.

Soon after *Iernut* (45 km—28 miles) D.N.15 is joined by D.N.14A from Tîrnăveni (see Itinerary 13), and then passes through the village of **Cipău** (49 km—31 miles), an important archaeological site with a continuous record of human occupation.

Excavation here has yielded linear pottery of the early Neolithic period (5500–3500 B.C.), Iron Age material, 15th century pottery, a hoard of Roman coins and 10th century silver buckles, and 8th and 9th century pottery.

Farther along the Mureş valley, near the village of *Ungheni*, are other important archaeological sites. On the south bank, at the village of **Cristeşti,** a whole series of levels were found—a Scythian settlement (Iron Age), a Dacian settlement, a Roman *castrum* and a large pottery of the same period, along with a settlement which continued to exist after the departure of the Roman administration (3rd century). On the north bank, at **Moreşti,** many discoveries have been made, including a citadel defended by earthworks and palisades built by the Rumanian population in the 11th and 12th centuries.

Tîrgu Mureş (75 km—47 miles; 106,000 inhabitants), chief town of the Mureş region, is the most important town in the upper Mureş valley. Its Hungarian name is *Maros Vasarhély.*

Situated on a terrace above the river, it is a picturesque town and also an active industrial and cultural centre which has developed considerably since 1955 as a result of the building of many new factories and housing areas. The main industries of the town are metalworking, chemicals, woodworking and foodstuffs. It contains a Medico-Pharmaceutical Institute, an Institute of Dramatic Art, a State Theatre and a Lyric Theatre, and many middle schools and technical schools.

History of the town. Tîrgu Mureş is first recorded in the 14th century under the names of *Agriopolis* and *Novum Forum Siculorum*. All round, however, there were older settlements: for exemple at *Sîntana de Mureş*, on the right bank of the Mureş, where a huge 4th century cemetery was found, and—a little farther away—the sites of Cristeşti and Moreşti, already mentioned, with origins going back to the remotest times. In the first half of the 16th century the township on the banks of the Mureş came under the protection of Petru Rareş, Voivode of Moldavia, and in 1610 was granted the right to have a mill for making gunpowder. It was at this period that the town took the name of Tîrgu Mureş. Between 1439 and 1707 the Diet of Transylvania met here on more than 13 occasions; and in 1848 it was from here that the Rumanian revolutionaries Avram Iancu and A. Papiu Ilarian set out for Blaj.

As evidence of the cultural activity of the mediaeval town, it may be noted that as early as the 14th century the town possessed schools where the teaching was given in Latin. Prominent representatives of Rumanian culture in the 19th century like Gheorghe Sincai, Petru Maior and A. Papiu Ilarian studied here; and here too worked Farkas Bolyai and his son Ianos Bolyai, one of the founders of non-Euclidean geometry.

Things to See

The **Palace of Culture** is a monumental building of the early 20th century, which has a magnificent reception room, the Hall of Mirrors, with fine stained glass windows. The Palace contains a *Museum of Art* with a valuable collection of pictures, an art school and the local artists' unions. The offices of the *Regional Committee of the Rumanian Communist Party* are in a building of the same style and period.

Other things of interest: the *Museum of History and Ethnography;* the *ruins of the mediaeval citadel*, mainly built in the 14th century and enlarged in the 17th century; the **Evangelical Church**, inside the citadel, built as a Franciscan church. Completed in 1442, it continued to be embellished up to the end of the 15th century; the *Teleki Documentary Library*, containing over 40,000 volumes (including many first editions), rare manuscripts, and many incunabula. It is in an 18th century building which also houses the *Bolyai Museum*.

Excursions in the district: to the *Zootechnical Research Station* in a forest near the town, with an interesting fox-breeding farm (blue, silver and platinum foxes); to the small bathing resort of *Sîngeorgiu de Mureş* (8 km—5 miles; water containing sodium chloride).

Tourist Office: 31, Piaţa Trandafirilor (tel. 35.60).

Beyond Sîngeorgiu de Mureş the road enters an attractive hilly region. Among the villages on its route may be mentioned **Gorneşti** (93 km—58 miles), where Bronze Age pottery has been found.

In the middle of the village is an 18th century *manor* in the Baroque style, with a fine park containing statues. It now houses a preventorium for children. There is a *church* with a Romanesque nave, built in the second half of the 13th century and altered in the late Gothic period, and with a belfry added in the 18th century.

Reghin (107 km—67 miles), in the Mureş valley, is an important centre of the woodworking industry (musical instruments factory, factory producing small boats).

The town has a long history behind it. A Dacian settlement has been found here, and coins of the 3rd and 4th centuries. The feudal town is mentioned in documents of the 12th century as a community of craftsmen and farmers.

The **Evangelical Church** was built at the beginning of the 14th century on the plan of a Romanesque basilica; but since building continued into the 15th century there are clear signs of Gothic influence. The *Ethnographical Museum.* The *Zoological Museum* of Middle School N⁰. 2 contains a collection of the birds of North America and a collection of owls from the Urals.

Near Reghin is the *ancient oak forest of Mociar,* designated as a nature reserve, containing some trees which are 500 years old.

From Reghin a country road runs east to *Lăpuşna* (40 km—25 miles), a timber processing centre and the starting point for excursions in the *Gurghiu Mountains* (5,830 feet).

Beyond Reghin the road runs through a district of vineyards and orchards to *Suseni,* an archaeological site (Bronze Age and Iron Age remains), and the village of **Brîncoveneşti** (117 km—73 miles).

Here there is a *castle* with five towers built in the 14th century and considerably altered between 1537 and 1558, which in 1599–1600 came into the possession of Sava Armaşul, a lieutenant of Michael the Brave. The village occupies the site of a Roman *castrum.*

Beyond *Deda* (133 km—83 miles) D.N.15 enters the wild defile which the Mureş has carved out between the Căliman range (6,897 feet) to the north and the Gurghiu Mountains to the south. The defile is so narrow that there is little room for any human habitation, apart from a few small forestry villages. The area is rich in game and in trout.

Emerging from the defile, the road comes almost at once to the thermal resort of **Topliţa,** which is also an important centre of the timber industry.

Beyond Topliţa the road forks, D.N.15 running east to Borsec and the Bicaz reservoir (p. 260), D.N.12 heading south towards Gheorgheni, from which the traveller can either continue to Miercurea Ciuc and Braşov or turn off towards Lacu Roşu and Bicaz (p. 259).

A. TO BORSEC
(26 km—16 miles; altitude 2,840–3,120 feet)

D.N.15 passes through a stretch of wooded country and comes to **Borsec,** a well known health resort in the middle of a large fir forest.

According to legend it was a shepherd from Sălişte who first discovered the therapeutic virtues of the mineral springs of Borsec. Whether this is true or not, their reputation had certainly reached Vienna by 1770, and in the 19th century there was a constant stream of rafts floating down the Mureş and the Olt laden with earthenware jars filled with the "bitter water" of Borsec. The first bathing establishments were founded at the beginning of the 19th century; they have been enlarged and modernised since 1948, and the resort is now open throughout the year. In the last few years new pipes have been laid from the main springs, giving an increased flow of water and raising the carbon dioxide content.

The mineral springs of Borsec (carbo-gaseous and ferro-alkaline) are recommended for the treatment of endocrine, cardiovascular and gynaecological conditions, diseases of the respiratory and urinary organs, and digestive disorders. The water of Borsec is also an excellent table water, stimulating the gastric juices and thus promoting digestion. A considerable proportion of the output of the springs (25 truck loads a day) is bottled and sent all over Rumania.

Situated as it is in a mountain pass, Borsec offers a variety of pleasant excursions within easy reach of the resort. The most popular objectives are the *Fairies' Glade*, the *Bears' Cave*, the *Ice Cave*, the *Owls' Lair*, the *Refreshing Waterfall*, the *Seven Springs*, and the *Beech Grove*.

From Borsec D.N.15 descends towards the Bistriţa valley at Poiana Teiului, where it crosses the new artificial lake of Bicaz (p. 260) on a viaduct. From this point the traveller can either turn down the valley to Bicaz or continue to Piatra Neamţ.

B. TO GHEORGHENI (37 km—23 miles)

D.N.12 runs south through beautiful forest scenery, passing through occasional villages (Remetea, *Ditrău*, Lăzarea). **Gheorgheni** is an important timber and textiles centre, as well as a nodal point for road and rail communications.

The existence of Gheorgheni is recorded in the 15th century. In the 17th century many Armenians, fleeing from the Turks, settled here. The town was set on fire by the retreating Nazis in 1944 but was rapidly rebuilt.

To Lacu Roşu and Bicaz, see p. 259.

As far as the little health resort of *Izvorul Mureşului* (altitude 2,950 feet) D.N.12 runs through the Giurgeu depression; thereafter it enters the Ciuc depression.

To the west there is a great area of volcanic mountains; to the east, beyond the limestone massif of the Cetatea Apelor pass (5,883 feet) in which both the Mureş and the Olt rise, the Ciuc Mountains stand against the horizon.

At *Cîrţa* there is a 14th century church, fortified in the 15th century; at *Mădăraş* a cooperative which produces a black pottery with a tradition going back to Dacian times.

In the centre of the Ciuc depression is **Miercurea Ciuc,** a local industrial centre (woodworking and foodstuff factories, mining).

The archaeologists have discovered remains of human settlement here dating from the first Iron Age. Near the town, on the hill of Şimleul Mare, are the remains of a Bronze Age fortress (the "*Citadel of Salt*") which was also used by the Dacians. Miercurea Ciuc is referred to in documents of the 15th century as a centre of Szekler administration.

Things to see: the *District Museum;* the *Municipal Baths* on the banks of the Olt (altitude 2,165 feet); and, 22 km (14 miles) west of the town, the resort of *Harghita* (altitude 4,430 feet) in the Harghita Mountains.

Running west from Miercurea Ciuc, D.N.13A passes through the Harghita Mountains by the Vlăhiţa pass and comes to *Odorheiu* (50 km — 31 miles).

Running south from Miercurea Ciuc, D.N.12 passes through several villages with small bathing establishments using the mineral springs which are so numerous in this district (Jigodin, Sîncrăieni, etc.). These places have a long history, as is shown by the Dacian hoard of silver recently found at Sîncrăieni and now in the Museum at Miercurea Ciuc, or the citadel of earthworks and timber, dating from the 1st century B.C., discovered at Jigodin.

The road now reaches the southern end of the Ciuc depression and enters the defile cut by the Olt through the volcanic mountains of the Harghita range.

In the middle of the defile, surrounded by an ancient forest of fir and larch, is the health resort of **Tuşnad,** which has grown up within the last hundred years.

Frequented in winter as well as in summer, Tuşnad owes its reputation to the beauty of its surroundings and to the therapeutic virtues of its mineral springs.

Its mineral waters (carbo-gaseous, containing sodium, calcium and magnesium, and slightly radioactive) are recommended for the treatment by internal application of affections of the digestive passages and the associated glands and affections of the urinary passages. Carbo-gaseous baths are indicated for the treatment of varicoseveins, debility, asthenia and nervous strain. Tuşnad has also a lake (Lake Ciucaş) with facilities for boating and bathing.

In addition to pleasant short walks within the immediate surroundings of the resort and along the banks of the Olt, there are easy excursions to the *Falcons' Crag*, the *Tower Rocks* and *St Anne's Lake*, the only volcanic lake in Rumania, lying at an altitude of 3,100 feet in the crater of an extinct volcano. On the shore of the lake is a tourist hut, which can be reached by a signposted footpath (1½ to 2 hours' walking).

The defile begins to widen out at the little resort of *Malnaş-Băi* (altitude 1,850 feet). Then, still following the Olt, the road passes through *Olteni*, a village occupying the site of a former Roman *castrum*, and comes to *Sf. Gheorghe* (p. 168).

15.   CLUJ

Cluj, chief town of the region of the same name, is an important industrial, commercial and cultural centre. Its main industries are engineering and metal processing (the Unirea plant, producing machinery for light industry, and the Technofrig plant, producing machinery and equipment for the foodstuffs industry), foodstuffs, boots and shoes (the largest factory in Rumania), furniture, china and chemicals.

As a cultural centre Cluj is notable for its institutions of higher education (five institutes with 22 departments and over 15,000 students). The town has also a branch of the Rumanian Academy, with 11 institutes and research groups, and three theatres, two opera houses, a symphony orchestra, several libraries and museums, the oldest botanic garden in Rumania, etc.

In recent years the town has been modernised on a large scale, with the building of many new housing areas, commercial buildings, social and cultural institutions, etc. Population 208,000. The German name of Cluj is *Klausenburg*, the Hungarian *Koloszvar*.

History of the town. The long history of Cluj is attested by the discovery within the town of remains of the Stone, Bronze and Iron Ages. It is first recorded under the name of the Dacian city which stood on the site — *Napoca*, mentioned by Ptolemy in the 2nd century B.C. Under this name, too, it achieved considerable prosperity in the Daco-Roman period, when, alongside a powerful *castrum*, there grew up a town which was at first a *municipium* and later a colony. The native population of this town left traces of their presence in the area at the period of the great migrations.

In the 9th, 10th and 11th centuries Cluj was the centre of the voivodate of Gelu, which waged war against the Hungarians who came from the west to conquer Transylvania (the "land beyond the forests"). As the Hungarians extended their sway in

Transylvania (11th and 12th centuries) the Hungarian military organisation was superimposed on the economic, social and political structure of the local Rumanian population. As part of this process a military stronghold was established at Cluj, the *Castrum Clus,* first mentioned under this name in 1213, which became the military and administrative centre of the comitat of the same name.

In the 11th century Cluj begins to appear in the documents under its present name. The growth of the town as a centre of trade and craft production was favoured by its position at the junction of important trade routes, and also by the privileges granted by the Kings of Hungary—privileges temporarily lost after the rising of 1427, in which the town took the side of the rebellious peasants. Later Iancu of Hunedoara restored its privileges, and the town quickly became a considerable centre of craft production, with many craft guilds.

After the constitution of the autonomous Principality of Transylvania in 1541 Cluj became its main economic, political and cultural centre. Michael the Brave, having become Prince Regnant of Wallachia, Transylvania and Moldavia, confirmed the city in all its ancient privileges. From 1790 to 1848, and again from 1861 to 1867, Cluj was capital of the Principality of Transylvania, then under Austrian control. Then from 1867 to 1918 Transylvania fell under the Hungarian yoke. Since the reunion of Transylvania with Rumania in 1918 Cluj has made great strides economically.

Tour of the Town

In the centre of the town is the large **Piața Libertății,** at the south-west corner of which (1, Str. Napoca) is the Continental Hotel.

The square is laid out with flower beds. In the centre is the *equestrian statue of Matthias Corvinus* (Matei Corvin), by the sculptor Jan Fadrusz. All round the square are 16th, 17th and 18th century buildings. On the west side there are shops selling traditional arts and crafts (N°. 13).

In the Piața Libertății is the large **Church of St Michael,** one of the largest Gothic churches in Rumania, built in the second half of the 14th century.

The church was altered at later periods, particularly after a fire in 1698. The tower was added in the 19th century. It alternated between different denominations (Catholic and Protestant), but finally returned to the Catholics in the 18th century.

The nave is 160 feet long and 70 feet high; the tower is 260 feet high. To the main Gothic structure have been added many later features, mainly decorative elements, in the Baroque style, as well as a number of Renaissance features (sacristy door, 1528).

In the main doorway is a figure of St Michael (15th century), with the arms of King Sigismund.

On the east side of the square is the **Art Museum,** in a Baroque 18th century palace.

The Museum, recently established here, contains a fine collection of works of art of various periods, including particularly the Middle Ages, works by painters, sculptors and other artists of the Cluj region, works by painters of the Baia Mare school, and works by various Rumanian artists from the 17th century to the present day.

In a little street which runs north from the north-west corner of the square (Str. Matei Corvin) is the *birthplace of Matthias Corvinus*, the son of Ioan of

---

CLUJ

1 University
2 Art Museum
3 Ethnographical Museum of Transylvania
4 Historical Museum
5 Tower of Fortress
6 Tailors' Bastion
7 House of Matei Corvin
8 Benkö House (birthplace of Bolyai)
9 Statue of Matei Corvin
10 Bust of Mihail Eminescu
11 Church of St Michael
12 Reformed Church
13 National Theatre and State Opera House
14 Hungarian State Theatre
15 Botanic Garden
16 Public park
17 Babeş-Bolyai Park
18 Continental Hotel
19 Astoria Hotel
20 Siesta Hotel
21 Pescăruş Hotel
22 Bucureşti Restaurant
23 Summer Garden
24 Someşul Restaurant
25 Gambrinus Restaurant
26 Clujul Restaurant
27 Main post office
28 Telephones
29 Telephone office
30 Tourist Office
31 Rumanian Railways and TA-ROM Agency
32 Station

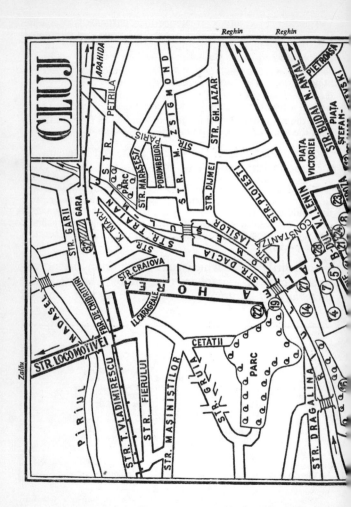

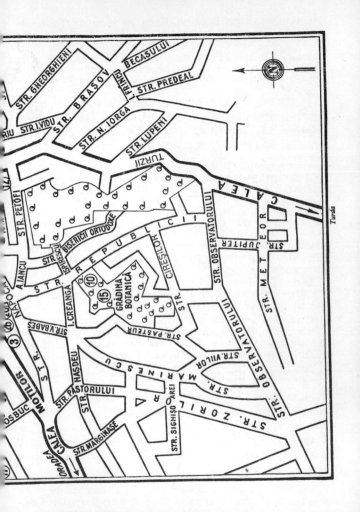

Hunedoara, who became King of Hungary (commemorative plaque).

Nearby, to the west, is the *Historical Museum*, and to the
north (Piaţa Carolina) the *Franciscan Church* (15th century; now
a music school).

In the Str. 30 Decembrie, which runs west from the
north-west corner of the square, is the **Ethnographical
Museum of Transylvania,** in the so called *Redoute*, a
building in the Empire style of the early 19th century.

Liszt played in this building in 1846. Here too, in 1894, was
held the trial of the "Memorandists" (a number of prominent
representatives of Rumanian cultural and political life who had
claimed equality of rights for the Rumanians and other oppres-
sed nationalities in the Austro-Hungarian Empire). The Museum,
established in 1923 and considerably enlarged in the last ten
years, contains over 50,000 objects and documents of ethnographical interest (pottery, textiles, clothing, tools, domestic usten-
sils, old prints, records of traditional customs, a library, etc.).

In the Hoia Forest on the outskirts of the town is an annex to
the Museum, an *open-air ethnographical park*, with traditional
peasant farms of the region.

Continuing west along the Str. 30 Decembrie and its continuation Str. Motilor, we come into the Calea Mînăşturului and so to
the *Mînăştur Monastery*, the existence of which is recorded in
1222. It was rebuilt in the 15th and 16th centuries in the late
Gothic style. The abbey, which possessed large properties, was
a target for attack during peasant risings.

Now return to the centre of the town by bearing
right into *Str. Miko*, which runs past the Faculties of
Medicine and Science and the Polyclinic and enters
Piaţa Gh. Sion. On the left of this square is Str. Sincai,
with the Tourist Office at N⁰ 2. On the right is Str.
Republicii, leading up to the **Botanic Garden.**

The *Botanic Garden* is in the University quarter, on the lower
slopes of the Feleac Hill. In an area of 25 acres it contains a collection of plants from all over the world, of great scientific value.

Of particular interest to the visitor are the decorative plants, the section containing plants grown for industrial use, the Japanese garden, a whole range of trees and shrubs from Rumania, and many species from other parts of the world. Note the group of new glasshouses built in 1960, covering an area of 2,150 square yards, and the 60 feet high palm house (containing banana plants). In addition to thermostats controlling the heat according to the species and the weather the glasshouses have an automatic watering system.

Now return down the Str. Republicii, turn right into Str. Napoca and come back to the Piaţa Libertăţii. Take the street next the Continental Hotel at the south-west corner of the square, then turn left into Str. Kogălniceanu, which leads to the **University.**

The University bears the name of the scholars Babeş and Bolyai, who were born in Cluj. Next to it is the **Church of the Piarists,** also known as the University Church (early 18th century Baroque; mahogany woodwork). At the east end of Str. Kogălniceanu is the little **Evangelical Church** (Gothic, late 15th and early 16th century), built in the time of Matthias Corvinus. In front of this church is a copy of the *equestrian statue* in the Hradčany Palace in Prague representing **St George and the Dragon** (by the sculptors Martin and George, 1373. According to tradition the sculptors came from Clussenberch, which is identified with the German name of Cluj, Klausenburg).

At the far end of Str. Kogălniceanu is the Piaţa Ştefan cel Mare (Stephen the Great). To the right is a fragment of the old fortifications, the *Tailors' Bastion* (built in the 15th century, altered in the 16th century, and restored some years ago). On the left is the *Rumanian National Theatre and State Opera House.* Still farther to the left, in the Piaţa Victoriei, is the *Orthodox Cathedral* (modern Byzantine style, 1933). From here return by way of the Bulevard Lenin to the Piaţa Libertăţii.

Other things to see. The Hungarian State Theatre and Opera House. The *Citadel*, on the north bank of the Someş, standing

some 200 feet above the river; from the top, where there are remains of early 18th century fortifications, there is a wide-ranging
view over the town and the surrounding countryside. *Collection
on the History of Pharmacy*, at 28 Piata Libertăţii.

The *public park*, with a boating lake, and the *Babeş-Bolyai
Park*, with a public swimming pool and sports facilities. The
Young People's House of Culture, a new building (1960) close to
the new halls of residence for students. It contains a hall seating
1000 people, rehearsal rooms for amateur drama groups, orchestras, choirs, folk dancing teams, etc.

Excursions in the district: the *Beech Grove*, on the wooded
hills south of the town. Two tourist huts and a camping site.

Tourist Office: 2, Str. Gheorghe Sincai (tel. 13.778).

16. FROM CLUJ TO ORADEA

152 km (95 miles) by D.N.1, following much the same route as the railway along the foot of the Apuseni Mountains.

Leave Cluj on the west, by way of Calea Mînaşturului. The road runs up the gently sloping valley of the Someş Mic, dominated to the south by an outlier of the Apuseni Mountains, the Gilăul range (5,994 feet).

At *Luna de Sus* (15 km—9 miles) a country road goes off on the left, passing through Săvădisla and Băişoara, to the village of Muntele Băişoara (36 km—23 miles), from which it is an hour's walk to the Băişoara hut (4,540 feet).

Gilău is an old established settlement where remains from the Neolithic period and the Bronze and Iron Ages have been found.

In the park attached to the school are the remains of a Roman *castrum*, which continued to be occupied after the Roman administration had left Dacia. After the peasant risings of 1437 the Catholic bishop who had a large property in the area had a *fortress* built here; it was rebuilt and modernised in the 18th century but was destroyed by a fire in 1861. The few architectural features which have survived show that this was the first appearance of the Renaissance style on Rumanian soil. (15th century).

After passing through a number of small villages and climbing over the summit of a hill the road descends into the *Criş Repede valley*. Near the source of the river a small restaurant provides an attractive halting place in a picturesque setting.

The road now enters the Huedin depression and passes through **Huedin,** a centre of local industry (km 51—32 miles).

There is an *Ethnographical Museum* displaying the peasant costumes of the Apuseni Mountains.

13 km (8 miles) north of Huedin, in the village of *Fildul de Sus*, is one of the finest wooden churches in northern Rumania, with a very tall belfry.

At the entrance to the defile which the Criş Repede has cut between the Apuseni and Mezeş Mountains is **Bologa.**

This is a place with origins going back into the remote past. The Romans built a *castrum* here to watch over the road from *Napoca* (Cluj) to *Porolissum* (Moigrad), lying in the Mezeş Mountains to the north. At the beginning of the feudal period a *fortress* was built at Bologa, and this has survived to the present day. First mentioned in 1322, the fortress—along with the 18 villages under its control—fell into the hands of Mircea the Old, Voivode of Wallachia, at the beginning of the 15th century.

From Bologa a signposted footpath runs south to the *Vlădeasa hut* (4,690 feet), under Mount Vlădeasa (6,020 feet).

At *Poieni* (69 km—43 miles) a country road branches off up the Drăgan valley to the tourist hut of Poieni (8 km—5 miles). Soon after this D.N.1 passes through the village of *Cincea*, with a small manor house which belonged to the poet Octavian Goga (1881–1938), who is buried here. The house is now a memorial museum.

After Ciucea the road passes through the villages of *Negreni* and *Bucea* (timber and woodworking). Just beyond Bucea a country road goes off on the left, running up the Valley of Hell to the small health resort of **Stîna de Vale** (the "sheepfold in the valley"; 44 km— 28 miles; altitude 3,610 feet). The Valley of Hell is strikingly picturesque, with a greatv ariety of karstic features which give it an air of wild grandeur.

The Apuseni Mountains

The road to Stîna de Vale is one of the main approaches to the Apuseni Mountains, which lie above D.N.1 as it runs north from Alba Iulia and then west. Although not particularly high (the highest peak, Cucurbăta Mare, does not exceed 6,070 feet), the

Apuseni range holds many surprises for tourists looking for magnificent scenery and interesting natural features.

The mountains, which cover a total area of some 8,000 square miles, have usually easy slopes and rounded summits covered with forest. In the valley, however, there are many gorges–such as, for example, the *Turda Gorges* (p. 196) and the gorges of *Rîmeţilor*, *Runcoul*, *Pociovalişte* and *Galbena*. There are also many caves, swallow-holes and underground rivers. The *Scări-şoara Glacier* (a natural glacier in the entrance to a swallow-hole), the *Meziad Cave* with its maze of passages, and the *Vadul Crişului Cave* are very easy of access, and so — at least in part — are the *Citadels of Ponor*, the most important feature on the *karstic plateau of Padis*.

But the attractions of the Apuseni Mountains are not confined to their underground caves or their karstic features. There are also, for example, the impressive *basalt columns of the Detunate* and the *Citadel of Gold* of Roşia Montană, a mountain pierced by a network of tunnels hewn by the miners of Roman Dacia in their quest for gold. And in this fantastic landscape of weathered rock there is an abundant flora. The edelweiss *(Leontopodium alpinum)* grows as low as 1,800 feet, near fields of daffodils; and the wild lilac is also found, along with some plants which in other areas are never found alongside the Alpine flora. It is not surprising, therefore, to find many nature reserves in the area.

Man too has made his contribution to the beauties of the Apuseni range, in the form of the many villages scattered about the high plateaux at altitudes of up to 4,000 feet or more. The houses in these villages are not built side by side, but may straggle over several miles. They are extremely picturesque, in their characteristic architecture with roofs twice the height of the houses. The traditional fairs held in this area are occasions for popular rejoicing, regular parades of folk art and traditions. One of the most interesting of these is the *Găina Fair*, which takes place each year (about 20th July) on the plateau of Mount Găina, at a height of nearly 4,900 feet. Thousands of peasants come to the fair from every corner of the Apuseni range; it is opened by prolonged blasts on the shepherds' horns, and the singing and dancing goes on all day, from dawn to dusk. Including the tourists who come from all over Rumania, there are often as many as twenty or thirty thousand people at this unusual mountain fair. It is a regular festival of singing and dancing.

Soon after the Stîna de Vale road D.N.1 leaves the Criş Repede defile, crosses the hill of Piatra Craiului and descends into the *Vad depression*. At first this is narrow, but it soon broadens and merges in the extensive Tisza plain.

At the village of *Topa de Criş* a country road branches off on the left to the commune of **Vadu Crişului** (the "ford on the Criş"), renowned for its unglazed pottery with brown patterns on the natural white clay. From Vadu Crişului a footpath runs through the finest part of the Criş Repede defile, reaching in 2 km (1¼ miles) the *Vadu Crişului Cave*, where there is a tourist hut.

Aleşd (114 km—71 miles), the chief town of the district and an industrial centre (woodworking, manufacture of fireproof bricks) is the largest place in the Vad depression. In the main square is a *monument* to the memory of 33 peasants who were killed here during the 1904 rising.

At km 150 (94 miles), Oradea (see below).

17. ORADEA AND ITS SURROUNDINGS

Oradea (population 145,000) is the chief town of the Crişana region and an important industrial and economic centre. It lies on the banks of the Criş Repede, at the beginning of the Tisza plain. The town has developed considerably in the last twenty years, acquiring a number of large new factories, and its appearance has been transformed by the building of new blocks of flats, commercial buildings, etc. It now contains a variety of modern industrial establishments (metal processing, chemicals, leather and skins, furs, foodstuffs, a large thermo-electric power station, etc.). It is also an important cultural centre, with two theatres, a People's Art School, a Regional Library, many schools, etc. The German name of the town is *Grosswardein*, the Hungarian *Nagyvárad*.

History of the town. The archaeologists have found at Oradea the remains of several very ancient settlements. In the Seleuş district, for example, tools of the Neolithic period were discovered; at Salca and in the Rulikovschi cemetery material belonging to the last stage of the Neolithic. The Scythians, and after them the Dacians, left their mark here. Remains dating from the Roman period have also been found, for even though this was not part of Roman Dacia the Romans used the roads which passed through the area. There are also many remains from the period of the great migrations, the most important being the Slav citadel which was identified under the ruins of the monastery on the Promontor Hill. When the Hungarians arrived in this region they found a feudal state organised by the native population, the princedom of Menumorut, with its capital in the *citadel of Bihara*, a fortress of earthworks and timber 9 km (6 miles) north-west of Oradea.

The feudal town grew up round the monastery founded in the 11th century, on the site now occupied by the citadel. In the following century the fortress of Oradea—which had now be-

come the residence of a bishop—was built on this site. Destroyed
in the Tatar invasion of 1242—which was described by an eye-
witness, the Italian monk Rogerius, in his memoirs under the
title "Carmen Miserabile"—and later rebuilt, Oradea prospered
in the 15th century, in the reign of Matthias Corvinus (who had
been brought up at the court of the Bishop of Oradea), when the
Diet of Transylvania met at Oradea to receive the envoys of
Stephen the Great and sign the peace treaty with Sultan Murad II.

After withstanding two assaults by the Turks—who did,
however, destroy the town—the citadel of Oradea fell in 1660,
and for 32 years the town and surrounding district remained
under Turkish control and became a pashalik.

In 1848 the town was one of the centres of the revolutionary
movement in Transylvania.

Things to See

The *People's Council* (town hall) is a neo-classical
building dating from the beginning of this century
(1902–03). The *Palace of the Regional Library*, built in
1905, occupies the site of a house in which the revolutionary General Bem had his headquarters in 1848.
(In addition to the Library, the building also houses
a People's Art School.)

The *Church of St Ladislas* dates from the beginning
of the 18th century. The **Moon Church,** built in 1784
in a transitional style (Baroque and neo-classical),
contains some fine frescoes. On the church tower is a
sphere 10 feet in diameter, worked by clockwork,
which shows the various phases of the moon.

The **Citadel of Oradea** was constructed in the 16th
and 17th centuries on the principles developed by
Vauban, replacing earlier fortifications.

Seriously damaged in 1692 when the Turks evacuated it, the
citadel was later turned into a barracks. All round the walls can
be seen the defensive ditches, which were filled with water from
a stream, the Peţa. Since the water came from warm springs it

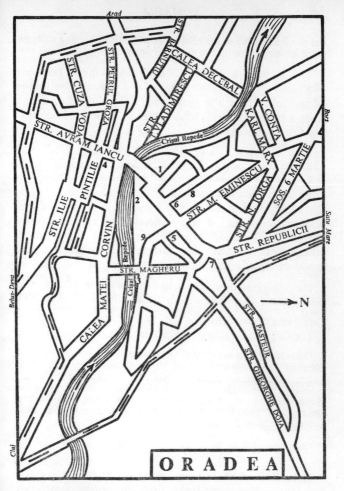

1 Tourist Office
2 Transilvania Hotel
3 Transilvania Restaurant
4 Victoria Hotel
5 Răsăritul Hotel
6 Bureau de change
7 Petrol pump
8 Garage (car repairs)
9 Post office

did not freeze even in the coldest weather, thus forming a formidable obstacle even in the depth of winter.

The **Roman Catholic Cathedral** was built between 1752 and 1780, on the model of the Baroque buildings of northern Italy; the money for its construction came from a tax on the serfs who worked on the land belonging to the diocese.

The *Bishop's Palace* was built between 1762 and 1777 on the pattern of the Belvedere Palace in Vienna. It houses the **"Tare Crişurilor" Museum,** established in 1872, wich contains a valuable collection of material in the fields of archaeology, history, art and the natural sciences, including a fine collection of engravings by Dürer (1471–1528), whose father was born in a village near Oradea, an ornithological collection, and a collection of eggs (10,000 items).

The palace, the most important example of the final phase of the Baroque style in Rumania, stands in a fine park containing many rare species of trees, including three specimens of the Californian *Sequoia gigantea*.

The *Canons' Corridor* is a Baroque structure built in 1773.

Other things to see: the *Zoological Garden* in the Nicolae Bălcescu Park; the *Iosif Vulcan Museum*, in the house in which Vulcan lived, and which was the office of the magazine "Familia" from 1880 to 1906; the *Ady Endre Museum*, commemorating the Hungarian poet, known for his progressive ideas, who lived in Oradea from 1900 to 1910; and the *State Theatre*, built in 1900 in the neo-classical style.

Excursions in the District

1. To **Băile 1 Mai** (9 km—6 miles; altitude 430 feet). This thermal resort, open throughout the year, lies south-east of Oradea and is reached by D.N.63. Its radioactive mineral springs are renowned for their therapeutic virtues.

The baths are mentioned for the first time in 1221. In the 15th century they became well known under the name of *Băile Episcopiei*. The resort, which has been enlarged and modernised since 1948, uses warm water from several springs; the principal spring, an artesian well, has a temperature of 42 °C. Some springs which are not used for either bathing or drinking flow into the Gipsies' Lake, from which the Peţa is an outlet. In the lake and on the bed of the stream there is a layer of sapropelic peat mud, which is also used by the bathing establishments. On the lake and in the stream grows a species of water lily *(Castalea thermalis)*, a relic of the Tertiary period which has managed to survive in the warm water. This species is designated a "natural monument" and is protected by law.

The mineral waters of Băile 1 Mai are indicated in the treatment (by internal application) of chronic gastritis accompanied by spasms, chronic cholecystitis, renal lithiasis and gout, and in the treatment (by external application) of affections of the locomotor system, the genital organs and the peripheral nervous system, functional disorders of the nervous system, disease of the cardiovascular system and skin conditions.

There is a camping site in the resort.

2. To Băile Felix (8 km—5 miles; altitude 460 feet). Near Băile 1 Mai, in the valley of the Şimleu, in the middle of an oak and beech forest, is another thermal resort, Băile Felix, which is also open throughout the year.

The existence of Băile Felix is mentioned for the first time in 1763, when a wooden swimming bath was built. The resort began to develop in 1885 and rapidly became well known. Since 1948 it has been enlarged and modernised, the most recent improvements being the provision of a publics wimming bath, a pool for open-air bathing in winter, a hotel complex, etc.

The bathing establishments use warm water (slightly radioactive and with a low mineral content), from an artesian spring drilled in 1885. The water (containing bicarbonates, sulphates, calcium, magnesium and sodium, and hypotonic) is used by external application both for its soothing effect on the nervous system and spasms of organs with unstriped muscle, and for its resorbent action on chronic inflammatory processes, for it accelerates the metabolism. Moreover since it also contains silicon it is effective in the treatment of skin conditions and affections of the mucous membranes.

The water is recommended for the treatment of various disorders of the locomotor and nervous system, particularly in sufferers from neuroses and in old people and children suffering from the after effects of poliomyelitis. It is also indicated in the treatment of urological disorders—prostatitis, vesiculitis, etc.

Tourist Office: 1, Aleea Strandului (tel. 1.18.83).

To *Borş* (14 km—9 miles). From Oradea D.N.1 continues west to the frontier post of Borş. Beyond here the road enters Hungary, connecting Rumania with the capital cities of central Europe (Budapest, Vienna, Prague). The frontier post is open day and night. See the Nagel Guide *Hungary*.

18. FROM CLUJ TO BAIA MARE AND THE MARAMUREŞ

151 km (94 miles) by D.N.1C, by way of Gherla and Dej. Between Cluj and Dej the road runs on the same line as D.N.17 to Bistriţa and Vatra Dornei in northern Moldavia (p. 239).

Leaving Cluj by the *Someşeni* district, with the town airport, the road passes through a small bathing resort (salt and bicarbonated water, mud). Remains of a settlement belonging to the 4th and 5th centuries have been discovered here.

At *Apahida* (13 km—8 miles), another important archaeological site, excavation has yielded a considerable amount of material from a Celtic settlement of the 3rd and 2nd centuries B.C., Christian material of the 5th century, and grave goods of the 6th to 10th centuries.

Gherla (45 km—28 miles) has developed since 1950 into an active industrial centre, with a large woodworking plant, a brickworks and carpet workshops.

It is a town with a long history. The Romans built a *castrum* here. In the 16th century a powerful fortress was erected, apparently on the site of an earlier fortress. In the 18th century a *colony of Armenians* settled here, building a monumental Baroque *church* which still dominates the town.

Things to see: the *District Museum* (a historical museum); the *Armenian Church;* the *carpet workshops.*

Dej (60 km—38 miles; altitude 1,020 feet; 32,000 inhabitants), chief town of the district and an industrial centre, lies at the junction of the Someş Mare and the Someş Mic (the Great and Little Someş). In the last few years a new furniture factory has come into production, together with a new paper and cellulose plant.

The existence of Dej is mentioned in the 13th century; later it became a centre of craft production. Near the town, at Căşeiu, the remains of a Roman *castrum* were discovered, and at Ocna Dejului (4 km—2½ miles) are salt mines which were worked in Roman times.

The *Historical Museum* contains much archaeological material from the *castrum* at Căşeiu. The *Calvinist Church* is a 15th century Gothic building. The *Franciscan Monastery* dates from the 18th century.

In the neighbourhood, at *Ocna Dejului*, are large salt mines with an underground salt mill. Lying only 7–10 feet deep, these deposits have been worked continuously since Roman times. A lake containing water with a high salt content, formed in the abandoned workings, now supplies a small bathing resort.

At *Bobîlna*, on a hill 14 km (9 miles) west of Dej, the rebellious peasants pitched their camp and won a resounding victory over the army of the nobles (1437).

D.N.1C now runs north-west from Dej along the Someş valley towards Baia Mare (94 km—59 miles) and Satu Mare (146 km—91 miles), the two biggest towns in north-western Rumania.

The road passes through *Căşeiu* with its Roman castrum, and then comes to *Cîţcău*.

3 km (2 miles) from here is **Vad,** with a church built in the time of Stephen the Great. Until the end of the 16th century the monastery of Vad was the seat of a bishopric within the Metropolitanate of Suceava.

On the right of the road are the Lăpuşului Mountains (6,043 feet). At km 40 (25 miles), *Ileanda*. After Răstoci the road leaves the Someş valley and crosses into a secondary valley leading to Baia Mare by way of Şomcuta and Satulung. At km 94 (59 miles), Baia Mare.

Baia Mare, with a population of over 84,000, is the chief town of the Maramureş region. It is the largest centre of the non-ferrous metals industry in

Rumania, and has developed considerably since 1955. It also has other industries (chemicals, mining machinery, foodstuffs). The building of large new housing areas, blocks of shops and offices, and social and cultural facilities has considerably altered the appearance of the town.

The existence of Baia Mare, as a mining community, is first recorded at the beginning of the 14th century. Throughout the centuries it has known the uncertainties and the ups and downs characteristic of areas in which "gold fever" waxes or wanes according to the abundance or scarcity of the precious metal from time to time. Then, having become a town of craftsmen, Baia Mare developed at a very slow pace until 1944.

St Stephen's Tower, a 14th century structure, dominates the old centre of the mediaeval town. The main sights of Baia Mare are the *Historical Museum*, the *towers* of the mediaeval walls and the *studios of the School of Painting*, the traditions of which are maintained by an Artists' House.

Tourist Office: 5, Bd. Bucureşti (Tel. 14.77 and 10.59).

Excursions in the district: In the *valley of the Firiza* a hydroelectric station has recently been built, with a reservoir at Strîmtori.

To *Lake Bodi* and the Mogoşa hut, in the Gutîi Mountains (altitude 2,400 feet; 15 km—9 miles—from Baia Mare).

In the villages of *Siseşti* (14 km—8 miles), *Bineşti* (16 km—10 miles), *Păuliş* (18 km—11 miles), *Surdeşti* (20 km—13 miles), and the neighbouring villages of *Plopiş* and *Rogoz*, near Tîrgu Lăpuş, are unusual **wooden churches.** They date from the 18th century, except the church at Rogoz, which was built in the 16th. They are built of oak and have a shingle roof; they often have a carved wooden porch, and the interior is decorated with carved wood ornament and wall paintings. The tall spires of these churches— the one at Surdeşti attains the impressive height of 180 feet— give them a striking and distinctive appearance. Most of them have been restored by the Directorate of Historical Monuments.

To **Sighetu Marmaţiei** (66 km—41 miles—from Baia Mare), on D.N.18 through the Tibleşului Mountains, by way of the villages, all with fine wooden churches, of *Deseşti*, *Şugatag*, *Giuleşti* and *Vad*.

Sighetu Marmaţiei (35,000 inhabitants) is situated in the Maramureş depression, a region noted for its fine timber building (carved porches, wooden churches) and its picturesque local costumes. Woodworking, foodstuffs industries. The town, which appears in the records as early as the 14th century, has a very interesting *Ethnographical Museum* with a fine collection of folk arts and crafts of the Maramureş region.

The **Maramureş** consist of four depressions, the territories of Oaş, Maramureş proper, Chioaru and Lapuş, each with its characteristic customs. Wood is the material principally used by the craftsmen of the Maramureş. The houses, with pine or oak beams, have steeply pitched roofs, attractive balustrades with carved pillars and richly decorated wooden porches which have something of the aspect of rustic triumphal arches. Picturesque interiors (woollen blankets, pitchers, icons on glass). The local peasant costumes are also very picturesque; the women wear embroidered blouses and flowered kerchiefs, the men wide trousers and homespun jackets.

The wooden churches are in the same style as the houses, built of massive timbers joined by wooden pegs. "The high and steeply pitched roof reaches down almost to the ground. The open external gallery, resembling the balcony of a peasant house, is surrounded by a balustrade and carved pillars. From the high roof soars up the slender tower, round the top of wich is a gallery, like some giant bird's nest... The richness of the carving on the beams, the pillars, the ribs of the vaulting and doorways... and the carved or pokerwork decoration of the iconostasis, similar in pattern to the carving on the doorways, show a masterly decorative sense" (I. Balos).

Tourist Office in Sighetu Marmaţiei: 18 Piaţa Libertăţii (tel. 815).

To Iacobeni and Vatra Dornei. D.N. 18 runs for 157 km through magnificent wooded country, between mountains rising to 6,500 feet in the north and 7,900 feet in the south, where there was bitter fighting between the Russians and the Germans and Austrians in 1914-16. The largest places are *Vişeu* (woodworking) and *Borşa* (mining), near which a tourist complex catering for both summer and winter visitors has been built. Beyond this the road climbs in sharp bends to the *Prilop pass* (4,635 feet) and then runs down the Bistriţa valley towards Iacobeni (p. 278).

The most interesting route to Borşa is by the little road through the *Iza valley* (leave on the Baia Mare road and turn off at Vad): very beautiful wooden churches at *Naneşti, Rozavlea* (18th century), **Ieud** (churches of 1364 and 1717), *Bogdan Vodă* (formerly Cuhea: church of 1718) and *Dragomireşti.*

To Satu Mare. The road runs down the Tisa valley. 18 km (11 miles): *Săpînţa,* with a picturesque cemetery (humorous verses and drawings on wooden crosses). At *Negreşti* a road goes off to the spa resort of *Bixad* (rheumatism, cardiac, renal and intestinal conditions, gynaecology). Then by way of *Vama* (pottery) to *Livada.* Soon afterwards a road goes off on the right to *Halmeu* (entry point to Soviet Union). To the left is a road to Satu Mare (below).

West of Baia Mare, the road to Satu Mare follows the Someş valley, with thriving vineyards (Ciclău, Seini). 65 km (40 miles): **Satu Mare,** only 7 ½ miles from the Hungarian frontier.

The town was founded by the boatmen who carried salt from the mines at Ocna Dejului (p. 234) down the Someş. Its fortress, first mentioned at the beginning of the 13th century, was destroyed by the Mongols in 1241. The town grew up as a market for the agricultural produce of the rich surrounding area (vegetables, wine, fruit). In recent years some industry has established itself at Satu Mare (textiles, timber, machinery).

The *main square,* laid out with flower-beds and fountains, is surrounded by large buildings, including the *Roman Catholic Cathedral.* The *Regional Museum* at 21, Piaţa Libertăţii, housed in a historic 18th century building, was founded in 1891 and reorganised in 1961; it contains historical and ethnographical material.

16 km (10 miles) south is *Ardud,* with the ruins of an old fortress dating from the end of the 16th century.

37 km (23 miles) south-west is **Carei,** an important agricultural and industrial centre with a number of interesting buildings (the 15th century *Karolyi Castle,* altered several times; the Church of the Piarists, a Catholic church in the Baroque style). Beyond Carei D.N.19 runs south-west to *Oradea* (p. 227), by way of Valea lui Mihai, Săcueni with its vineyards, Diosig and Roşiori.

19. FROM CLUJ TO VATRA DORNEI
(From Transylvania to Moldavia)

An itinerary of outstanding interest, very strongly recommended, taking in the monasteries of northern Moldavia, and passing through the magnificent scenery of the Northern Carpathians, with varied and wide-ranging views of the mountains.

From Cluj to Dej: see above, Itinerary 18.

Starting from Dej, D.N.17 runs east towards Bistriţa, Vatra Dornei and Suceava. The road follows the valley of the Someş Mare, passing through a pleasant rolling countryside, and comes to **Beclean**, 25 km (16 miles) from Dej and 85 km (53 miles) from Cluj, with an 18th century *church*.

From Beclean a minor road runs north-east to *Salva* (22 km— 14 miles), where it forks. One fork continues north-east to *Coşbuc* (so named after the poet Gheorghe Coşbuc, who was born there) and Viseu de Sus in the Maramureş (p. 236). The other fork runs east to *Năsăud* (a small town founded in the 13th century, with a church and an interesting museum), *Ilva Mică, Sîngiorz Băi* (a thermal resort) and *Rodna*. **Rodna** (68 km— 43 miles—from Beclean) has two interesting churches and the remains of a third. In the 15th and 16th centuries it was an active mining centre. It is now a tourist resort, set among the imposing mountains which dominate the valley, with many excursions to Valea Vinului, the summit of Mount Ineu (7,809 feet), Lake Lala, and Mount Pietrosu (7,563 feet). The whole of this area shows clear evidence of ice action, and contains some of the wildest and most impressive scenery in Rumania.

After Beclean D.N.17 comes to **Bistriţa**, 65 km (41 miles) from Dej and 125 km (78 miles) from Cluj. Bistriţa, chief town of the Bistriţa-Năsăud region, is one of the principal towns in north-eastern Transylvania and an active industrial centre (foodstuffs, building materials).

History of the town. The archaeologists have discovered Bronze Age tombs in the town itself and remains of later periods in the surrounding district. Among these are a Dacian citadel (1st century B.C. to 1st century A.D.) near Sărăţei, the most northerly of the many Dacian citadels discovered in Rumania.

The mediaeval town of Bistriţa is first mentioned in the documents in the 12th century, when settlers from Germany were brought here. In 1353 it obtained the right to hold a fair once a year and to have its own seal, thus becoming a free city. A town of craftsmen and merchants, Bistriţa developed mainly as a result of its busy trade with Moldavia. In 1530 Ioan Zapolya, Voivode of Transylvania, made a present of Bistriţa and its citadels at Rodna and Unguraş to Petru Rareş, Voivode of Moldavia. The recipient did not long enjoy the gift, but relations between Bistriţa and Moldavia continued to develop. Many of the craftsmen of the town went as far afield as Iaşi to sell their wares, and the stone masons of Bistriţa were renowned. In those days Bistriţa played the same role in relation to Moldavia as Braşov in relation to Wallachia.

In 1713 the Rumanian population of the town was expelled by order of the Saxon magistrates. The Rumanians later returned, and in 1918 the town was restored to Rumania.

The district round Bistriţa is renowned for the quality of its wines.

Tour of the Town

The main things of interest in the town are in or near the town square. The *Local Museum* (historical section and science section) is in a house which formerly belonged to the guild of silversmiths.

The **Evangelical Chuch** (15th century) has a tower 250 feet high.

Originally built in the Gothic style, it was altered in later periods (Renaissance and Baroque features). It contains 16th century carved furniture and 16th and 17th century Oriental carpets.

The **Sugălete** are a row of 16th century houses on the north side of the main square, with porticoes under which the craftsmen sold their wares.

In the main streets of the old town are many houses between 300 and 400 years old, with *stone doorways* and quaint window frames which carry the visitor back to mediaeval times. The *Franciscan Church* is a 15th century building, and near it are the ruins of the *wall* which surrounded the town in the 15th and 16th centuries.

Tourist Office: 1, Piața Centrală (tel. 684).

Beyond Bistrița D.N.17 runs along the valley of the River Bistrița, passing through the villages of the *Bîrgăul* district, ancient communities in which folk art and traditions are still practised. The centre of this picturesque area, dominated by the pyramidal bulk of a volcanic mountain, Heniul Mare (5,289 feet), is *Prundu Bîrgăului*, a small town with a paper-mill.

Here a country road branches off on the right to *Colibița* (18 km — 11 miles; altitude 2,720 feet), a health resort and the starting point for excursions and shooting parties in the Căli-mani massif (6,896 feet), the largest massif of volcanic origin in Rumania.

At the **Tihuța Pass** (175 km—109 miles; altitude 4,026 feet), between the Călimani and the Bîrgăul Mountains, D.N.17 leaves Transylvania and enters Moldavia, in the Dorne depression.

The Tihuța is undoubtedly one of the finest passes in the Ru-manian Carpathians, with magnificent views of the peaks of the Rodna (7563 feet) and Călimani Mountains and the "Obcinele" ("crests") of Bukovina. Here and there in the midst of the vast coniferous forests are beautiful clearings, which become larger as we approach the Dorne depression.

At **Vatra Dornei** (206 km—129 miles; altitude 2,790 feet), an important health resort, the Cluj-Bistrița-Vatra Dornei itinerary joins the Suceava-Cîmpulung Moldovenesc-Vatra Dornei itinerary through northern Moldavia (see p. 274).

20. FROM BUCHAREST TO BACĂU

The motorist travelling from Bucharest into Moldavia takes D.N.2, which heads for the north-east corner of the Rumanian Plain, runs through the whole length of Moldavia along the Siret, Moldova and Suceava valleys, and finally reaches the Soviet frontier at Siret in Bukovina.

Throughout its length Ş.N.2 sends out a large number of offshoots, the most important of which are the following: near Urziceni (km 56—35 miles), D.N.2A, for Constanţa and the Black Sea coast; at Buzău (km 110—69 miles), D.N.2B, for Brăila (105 km—66 miles) and Galaţi (136 km—83 miles); near Mărăşeşti (km 199—124 miles), D.N.24, for Bîrlad (68 km—43 miles), Vaslui (123 km—77 miles) and Iaşi (195 km—122 miles), with an important branch road at Crasna (km 105—66 miles), D.N.24B, running via Huşi (31 km—19 miles) to Albiţa (50 km—31 miles), on the frontier with the U.S.S.R.; at Adjud (km 228—143 miles), D.N.11, for Gh. Gheorghiu-Dej (38 km—24 miles) and Braşov (163 km—102 miles); at Bacău (km 225—141 miles), D.N.15, for Bicaz (88 km—55 miles) and Topliţa (184 km—115 miles); at Săbăoani (km 339—212 miles), D.N.28, for Iaşi (73 km—46 miles); at Suceava (km 434—271 miles), D.N.17, for Vatra Dornei (109 km—68 miles), D.N.29, for Botoşani (43 km—27 miles), and D.N.29A, for Dorohoi (41 km—26 miles).

The main railway lines serving this part of Rumania are the following:

1. Bucharest – Ploieşti Sud – Buzău – Mărăşeşti – Adjud – Bacău – Roman – Suceava – Vicşani (railway frontier point with the U.S.S.R.), the route also followed by the Carpaţi Express between Bucharest and Warsaw.

2. Bucharest – Ploieşti Sud – Buzău – Mărăşeşti – Tecuci – Bîrlad – Vaslui – Iaşi – Ungheni (railway frontier point with the U.S.S.R.), the route also followed by the Danubius Express between Moscow and Sofia, via Kiev and Bucharest.

3. Bucharest – Urziceni – Brăila – Galaţi.

The most important branch lines are from Adjud to Oneşti, and through the Eastern Carpathians into Transylvania; and from Dărmăneşti to Cluj, via Vatra Dornei and Năsăud.

Between Bucharest and Bacău (285 km—178 miles) D.N.2 (described as far as Urziceni, p. 298) runs for the most part in a north-easterly direction towards the meeting place between the Rumanian Plain and the Subcarpathian hills.

Buzău (km 111—69 miles; 75,000 inhabitants) is the first town encountered since leaving Bucharest. An old-established community in the valley of the River Buzău, mentioned in documents of the 15th century, Buzău is now the chief town of the region, an industrial centre (foodstuffs, plastics, metalworking) and a junction point of road and rail communications.

The town has recently expanded, with many new buildings and housing areas, including one—Crîngul, "the Copse"—situated on the edge of an unspoiled park.

An attractive tree-shaded avenue leads to the *Episcopal Church* and the Bishop's Palace, both built in the 17th century and altered in the 18th.

15 km (9 miles) west of Buzău is the small thermal resort of *Sărata Monteoru.*

From *Buzău to Ploieşti* (65 km–41 miles–west), D.N. 1B and the railway run along the foot of the Carpathian outliers, through a rich agricultural district. Urlaţi has an interesting church and small museum.

From *Buzău to Braşov* (146 km–91 miles), D.N. 10, through the Carpathians, with beautiful wooded scenery. The road passes through Măgura (Ciolanu Monastery, founded 1650; a church built in 1818) and Nehoiaşu (ascent of Mount Penteleu, 5,810 feet).

Tourist Office: 176, Str. Unirii.

Leaving Buzău, D.N.2 runs alongside the fields and buildings of a viticultural research station, passes through the wide Buzău valley, and then bears northeast to reach in 32 km (20 miles) the Rîmnicu Sărat valley.

Rîmnicu Sărat (km 143—89 miles; 26,000 inhabitants) is situated on the river of the same name.

Cigarette factory, local industries. In 1481 Stephen the Great, Prince Regnant of Moldavia, won a victory over the Turks here. The visitor should see the *Mănăstirea Church*, built between 1691 and 1697, with some fine frescoes.

From Rîmnicu Sărat to beyond Mărăşeşti the road is flanked on the left by hills covered with flourishing vineyards. This is the largest vine-growing area in Rumania.

After *Goleşti* (km 177—111 miles) the road crosses the River Milcov, which from 1473 to 1862 was for considerable stretches the frontier between Moldavia and Wallachia.

Focşani (km 181—113 miles; 44,000 inhabitants). After crossing the Milcov the road enters the town of Focşani, which was for some time the seat of the common institutions of the two Rumanian Principalities after their union in 1859. There is a monument commemorating this important event in the history of the Rumanian people.

Focşani is now a considerable industrial centre (wine production, dairy products, a large furniture factory, clothing). Things to see: the *Historical Museum*, with a rich collection, the *Museum of Ethnography*, the *Museum of Natural Science* and two churches, the *Domnească (Prince's) Church* and *St John's Church*, both built in the 17th century.

From Focşani a road and railway run north-west to *Odobeşti* (11 km–7 miles), an important wine-producing centre. From there the road continues westward and runs through the Milcov valley to Năruja (25 km–16 miles) in the Vrancea Country, a picturesque depression in the arc of the Carpathians.

Leaving Focşani, D.N.2 approaches the valley of the Siret, the large river which cuts Moldavia in two from north to south, fed by many tributaries coming down from the Eastern Carpathians and by a number of rivers from the Moldavian plateau.

In the valley of a small tributary of the Siret, the Suşiţa, which rises in the Vrancea Mountains, the road passes through the commune of *Tişiţa* (km 199—124 miles), where it is joined by D.N.24.

From Tişiţa a road runs westward to the Carpathians. It passes through *Pancin* (18 km–11 miles), a small vine-growing town, Cîmpuri (near the thermal resort of *Vizantea*, where there is a 16th century monastery), and *Soveja*, a health resort at an altitude of 1,700 feet in the midst of the forest (with a monastery in which the writer A. Russo lived for a time).

To Bîrlad, Huşi and Albiţa (U.S.S.R.)

Motorists seeking to enter the U.S.S.R. en route for Kishinev, Odessa, etc., take D.N. 24 as far as Crasna and D.N. 24A from there to the Soviet frontier. This route takes them through a number of old-established communities in the Bîrlad valley. First comes **Tecuci** (km 20–13 miles), mentioned in 1435, and now containing a large tinned fruit and vegetable factory and an important school of agriculture. There is a Local Museum (history and science). From Tecuci D.N. 25, recently modernised, runs to Galaţi (78 km–49 miles) and Brăila (107 km–67 miles).

Bîrlad (km 68–43 miles) contained from the second half of the 14th century a residence of the Princes of Moldavia. Formerly a town of no particular importance, Bîrlad has been modernised in recent years, acquiring a State Theatre, a large educational establishment (2,000 pupils) and a large ball bearings factory. Things to see: the Prodana Park and the park in the north of the town, the Museum of History and Science, and two old buildings, the *Church of St Dumitru*, built in 1600, and the *Domnească (Prince's) Church*, built in 1636.

The road runs along the Bîrlad valley and comes to *Crasna* (km 105–66 miles). From here D.N. 24B runs east through a vine-growing region to Huşi (31 km–19 miles) and Albiţa, on the Soviet frontier (304 km–246 miles–from Bucharest).

D.N. 24 passes through the town of *Vaslui* (km 123–78 miles), near which, in 1475, Stephen the Great with 40,000 men routed a Turkish army three times the size. The road then crosses the Bucium hills and descends to Iaşi (394 km–246 miles–from Bucharest). See p. 281.

Continuing northward, D.N.2 enters **Mărăşeşti** (km 202—126 miles), a centre of the chemical industry and a railway junction, after passing a huge *mausoleum*.

This contains the remains of the Rumanian soldiers who were killed in the great battle fought here in the summer of 1917 with the German forces. In spite of the efforts of von Mackensen the German offensive failed, notwithstanding its superiority in numbers and in armament.

Beyond Mărăşeşti the road enters the Siret valley, following the line of the old trade route which ran from "Upper Moldavia" (as the north of Moldavia was then called) to the river port of Galaţi.

At the junction of the Siret and the Trotuş is the town of **Adjud** (km 228—143 miles), also known as *New Adjud*, so called because it was founded in 1795 by the citizens of the old town, which was nearer the Siret and continually subject to flooding.

From Adjud D.N. 11A runs westward. At Gh. Gheorghiu-Dej (Oneşti) (km 38–24 miles), it forks, and one branch, D.N. 11, crossing the Carpathians at the Oituz Pass (2,846 feet), runs on to Braşov (125 km–78 miles–from Gh. Gheorghiu-Dej); the other, D.N. 12A, also goes through the Carpathians, by way of the town of Ghimeş (3,300 feet).

The road then comes to *Sascut* (km 242—151 miles) and to the town of **Bacău,** at the junction of the Siret and the Bistriţa, 285 km (178 miles) from Bucharest. (See the next Itinerary.)

21. FROM BACĂU TO BRAŞOV

Bacău (100,500 inhabitants) is the chief town of the region of the same name—a region which since 1950 has developed into a busy industrial area. The town has an active and varied industry (metalworking, textiles and clothing, woodworking, paper, building materials, foodstuffs, leather and skin working, boots and shoes) and is also the commercial and cultural centre of the district.

Situated at a crossing of old trade routes, Bacău is mentioned in 1408 as a customs post, and at the end of the 15th century as the Prince's residence and the seat of his court; to this period also belongs the *Precista Church* (dedicated to the Virgin), subsequently restored on a number of occasions. The town possesses a *Historical Museum*, with interesting collections of Dacian pottery and idols of the Neolithic period, a *Museum of Natural Science* and a *Museum of Art*. The Park of Liberty, the Park of Roses and the Gherăeşti Natural Park on the banks of the Bistriţa are among the other tourist attractions of the town.

Bacău is also a junction point for road and rail communications. There is a railway line from here to Piatra Neamţ and Bicaz, and a number of main roads—to Topliţa, on the far side of the Carpathians, via Bicaz; to Braşov, also beyond the Carpathians, via the town of Gh. Gheorghiu-Dej; and to Suceava via Roman.

Tourist Office: 10, Calea Mărăşeşti.

On leaving Bacău D.N.11 turns south-east.

On the first part of its course the modern road follows the line of the old "salt road", so called because for centuries salt from Tîrgu Ocna was transported along it to the principal towns in Moldavia.

After running for some distance along the Trotuş valley, and passing through Gh. Gheorghiu-Dej, D.N. 11 crosses the Carpathians by the *Oituz Pass* (2,835 feet) and then descends to Braşov. For most of the way the road runs through picturesque scenery, amid mountains covered with great forests. It also

BACĂU

1 Town hall
2 Police office
3 Precista Church

4 Historical Museum
5 State Theatre

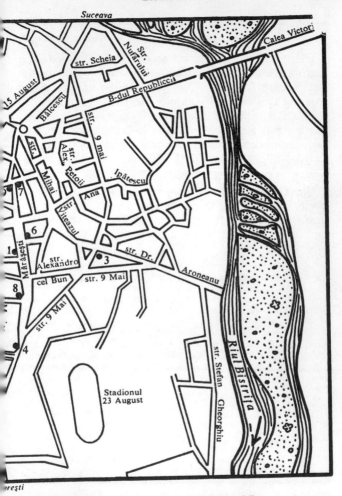

6 Hotel Bistriţa
7 Tourist Office

8 Post Office
9 Hotel Central

introduces the visitor to a recently established new town and to a large oil-processing plant at *Oneşti-Borzeşti*, also quite new.

D.N.11 leaves Băcau by way of the railway station and makes for the Petricica Hills which separate the Siret valley from the Tazlău-Caşin depression. After crossing the wooded summit, the road descends into the Tazlău valley and runs southward along the river. Farther on, a reservoir gives the first indication that the visitor is approaching the new industrial area in the Trotuş valley. At km 52 (33 miles) is Gh. Gheorghiu-Dej.

Gh. Gheorghiu-Dej (Oneşti), one of the youngest towns in Rumania, has grown up since 1955 on a terrace overlooking the junction of the Oituz and the Trotuş. Its development is a consequence of the establishment in the Trotuş valley of a huge complex of oil-processing and chemical plants designed to exploit the mineral resources of the area (oil, salt and methane).

The new town is sited between the village of *Oneşti* and *Borzeşti*, the birthplace of Stephen the Great, Voivode of Moldavia. Between 1953, when the foundations of the first buildings were cut, and 1964 more than 6000 houses were built, along with schools, commercial buildings and social and cultural facilities which provide the inhabitants with all the amenities of a modern town. There is an interesting local museum.

Environs of Gh. Gheorghiu-Dej

In the village of **Borzeşti**, 5 km (3 miles) to the south-east, is a *church* built in 1493 by Stephen the Great, a building of modest size but an interesting example of the style of Moldavian architecture which crystallised during the long reign (47 years) of this Voivode who transformed Moldavia into a centralised feudal state. The road to Borzeşti also allows the visitor to see part of the large *oil-processing installations* which extend for a distance of 5 miles along the Trotuş valley.

The fortified *Caşin Monastery* was built in the 17th century and restored at the beginning of the 19th century.

Tîrgu Ocna (15 km–9 miles; altitude 919 feet) is a centre of the salt industry and a health resort (springs of water containing sodium chloride, with a low bicarbonate content, and sulphurous water). 18 km (11 miles) farther on, at an altitude of 1,739 feet, is **Slănic-Moldova,** a health resort reputed for the therapeutic virtues of its water. Situated in a heavily wooded area, this resort enjoys a mild climate and picturesque surroundings which fully justify the name, "Pearl of Moldavia", that has been given to it. Its springs—discovered in 1800, 1839 and 1844—are of two types, alkaline and ferruginous, with compositions and concentrations varying from one spring to another. They are particularly recommended for affections of the respiratory passages.

Tourist Office in Gh. Gheorghiu-Dej: Piaţa Magistralei, Block G4 (tel. 1085).

Beyond Oneşti D.N.11 enters the **Oituz valley,** which gradually becomes narrower and more thickly wooded. Here and there small white patches on the ground indicate the presence of large deposits of salt under the ground.

After the village of *Oituz,* a centre of the timber industry, the road goes over a wooded pass and descends again into the large Braşov basin within the Carpathians, passing through the town of *Breţcu.*

This is a centre of the timber industry, and is also a popular centre for excursions.

D.N.11 now crosses the plain of *Şesul Frumos* which forms the eastern part of the Braşov basin. In the centre of this is **Tîrgu Secuiesc,** the chief town of the district.

This town is of very ancient origin, having grown up on the ruins of the Roman colony of *Praetoria Augusta.* In the Middle Ages Tîrgu Secuiesc became a centre of craft production, and in the 15th century rose to the status of a town. Today it is an industrial centre, with metalworking, foodstuffs and timber works. There is a small local museum.

Just beyond Tîrgu Secuiesc a country road branches off to the health resort of **Covasna** (22 km–14 miles; altitude 1,850 feet), known for its abundant supply of carbon dioxide, which the thermal establishments use along with the water from the mineral springs.

Continuing across the plain of the Braşov basin, the road passes through a number of villages, is joined at Chichiş by D.N.12 from Tuşnad and Miercurea Ciuc (see p. 213), and then passes the trout hatchery of *Prejmer*.

The town of **Prejmer,** lying to the left of the road, has a large agricultural producers' cooperative and a textile mill. In the centre of the commune is the most imposing **peasants' citadel** in the Braşov basin (described on p. 168).

At km 177 (111 miles) is **Braşov** (see p. 161).

22. PIATRA NEAMŢ AND ITS SURROUNDINGS

FROM BACĂU TO PIATRA NEAMŢ (60 km—38 miles), **BICAZ** (87 km—55 miles), **LACU ROŞU** (119 km—75 miles), **AND TÎRGU NEAMŢ** (227 km—142 miles).

An important tourist route runs north-west from Bacău, up the Bistriţa valley to the new town of Bicaz, cuts through the Eastern Carpathians by way of the impressive Bicaz Gorges, and reaches the famous health resort of Lacu Roşu. Thereafter the road passes into Transylvania by the Pîngăraţi pass (3,855 feet) and comes to Gheorgheni (p. 212). As far as Bicaz this itinerary follows D.N. 15; after Bicaz it is on D.N. 12A and D.N. 12. The route is one of outstanding scenic beauty, particularly at Bicaz (with the dam supplying the hydro-electric station on the Bistriţa), in the Bicaz Gorges and at Lacu Roşu.

This itinerary can readily be combined with the trip from Bacău to Suceava and the monasteries of Bukovina (Itinerary 23, p. 263). In that case, instead of following D.N. 2 the visitor should take the route Bacău-Piatra Neamţ-Bicaz as indicated below; make a trip from Bicaz to the Bicaz Gorges and Lacu Roşu; then from Bicaz take D.N. 15 along the artificial lake, followed by D.N. 15B to Neamţ and Tîrgu Neamţ, before rejoining D.N. 2. It is a long day's run from Bacău to Suceava, but the additional distance is well worth while. Total mileage: 180. This is the route described below.

Between Bacău and Piatra Neamţ D.N.15 runs through a large depression in the Subcarpathians of Moldavia, the Cracău basin. This is a fertile and highly cultivated plain lying at some altitude among the mountains.

There are many villages, particularly along the Bistriţa. In some of these (Costişa, Zăneşti) and in a number of industrial centres (Buhuşi, Roznov, Săvineşti) are hydro-electric stations built after the construction of the artificial lake of Bicaz had regularised the flow of the river. This series of hydro-electric stations (altogether there are 12 below Bicaz) justifies the name "river of light" now given to the Bistriţa.

The first place of any importance on the route is the town of *Buhuşi*, an industrial centre with a large textile mill built in 1885 but considerably enlarged and modernised since 1948. It is a town of fairly recent growth, founded in 1831 round an area which was used as a halting place by grain merchants.

Roznov is a centre of the timber industry. Beyond this town the road runs alongside two large and recently built industrial establishments—the nitrate fertiliser factory of Roznov and the *Săvineşti* synthetic fibres factory.

Piatra Neamţ (60 km—38 miles; altitude 1,020 feet). Just where the Bistriţa emerges from the mountains, between Mounts Cozla, Pietricica and Cernegura, is the town of Piatra Neamţ, the chief town of the district of Neamţ, an industrial centre with timber processing works, a paper factory, an ironworks, etc. Since 1955 the town has developed considerably. It is also a pleasant climatic resort, situated in an area of great natural beauty.

History. Piatra Neamţ is one of the oldest settlements in Rumania. Objects have been discovered here dating from the transitional period between the Stone Age and the Bronze Age (1900-1700 B.C.), when the site was occupied by a settlement belonging to the "spherical amphora culture". Many remains from the Bronze Age have also been discovered. In addition excavation at Bîtca Doamnei, just outside the town, has recently revealed the ruins of a large Dacian city, *Petrodava*, which is mentioned by Ptolemy in 106 B.C. During the period before the formation of the mediaeval state of Moldavia there was a settlement *(poleis)* at Cozla, the centre of a tribe or group of tribes. In the 15th century the documents refer to Piatra Neamţ as a town where fairs were held; it also possessed a princely residence, of which some remains can be seen in the courtyard of the school.

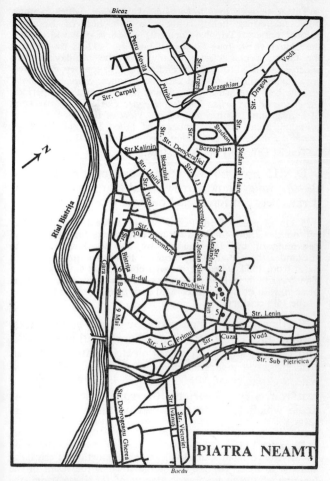

PIATRA NEAMŢ

1 Town hall
2 Police Office
3 Museum

4 Chuch of Sf. Ioan
5 Tourist Office
6 Hotel Ceahlău

Things to see: the *Archaeological Museum*, which, among other interesting items, contains a collection of Neolithic painted pottery (Tripolye-Cucuteni) which is of world repute; the **Church of Sf. Ioan** (St John), built in 1497-98 by Stephen the Great, a characteristic example of the Moldavian style which crystallised towards the end of the 15th century, decorated with niches and enamelled ceramic plaques; *Stephen's Tower*, a stone belfry in which a clock was installed at a later period; the *house of the writer Calistrat Hogaş; Cozla Park*, on a spur of high ground, with a magnificent view of the town and surrounding area; the *Caravanserai of Valea Viei* and the *Cupbearer's House*, two interesting specimens of local architecture.

Tourist Office: 1, Str. Karl Marx.

D.N.15 now turns westward and continues up the *Bistriţa valley*, now narrower and more picturesque as it runs between forest-clad mountains.

5 km (3 miles) from Piatra Neamţ a local road branches off on the right to the **Bistriţa Monastery**, founded at the beginning of the 15th century by the Moldavian Voivode Alexander the Good, who is buried there. The present *church* dates from 1554, when the original church was entirely rebuilt. The *tower* built in 1498 by Stephen the Great can still, however, be seen, with its oratory decorated with *frescoes* of the beginning of the 16th century.

Farther on D.N.15 passes through two small places, Vaduri and Pîngăraţi, where there are timber works and two recently built hydro-electric stations. It then runs close to the large hydro-electric station of *Stejarul*, with a capacity of 210,000 kW, supplied by the Bicaz reservoir. Beyond Stejarul the road enters a narrow defile which leads to the town of **Bicaz** (87 km—55 miles).

Bicaz (altitude 1,420 feet) is a town of recent growth which has developed from a small village at the junction of the Bicaz and the Bistriţa. The growth of the town is the result of the building of the hydro-electric station of the same name, the reservoir for which extends to the north-west of the town. There is a modern cement works and a factory for the production of asbestos cement panels and pressure tubes. A climatic resort, with a small museum, Bicaz attracts large numbers of tourists who come to see its large artificial lake (170 square miles) and the picturesque scenery of its surroundings.

From the centre of Bicaz D.N.12C runs westward through the *Bicaz valley* dominated by Mount Ceahlău, passing through some picturesque *mountain villages* with handsome wooden houses in characteristic peasant architecture.

25 km (16 miles) from Bicaz, before reaching Lacu Roşu, the road passes through the **Bicaz Gorges,** an impressive feature of karstic geology, now designated as a "natural monument".

The very narrow gorges (sometimes no more than 15 to 20 feet wide) are formed of walls of limestone ranging from 650 to 1000 feet high, between which the river and the road have to find their way as best they can. At *Gîtul Iadului* (the "Gorges of Hell") the road is hewn directly out of the rock face. There are many paths, for experienced climbers only, leading up the slopes and rock faces.

Lacu Roşu (119 km—74 miles; altitude 3,150–3,300 feet). The climatic station of Lacu Roşu is situated 32 km (20 miles) from Bicaz, round the lake of the same name (the "Red Lake"), formed in 1838 by a landslide which dammed the river Bicaz, swallowing up the forest which formerly grew here. The tips of a few fir-trees can still be seen emerging from the lake, which is rich in trout.

Lacu Roşu is a particularly attractive resort, thanks to the natural beauty of the surroundings, the high ozone content of the air, and the peaceful atmosphere it offers the visitor. There is skiing and skating in winter. Many paths (signposted) lead up through the forests to the summits of Mounts Curmătura (5,883 feet) and Giurgeu.

From Lacu Roşu the road climbs through a fine coniferous forest to the *Pîngăraţi pass* (3,855 feet) and then descends, to *Gheorgheni,* in the Giurgeu basin (see p. 212).

From Lacu Roşu, return to Bicaz through the Bicaz Gorges; then take D.N.15, which runs northward and comes in a mile or two to the *dam* and the *reservoir*.

The road passes along the top of the dam, which is 300 feet high, and reaches the east shore of the great artificial lake, 22 miles long. From here there is a succession of magnificent views, particularly on the west shore, dominated by the mighty bulk of Mount Ceahlău (6,247 feet). There is a service of motor launches on the lake, which is also used for floating timber from the forests.

At *Poiana Teiului* the road forks.

To the left D.N. 15 crosses the lake on a viaduct (upstream is a picturesque crag standing by itself in the middle of the water), and comes to the village of *Ceahlău* and the thermal resort of Borsec (p. 211). From the village of Ceahlău a number of signposted paths lead up into the range, particularly to the Dochia hut, situated at a height of 5,750 feet on a plateau dominated by the peak of Ceahlău (6,247 feet). The limestone mass of Ceahlău has weathered into a variety of contorted shapes of great picturesqueness, which have given rise to a whole series of folk tales and legends. The slopes of the mountains are clothed with great forests.

To the right—which is the route described here—D.N.15B crosses the Stînişoarei Mountains (5,023 feet), passing through fine forest scenery. On the eastern slope a track (4 km—2½ miles) branches off on the left to **Neamţ Monastery.**

Neamţ Monastery, the oldest and most important focus of culture in Moldavia in the feudal period, consists of a complex of cells, galleries and towers, in the middle of which is the *church built by Stephen the Great* in 1497. In the course of centuries the monastery has undergone many alterations, as can be seen from the great variety of styles which it displays.

The first restoration work, carried out between 1917 and 1934, was concerned solely with the church, and in particular with restoring its original exterior, the stone and brick facing of which had been plastered over during the 19th century.

The second stage of the work, begun in 1954 and completed in 1961, was concerned with the whole structure of the monastery. In the church the flat 19th-century roof was replaced by a high pitched roof of Moldavian type, the form of which was known from an old engraving, from a number of frescoes, and from the traces found on the bases of the towers. The windows of the tomb chamber and the apse, with frames dating from the 19th century, were replaced by small windows copied from the old ones with the help of a few surviving fragments. The sacristy which was built against the south side of the apse in the 18th century was retained in view of its high architectural quality. And finally the clearance of the base of the church restored its true proportions.

The archaeological investigation showed that the *Church of St George*, built in 1794 beside Stephen the Great's church and partly concealing it, incorporated no part of the first stone-built church which according to tradition was destroyed by the earthquake of 1471. In consequence the Church of St George was dismantled and re-erected in the cell block on the east side of the monastery precinct. The lines of the original walls are clearly visible in the courtyard.

The cells which form the four sides of the precinct have been restored. The original roof shape has been reproduced, and the wooden galleries dating from 1883 have been replaced by new ones, built in stone on the ground floor and in wood on the upper floor. The roof of the tower at the north-east corner has similarly been rebuilt in its original form.

Finally, outside the main precinct, the 19th-century pavilion intended for the blessing of the water *("aghiasmatar")* has also been restored, following the destruction of its onion-shaped dome in a storm in 1954.

In association with this restoration work, and with the concurrence of the Ministry of Forestry, a "protective zone" was marked out round the monastery, and special provisions were laid down for the felling of trees in the forests on the surrounding hills.

There is an interesting *Museum of Religious Art* in the monastery.

Shortly before reaching Tîrgu Neamț the traveller sees on the left the **Fortress of Neamț**, on a crag on the north side of the valley. Founded in the 14th century by Voivode Petru Muşat, the fortress was enlarged in the following century by Stephen the Great, and was destroyed by the Turks in the 17th century. It is now under the care of the Directorate of Historical Monuments.

Tîrgu Neamţ is an important market for agricultural produce, serving both the mountains and the plain areas. In the Humuleşti district of the town is the *birthplace* of the great Rumanian writer *Ion Creangă* (1837–89).

To the south of Tîrgu Neamţ, reached from the Piatra Neamţ road, is the *Agapia Monastery* (a mile or two from the road, on a country track running west from the road). Built in the 17th century, the monastery contains a fine church decorated in the 19th century with paintings by N. Grigorescu. There is an interesting museum of religious art. It is possible also to continue to the thermal resort of *Bălţăteşti*, 7½ miles south of Agapia, and to the 18th century monastery of *Varatec*.

Beyond Tîrgu Neamţ D.N.15B continues for 18 km (11 miles) and then runs into D.N.2. Turn left for *Suceava* (Itinerary 23).

23. FROM BACĂU TO SUCEAVA
(D.N. 2)

From Bacău D.N.2 runs north between the wooded Siret valley on the right and the hills sloping gently up to the Eastern Carpathians on the left.

At the junction of the Siret and the Moldava is *Roman*, a rapidly developing industrial centre. In addition to older enterprises (sugar refinery, etc.) there are now a large factory manufacturing steel tubes and factories producing building materials.

The new housing areas and public buildings have given a fresh lease of life to this ancient town which, in terms of a rescript of 1392 bears the name of Roman I, Prince Regnant of Moldavia. At first Roman was a small settlement on the trade route along the Siret valley, a favourable situation which led to its development in later centuries. In the 14th century it possessed a fortress built of logs, and in 1483 this was replaced by a citadel of stone, the "New Citadel". In the 17th century Roman became the seat of a bishopric; and it was here that the learned Metropolitan Dosoftei (1624-93) produced — in verse — the first work in the Rumanian language, a *Psalter*.

From this earlier period of Roman's history date the *Episcopal Church* (begun in 1542 by Prince Petru Rareş and completed in 1550) and the *Church of Precista Mare*, founded by Ruxandra, wife of Prince Alexandru Lăpuşneanu. The *Local Museum* also contains some interesting remains.

10 km (6 miles) beyond Roman D.N.2 leaves the Siret valley and follows one of its main tributaries, the Moldova. At this point, near the commune of Săbăoani (km 54—34 miles), D.N.28 branches off on the right, coming in 73 km (46 miles) to Iaşi (p. 281).

Beyond Săbăoani a country road leaves D.N. 2 on the right for the village of *Mirceşti* (4 km–2½ miles). Here Vasile Alecsandri (1821-90) lived and composed some of his works. His house, in a park in the Siret valley, is now a museum; his tomb can also be seen in the park.

At Moțca D.N.28A goes off on the right to the railway junction of *Pașcani* (7 km—4½ miles). Shortly afterwards another road, D.N.15B, goes off on the left, leading to *Tîrgu Neamț* (18 km—11 miles) and Poiana Teiului (67 km—42 miles). See Itinerary 22.

D.N.2 continues along the Moldova valley, passing a string of picturesque villages, then crosses the river, runs along the north bank, and soon leaves the valley.

At *Spătărești* a country road goes off on the left to Gura Humorului (35 km–22 miles): see p. 274.

2 km (1¼ miles) farther on another country road leads to the village of **Baia** (5 km–3 miles), the first residence of the Princes of Moldavia (middle of 14th century), where there are the ruins of a *church* in the Gothic style (15th century), a 16th century church, and the *White Church*, said to have been built by Stephen the Great.

Fălticeni (km 125—78 miles) is situated on a terrace between the Moldova and one of its tributaries, the Somuz. Formerly a modest village, Fălticeni has developed considerably in recent years. It now possesses a large timber works, a linen and hemp mill, and a local factory specialising in the production of carpets and costumes in traditional designs. There is also a District Museum.

To the east of Fălticeni a minor road branches off to *Dolhasca* (25 km–16 miles) by way of *Dolheștii Mari* (13 km–8 miles), where there is an interesting 15th century church built entirely of undressed stone). 6 km (4 miles) from Dolhasca is the fortified **Probota Monastery**, built in 1530 by Petru Rareș (who is buried here with his family); there is a church with external walls covered with *frescoes*, but these have been plastered over, and the only frescoes still to be seen are in the narthex and the pronaos.

Beyond Fălticeni D.N.2 descends the valley of the Somuz and then climbs the hill between the Moldova and the Suceava valleys. As it approaches the Suceava valley there is a view of the important town of **Suceava,** the chief town of the region of the same name (see below).

SUCEAVA
AND THE MONASTERIES
OF BUKOVINA

Southern Bukovina (Northern Bukovina now belongs to the Soviet Union), with its beautiful series of monasteries with frescoed exteriors, is a part of Rumania which must be included in the tourist's itinerary. Two days at least should be allowed for seeing the monasteries properly.

In the 16th century painting was used on the external walls of churches to illustrate Bible stories which otherwise would have remained unknown to the illiterate peasants. The paintings represent Biblical and historical scenes, rather like sequences from a film. Some of the scenes, painted in the style of the period, were intended to arouse popular hatred of the Turks who had so often invaded the country. Similarly in the scene "The siege of Constantinople" (Humor, Moldoviţa) the Moldavian artists distorted the historical facts and interpreted them after their own fashion, attributing the victory to the Rumanians. The scenes from the lives of saints (Voroneţ and Arbore) and the "Last Judgment" at Voroneţ show the same spirit of hostility to the Turks.

The cultural development of Moldavia in the 15th and 16th centuries, in the reign of Stephen the Great (1457-1504) made possible the growth of a regular school of native painters who produced some authentic masterpieces in a fresco technique which still retains all its freshness. Unfortunately the secret of the methods used by the painters died with them, and experts throughout the world have devoted their efforts to rediscovering them.

A. SUCEAVA

Suceava is situated at an altitude of 1,115 feet, at the crossing of important trade routes which favoured its development from an early period.

For a period of two hundred years (from the middle of the 14th to the middle of the 16th century) Suceava was the residence of the Princes of Moldavia. Even after they transferred their capital to Iaşi, Suceava continued to play an important economic and strategic role in virtue of its possession of a finely situated and strongly fortified citadel. In the reign of Stephen the Great the citadel successfully withstood two fierce assaults by the Turks, the first of which was led by Mahomet II, the conqueror of Constantinople. After they had succeeded in subjugating Moldavia in the 16th century the Turks set fire to the impregnable fortress, and its destruction was completed by an earthquake at the end of the 17th century. In view of its historical and architectural importance the citadel is to be restored, and work is at present in progress.

Throughout the first half of this century Suceava was a town of minor importance, but in recent years it has become increasingly industrialised (woodworking, paper and cellulose factory, oxygen factory, power station, etc.) and has in consequence rapidly developed. Between 1948 and 1963 its population multiplied almost sixfold (77,000 inhabitants in 1967).

Tour of the Town

The many modern buildings of Suceava harmonise with its surroundings and with its remains of the past. It has a number of sights of the greatest interest to the visitor.

The **Citadel of the Princes of Moldavia** is situated on a hill to the east of the town (from which there is a magnificent view of the surrounding countryside). The ruins have been cleared by the archaeologists, and parts of them have been consolidated or reconstructed.

The **Museum,** 33, Str. Ştefan cel Mare, contains more than 350,000 items.

There is a fine collection of pottery and terracotta, mediaeval weapons, fragments of architectural elements (arcades and window frames, keystones, etc.), old craftsmen's tools; coin collections; material dating from the 15th to 18th centuries; fine art collection; natural history section.

Another sight of interest to visitors is the **Church of the Monastery of St George,** also known as the church of the **Monastery of St John the Younger,** built between 1514 and 1522 in the Moldavian style to replace the former Metropolitan Church of Suceava.

The church contains a remarkable series of 16th century *frescoes* and a portrait of the founder, Prince Bogdan III. Of the external painting a few frescoes survive on the south wall. There is a fine *tower*.

The other monuments of Suceava include the *Prinely Inn* (Hanul Domnesc), 5, Str. Ciprian Porumbescu, a 17th century building which now houses an Ethnographical Museum; the **Church of St Dimitru,** built in 1534-35 by Petru Rareş in the traditional Moldavian style, with later renovations and alterations which have to some extent changed its original appearance; the *Invierea Church* (Church of the Resurrection, 1551); the *Church of St John the Baptist,* built by Vasile Lupu in 1643; the *fortified Monastery of Zamca* (15th century), on the plateau to the north-west of the town.

The older parts of Suceava still have something of the picturesqueness of the past, particularly on market days.

Tourist Office: 2, Str. N. Bălcescu (tel. 1.08.97).

B. TO BOTOŞANI AND DRAGOMIRNA

To the north of Suceava is the district of *Iţcani*, containing the main railway station (Suceava Nord). To the south is the *Burdujeni* district.

1. From Burdujeni D.N.29 runs east, crosses the River Siret and comes to **Botoşani** (43 km—27 miles).

Burdujeni is an industrial district of Suceava. Near here is the *Agafton Monastery* (18th century), with fine mural paintings. On the far side of the Siret a country road on the left leads to *Bucecea*, where there is a modern sugar refinery. Also in this district, near the commune of Cucorani, is the village of *Ipoteşti*, the birthplace of the great poet Mihail Eminescu. (The house where the poet was born is now a museum: manuscripts,

material associated with Eminescu, photographs, early editions
of his works.)

Botoşani (50,000 inhabitants), long known as a market
town for agricultural produce and wine, has now become an
industrial centre (textiles, clothing, etc.). The *Popăuţi Church*
was built by Stephen the Great in 1946 and altered in the 18th
and 19th centuries (16th century wall paintings). There is a
local museum with some pictures by Octav Băncilă, who was
born here. Botoşani was also the birthplace of the great historian
Nicolae Iorga.

Other interesting buildings in Botoşani are the *Monastery
of Stephen the Great* (1496, with fine frescoes) and the *Church of
St George* and the *Uspenia Church*, both built in the 16th
century by the wife of Petru Rareş but altered in the 18th
century. In the neighbourhood are a number of monasteries,
the most important of which are *Coşula* (16th century) and
Vorona (1600), lying to the south of the town.

2. **Dorohoi** is 36 km (23 miles) from Botoşani, and
41 km (26 miles) from Suceava by D.N.29A. To the
right is the Adîncata Forest (camping site).

At Dorohoi is a house converted into a museum in honour
of the great musician George Enescu, born in the commune of
Liveni (now called *George Enesco*), which is reached on a
country road (20 km–12 miles) branching off D.N. 29A. The
Church of St Nicholas (1495) was built by Stephen the Great;
it is very similar to the church at Botoşani.

3. A country road from Iţcani leads to one of the
most interesting mediaeval buildings in Moldavia, the
Dragomirna Monastery (12 km—8 miles), built in 1609
by Anastase Crimca, Metropolitan of Moldavia, a
skilful miniature painter and patron of the arts.

The monastery **church,** built entirely of dressed stone, is
remarkable for its narrowness (30 feet) and its tall slender
lines. It shows a number of architectural features first used
in Moldavia. The carved stone ornament on its towers is found
on a larger scale in the Church of the Three Hierarchs in Iaşi,
where it covers the whole external surface. The interior is

decorated with *wall paintings*, and there is a delicately carved wood *iconostasis* brought from the Socola Monastery in 1793.

Dragomirna possesses a massive range of **fortifications** built in 1627 by Prince Miron Barnovschi. Near the walls is a particularly graceful building, the Hermitage Church—known as the *Little Dragomirna*—erected by Crimca in 1602. There is a fine viewpoint near the lake.

Also worthy of mention is the *Mediaeval Museum* in the monastery: icons, liturgical objects, carved furniture, embroidery and a valuable collection of manuscripts decorated by illuminators trained in the school founded by Crimca.

C. TO THE FRONTIER (SIRET-RĂDĂUȚI)

D.N.2 runs north from Suceava, passing through the beautiful rolling countryside of Southern Bukovina.

A country road branches off on the right to **Pătrăuți** (church built in 1487 by Stephen the Great), and a road on the left leads to *Părhăuți* (church built in 1522, the narthex of which is thought to have been the model for Humor and Moldovița).

The road to Rădăuți (see below) branches off on the left. Then, at km 47 (29 miles) D.N.2 enters **Siret,** the terminal point within Rumania of the main road north, on the frontier with the U.S.S.R. From Siret it is possible to enter the U.S.S.R. by way of *Cernăuți* (Chernovtsy). See the Nagel Guide, *U.S.S.R.*

The documents show that Siret was one of the residences of the Princes of Moldavia in the 14th and 15th centuries. The town contains an important building of this period, the **Church of the Trinity,** built by Prince Petru I Mușat (1378-93), the organiser of the Moldavian church. Built on a trilobate plan of Byzantine origin and decorated externally with glazed ceramic panels, it is one of the prototypes in the development of the distinctive architectural style of mediaeval Moldavia.

Rădăuți, the chief town of the district, is situated in the middle of a depression which was at one time marshland but has been drained and transformed into a fertile plain. It contains two sights of particular interest, the *Bogdana Church* and the *Museum of Folk Art* which stands next to it.

The **Bogdana Church,** the oldest building in the region, was erected some time before 1365 by Prince Bogdan I, the founder of the independent feudal state of Moldavia. The church is built on a Romanesque plan with certain Gothic features. The interior contains paintings restored in the 16th century and some fine funerary slabs. The bell tower still has the bells dating from the time of Stephen the Great.

Like the Church of the Trinity in Siret, this church is of particular interest as an illustration of the beginnings of a characteristically Moldavian style of architecture, created by local craftsmen grafting Byzantine, Romanesque and Gothic features on to the old native style of architecture.

The *Museum of Folk Art*, in a building near the Bogdana Church, contains a rich collection of objects illustrating the way of life, the interests and the artistic skills of the country people of the area: black and coloured pottery, painted eggshells, furniture, domestic utensils, embroidery, local costumes, etc.

8 km (5 miles) west of Rădăuți is the commune of *Marginea*, well known for its black pottery, in a tradition which goes back to the Bronze Age. Of Celtic origin, this pottery, burnished with a whetstone, was later adopted by the Getae and the Dacians. It is produced by incomplete firing of the clay.

Through Marginea runs a country road which links the Suceava valley in the north with the Moldova valley in the south. Running north, it passes through *Vicovu de Jos* (13 km—8 miles), then bears west along the Suceava valley, and finally, by way of a side valley, comes to **Putna Monastery** (30 km—19 miles—from Rădăuți), built between 1466 and 1481 by Stephen the Great, who is buried here. The museum contains, among other things, an exceptionally fine collection of embroidery.

The church was built between 1466 and 1469, and the rest of the building was completed in 1481. The buildings were reconstructed after a fire in 1484, and again after the devastation caused by the wars of the 17th century and the earthquake of 1739. The latest restoration was carried out in 1902 (by the Austro-Hungarian architect Romstorfer).

The *walls*, 10 feet high, are topped with battlements and supported by buttresses. The **Great Church**, 120 feet long, is built on a trilobate plan. The narthex is the earliest example of this type in Moldavia. In the church are the *tombs of Stephen the Great*, his family and his descendants down to Petru Rareş.

The *Treasury Tower*, on the west side of the precinct, dates from 1481; the entrance tower dates only from 1757. The buildings in the courtyard were erected in the 19th century.

Now return to Marginea and follow D.N. 17A, which runs south-west to the **Suceviţa Monastery** (10 km–6 miles).

The monastery was built by the Movilă dynasty in the second half of the 16th century, and is the last building (1601) erected in Rumania with its outer surface entirely covered with **frescoes**. Careful examination and clearance of the cell blocks of the monastery, however, has led to the discovery of arches, niches, windows and staircases which show that there existed here, before the building of the church, a baronial hall of the first half of the 16th century.

The internal walls are decorated not only with large-scale paintings but also, in the pronaos, with many miniatures. The external paintings include, on the north side, a scene from the *Last Judgment* known as the *Ladder of Heaven* or the *Ladder of the Virtues*, one of the finest achievements of mediaeval Rumanian painting, in magnificent tones of blue and green.

The *walls* which enclose the monastery, like those at Dragomirna, are well preserved and of impressive thickness.

From Suceviţa return to Marginea and take the road on the right which runs south to Solca.

Just before Solca a country road goes off on the left and runs east to the church of **Arbore**, a mile or two away.

The church was founded in 1503 by Stephen the Great's general Luca Arbore. The ravages of weather have destroyed the *frescoes* on the north front, but those on the south and west fronts, protected by the overhanging eaves, have survived. They represent scenes from the lives of saints. Inside the church, which is very dark, are the remains of frescoes, and the tomb of Luca Arbore in the narthex.

Solca is a small health resort situated in the middle of the forest, with an old church. Farther on is *Cacica*, with salt mines which can be visited (cathedral hewn from the salt, underground lake).

Some 40 km (25 miles) from Marginea the road runs into D.N.17 from Suceava to Vatra Dornei (see below).

D. FROM SUCEAVA TO VATRA DORNEI

110 km (69 miles) by D.N.17, a good road linking Moldavia and Transylvania. Itinerary including the three fine monasteries of Humor, Voroneţ, and Moldoviţa.

Leaving Suceava through the new district in the west of the town, D.N.17 passes through the village of *Sf. Ilie* (15th century church founded by Stephen the Great; in the interior, votive picture representing the founder), and then crosses a plateau on which is the *fortified Zamca Monastery* (17th century). After the village of Ilişeşti the road runs through a fine forest of deciduous trees and then descends to *Păltinoasa* (27 km—17 miles), a small village from which a country road runs north to Cacica (12 km—8 miles), Solca (18 km—11 miles) and Arbore (25 km—16 miles): see above, p. 273.

After Păltinoasa D.N.17 enters the Moldova valley and runs along it in a westerly direction. At km 35 (22 miles) is *Gura Humorului*, a health resort and centre of the timber industry, from which a road runs north-east to **Humor Monastery** (6 km—4 miles), in the village of the same name. This monastery is one of the masterpieces of Moldavian art of the 16th century.

A monastery was built here at the beginning of the 15th century by Alexander the Good; some remains of its walls are to be seen in the centre of the village, but the cause of its destruction is unknown. The present monastery was built in 1530—as is attested by the inscription near the entrance to the church—by the boyar Theodor Bubuiog, a relative of the voivode Petru Rareş and a great dignitary of Moldavia. On his death in 1539 the founder was buried here.

In 1641 Vasile Lupu built a defensive tower and surrounded the monastery with a wall, but these were not sufficient to save Humor from the ravages of the wars of the 17th century. The monastery was closed by Joseph II in 1785 and became a parish church. It has been restored by the Directorate of Historical Monuments.

Humor is thought to be the first example of the use of an open portico in place of the closed narthex (an example followed at Moldoviţa but not at Suceviţa); it also offers the earliest example of a "treasury" above the tomb chamber, which is situated between the pronaos and the naos.

The **frescoes** date from 1535. Those on the north front are largely obliterated (*Tree of Jesse*), as are those on the apse, though here they are rather better preserved (the *Church in Heaven* and the *Church on Earth*). On the west front is a *Last Judgment*, and on the south front a *Hymn to the Glory of the Virgin*, who saved Constantinople from the Persians in 626. (Note that these scenes have been brought up to date, the Persians being transformed into Turks.)

In the interior, which is also decorated with 16th century frescoes, see the carved wood *iconostasis* and four 15th century *icons* (from the earlier church of Humor).

Just beyond Gura Humorului a country road turns south off D.N.17 to the village of Voroneţ (4 km—2½ miles) and the church of **Voroneţ Monastery,** built by Stephen the Great in 1488. In 1547 a completely closed narthex was added, and the external walls were covered from top to bottom with the **frescoes** which make Voroneţ one of the treasures of Rumanian art. The attractiveness of the church is still further enhanced by its setting, shaded by trees and surrounded by mountains.

The church was built by Stephen the Great in a few months in 1488; it thus comes between the churches of Putna and Neamț. According to tradition it was built on the advice of a hermit after a victory won by Stephen over the Turks. The narthex and the painting were added about 1547-50 by the Metropolitan Grigore Roșca.

A tribolate plan, massive walls with buttresses, blind arcades on the three apses, a windowless west front: these are the architectural features of Voroneț.

The **external frescoes,** with blue tones predominating, are devoted to the theme of the struggle against the Turks, and are remarkably well preserved after four centuries of weathering and damage. The intensity of the blues is due to the use of lapis lazuli powder.

Apses: "The Church on Earth and the Church in Heaven" (representing, according to A. Grabar, the Prayer of all the Saints). North front (largely obliterated): "Creation of the World". West front: a fine *Last Judgment*, in which the river of fire (Gehenna) is particularly striking; note the presence of Ottomans and Jews among the damned; see also the procession of animals, some of them yielding up the bodies of human beings whom they had devoured. South front: *Tree of Jesse* and scenes from the life of St Nicholas and St John the Younger.

In the naos and sanctuary are *paintings of the period of Stephen the Great*, now blackened by age. Particularly interesting is the picture representing Stephen, conducted by St George, offering the church to Christ. The paintings in the pronaos and narthex date from 1550.

Beyond Gura Humorului, in the Moldova valley, is *Vama*, a health resort and centre of the timber industry. Vama is mentioned in the documents as early as 1409 and, as its name indicates, was formerly a customs post on the old trade route between Transylvania and Moldavia.

From here a country road runs north-west (14 km— 9 miles) to **Moldoviţa Monastery,** with another church entirely covered with frescoes.

Although more than 400 years old, these frescoes have withstood the rigours of a harsh climate without losing any of the brilliant colouring which, along with their artistic quality and the unusual nature of some of the scenes represented, gives them their outstanding value and interest. The practice of covering the external surfaces of churches with painted decoration is a unique phenomenon not found anywhere else in the world. It appeared in Moldavia in the first half of the 16th century, and was initiated by the Metropolitan Roşca, who had the idea of transforming the outside of the church into a kind of illustrated Bible for the benefit of the peasants. The paintings on the church of Moldoviţa Monastery are among the best preserved, and from the artistic point of view are surpassed only by the frescoes of Voroneţ Monastery.

The church is part of a remarkable architectural ensemble built in 1532 on the site of an earlier monastery of the 14th century, which had been destroyed by a landslide, by the voivode Petru Rareş, son of Stephen the Great. Within the precincts there are also a *Prince's House* (recently restored), now containing a small museum of ancient religious art, and three defensive *towers* on the south side; the walls are 20 feet high.

External frescoes representing traditional themes. South front: *Tree of Jesse, Siege of Constantinople, Hymn to the Virgin.* Apses: *The Church in Heaven and the Church on Earth.* West porch: *Last Judgment.* Inside the church there are frescoes of the 16th and 17th centuries.

Returning to the Moldova valley, we continue along D.N.17, which at km 67 (43 miles) comes to **Cîmpulung Moldovenesc,** a very ancient settlement which is known to have existed before the establishment of the independent feudal state of Moldavia in the 14th century. In recent years Cîmpulung has developed into a small industrial town (building materials, timber products, foodstuffs). At 10, Str. 7 Noiembrie is a *Museum of Wood*, with a rich collection, mainly of ethnographic material.

A health resort renowed for its picturesque surroundings,
its wooden houses in traditional style and the beauty of its
local costumes, Cîmpulung is also the starting point for excursions on *Mount Rarău*, with a network of well signposted
paths. A country road runs from Cîmpulung to the *Rarău hut*
(altitude 4,987 feet), close to the *Pietrele Doamnei*, a group
of striking limestone rocks with a great area of scree and broken
fragments lying below them. It is an impressive sight and one
of the most remarkable pieces of scenery in the area. The
Pietrele Doamnei are classified as a "natural monument".
To the south-east of Mount Rarău (5436 feet) is Mount Todi-
rescul (4,895 feet), covered with an ancient larch forest, the
Slătioara Forest, now a nature reserve. It can be reached from
Cîmpulung by car by way of the commune of Slătioare (8 km–
5 miles).

3 km (2 miles) from Cîmpulung, in a beautiful fir forest,
is the *Deia hut* (2,231 feet), connected with Cîmpulung by a
country road which is useable by cars.

Tourist Office: 4, Str. 7 Noiembrie.

Beyond Cîmpulung D.N. 17 continues along the
Moldova valley to *Pojorîta*, a centre of the timber
industry, then skirts Mounts Rarău and Giumălău,
crosses the Mesteacăniş pass (3,606 feet), and descends
southward into the valley of the Golden Bistriţa.

Here, at *Iacobeni* (manganese mines and mineral springs),
the road is joined on the right by D.N. 18, coming from the
Maramureş by way of the Prislop pass. (Sighetu 157 km — 98 miles:
see p. 236).

D.N. 17, still following the valley of the Golden
Bistriţa, now descends into the Dorne basin.

Vatra Dornei (110 km–69 miles; altitude 2,789 feet)
is situated in the middle of the volcanic basin of the
Dorna, at its junction with the Golden Bistriţa.
An industrial centre (timber, cheese), Vatra Dornei
is also a health resort with a number of mineral
springs (carbogaseous), peat baths, a Subcarpathian

climate, and an air rich in therapeutic aerosols, containing in particular volatile pine essences.

The carbogaseous baths are specially recommended for the treatment of myocardial, valvular and vascular conditions, hyperthyroidism, etc. The Baths, built in 1895 but modernised in recent years, are open both in summer and winter. In addition to its *parks* (on the Black Hill and at Runc) and the *Local Ethnographical Museum*, Vatra Dornei offers the visitor a number of attractive excursions to the neighbouring villages, with their wooden houses built in traditional style and their beautiful local costumes, and to the mountains in the area, particularly Giumălăul (6,099 feet) and Pietrosul Bistriței (5,886 feet).

Beyond Vatra Dornei D.N. 17 crosses the Carpathians by the Tihuța pass (4,026 feet) and enters Transylvania. See Itinerary 19.

25. IAŞI (JASSY)
AND ITS SURROUNDINGS

At Iaşi (traditionally known in English as Jassy), chief town of the region of the same name, the visitor finds a city which is surprisingly young in spite of its long history, with an active and varied industry and an intense cultural life.

Character of the Town

Iaşi has some fine examples of contemporary architecture —for example in the Păcurari district, on Copou Hill (where there is also a series of halls of residence for students), in the Piaţa Unirii with its ring of tower blocks and its mosaic of flower beds and lawns, and in the industrial districts of Nicolina and Socola, where the visitor's eye will be caught by the simple and elegant lines of the Trade Unions' House of Culture (with a hall seating more than 1000 people).

The industry of Iaşi is largely of recent growth: a factory producing antibiotics, an ironworks, textile mills, a furniture factory, an oilworks, etc. Other enterprises (railway workshops, steelworks, various factories producing foodstuffs, etc.) have been enlarged and re-equipped.

As for scientific and cultural life, there are in Iaşi 8 research institutes of the Rumanian Academy, 6 institutes of higher education with a total of 28 faculties, two theatres, an opera house, a philharmonic orchestra and several museums. The town has a population of 200,000.

History

The name of Iaşi appears for the first time in a rescript of Voivode Alexander the Good at the beginning of the 15th century. At this period it was already a flourishing town and a customs post. In the middle of the same century it became one of the residences of the Princes Regnant of Moldavia; and in 1565 Alexandru Lăpuşneanu made it the capital of Moldavia. This gave a considerable impetus to the development of the town; and it would no doubt have prospered even more had it not been for its frequent changes of rulers in the 18th century and the devastating attacks by foreign invaders. Nevertheless Iaşi became the largest town in Moldavia, an active centre of production and trade, with a cultural life whose traditions are being continued and developed today.

Three great figures of the 17th century in Iaşi were the chroniclers Grigore Ureche and Miron Costin and the Prince Regnant, Vasile Lupu, who founded the "Vasilian School" in 1641 and established a printing press in the Monastery of the Three Hierarchs. In the 18th century a distinguished scholar, Dimitrie Cantemir, succeeded to the throne of Moldavia, and Iaşi had another great chronicler, Ion Neculce. Finally, in the 19th century, Iaşi produced great writers like the poets Vasile Alecsandri and Mihail Eminescu and the teller of fairy tales Ion Creangă; and these have been succeeded by later generations of talented writers and artists.

Tour of the Town

The remains of Iaşi's past are mainly to be found in the centre of the town, round the place where the residence of the Princes of Moldavia once stood. On the ruins of the palace a flamboyant neo-Gothic building was erected in 1907; and this, now the *Palace of Culture*, contains several museums.

The *Museum of the History of Moldavia* is devoted to the development of human society on the territory of Moldavia; the *Ethnographical Museum of Moldavia* displays tools and domestic utensils, farming equipment and the national costumes of the various regions of Moldavia; the *Museum of Plastic Art* possesses a rich collection of Rumanian and foreign art; the *Polytechnic Museum* is concerned with the development of the technology of power supply.

Behind the Palace, to the south, is the municipal swimming pool.

In front of the Palace, to the north, is a statue of Stephen the Great.

To the north of the Palace of Culture, in the Str. 6 Martie, is the Church of St Nicholas (the court church), built by Prince Stephen the Great in the Moldavian style of the 15th and 16th centuries.

Opposite this is a *two-storey house*, the only private building of the 17th century left in Iaşi. To the east the Str. 6 Martie runs into the Str. Ghica Vodă, in which is the *Barnovski Church*, of the 17th century (massive belfry; in the interior, mural paintings).

On the west side of the main artery of Iaşi, the **Str. Ştefan cel Mare** *(Stephen the Great)*, which runs north from the Palace of Culture, is the **Church of the Three Hierarchs**, built in 1638. The exterior is entirely covered with sculptured stone ornament; the interior is sumptuously decorated.

The church was the work of Prince Vasile Lupu, who in 1638, seeking to found a monastery more beautiful than any so far known, built the Monastery of the Three Hierarchs, which included in addition to the church a refectory (known as the Gothic Hall), the abbot's lodging, a belfry and a printing press. To these a Turkish caravanserai was later added.

All these buildings subsisted unchanged until 1882, when the belfry and the caravanserai were demolished. Later other old buildings within the precincts of the monastery were also demolished. At the same time the architect Lecomte du Nouy undertook the restoration of the church; then in 1893 he began the reconstruction of the Gothic Hall. The reconstruction work was interrupted for many years and was not completed until 1960, under the control of the Directorate of Historical Monuments.

Constructed on a trilobate plan, the *Church of the Three Hierarchs* consists of an exonarthex, a pronaos, a naos and an apse. Above the naos and pronaos are towers borne on vaulting in the Moldavian style. The most characteristic and striking features of the building are undoubtedly the façades and the towers with their sculptured stone ornament, delicately and meticulously carved; the carving was originally gilded.

The building known as the *Gothic Hall* contains on the ground floor a large room with stone vaulting and tracery; in

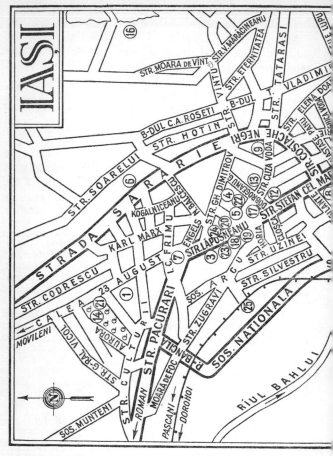

IAŞI (JASSY)

1 University
2 Palace of Culture
3 Museum of the Union
4 Museum of Natural History
5 House of Vasile Alecsandri
6 House of Ion Creangă

7 Statue of Mihail Eminescu
8 Church of the Three Hierarchs
9 Golia Monastery
10 Galata Monastery
11 Cetăţuia Monastery
12 National Theatre
13 Philharmonic Institute
14 Copou Gardens

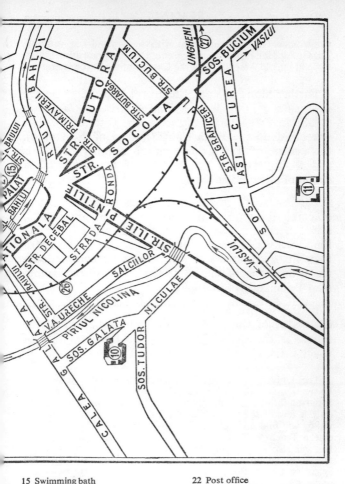

15 Swimming bath
16 Lake Ciric
17 Continental Hotel
18 Victoria Hotel
19 Moldova Restaurant
20 Iaşul Restaurant
21 Rarău Restaurant

22 Post office
23 Tourist Office
24 Agency for Rumanian Railways
   and TAROM
25 Main railway station
26 Nicolina station
27 Socola station

the basement is another room with semi-cylindrical vaulting. The Gothic Hall is now a *museum* containing, among other things, some of the old frescoes from the Church of the Three Hierarchs.

Farther along the Str. Ştefan cel Mare, also on the west side, is the *Metropolitan Church of Moldavia* (1883; in the interior, frescoes by Tattarescu). The street ends in the **Piaţa Unirii** (Square of the Union), the centre of Iaşi's life, with a number of hotels and restaurants. In the middle of the square is a statue of Alexandru Ioan Cuza.

Farther north is the **Str. Lăpuşneanu,** lined with official and commercial buildings (hotels, restaurants, travel agencies, the Tourist Office). A building in Empire style, formerly the residence of Alexandru Ioan Cuza, contains the *Museum of the Union* (documents and objects relating to the Union of the Rumanian Principalities in 1859).

In the square at the far end of Str. Lăpuşneanu is a statue of the poet Mihail Eminescu. Beyond the square is the *Calea 23 August*, on the west side of which is the **University.**

The University of Iaşi is called the Alexandru Ioan Cuza University, in honour of the prince who founded it in 1860. It moved into its present building in 1897, but this now contains only a few of the many faculties of the University. Here the visitor will find an Agronomical Institute, an Institute of Medicine, a Teachers' Training Institute and an Academy of Music. He will also see, in the Copou district, the modern students' residences which constitute a real "University city" and the extensive **Copou Park** where Eminesco used to come to rest under a lime-tree.

From this point the visitor can go on to the Ticăul district to see the "bojdeuca", the modest shingle-roofed cottage which was the home of Ion Creangă, well known for his humorously told tales.

In front of the University there are also statues of three famous representatives of Rumanian culture — M. Kogălniceanu, A.D. Xenopol and V. Conta.

Now return to the Piaţa Unirii and take the *Str. Cuza Vodă*, which runs south-east from the square. On the left of this street is the Moldova State Philharmonic Institute. A side street on the right leads to the *National Theatre* (in the neo-classical style, built in 1896), in front of which is a statue of Vasile Alecsandri.

Farther along the Str. Cuza Vodă, on the left (north) side, is the **Golia Tower**, from the top of which there is a magnificent view over the whole of the town and the surrounding country.

The tower, along with the nearby *Golia Church*, dates from the 16th century. Within the precincts of the church are the *State Archives* (established in 1832) and a modest house in which the writer Ion Creangă lived at one time, now arranged as a museum.

Other buildings worth seeing in the neighbourhood are the **Church of St Sava** in the Str. Costache Negri (built in the 14th century and renovated in the 16th), with low towers which give it the appearance of a mosque, and the *Bărboi Church* (16th century), near the Str. Elena Doamna.

Environs of Iaşi

At *Ciric*, to the north of the town, a fine park has recently been laid out. It has a boating lake.

On a hill to the south is a fortified monastery founded by Prince Duca, the **Cetăţuia Monastery** (1672). Another monastery, still older, is situated on a hill to the south-west of Iaşi: this is the **Galata Monastery**, built by Peter the Lame in 1584.

Pleasant excursions can also be made to the *Bîrnova Forest*, to the west of the town, and *Repedea Hill*, to the south-east, which is classified as a "natural monument" on account of its remarkable fossiliferous rocks.

Tourist Office: 12, Piaţa Unirii (tel. 52.36).

26. BRĂILA AND GALAȚI

From Buzău to Brăila (105 km–66 miles) and
Galați (136 km–85 miles)

The two large Danube towns of Brăila and Galați are reached from Buzău (p. 243) by D.N. 2B. As far as the railway junction of *Făurei* the road follows the winding course of the Buzău, and then crosses the north-eastern part of the Bărăgan plain. It then enters the Danube valley and soon reaches the town of Brăila (105 km–66 miles).

Brăila, 216 km (135 miles) from Bucharest (158,000 inhabitants), is an industrial town, the chief town of its region and one of the largest Rumanian ports on the Danube, which at this point is deep enough to take large ships, including sea-going ships.

The documents show that Brăila has existed as a town for six centuries. Its history during these centuries has been a troubled one, particularly during the period of Turkish domination (1554-1829). It was several times recaptured from the Turks, at the cost of fierce fighting which led to devastating fires. In 1829, when the town was restored to Wallachia, it was almost entirely destroyed, and it was therefore rebuilt in accordance with a regular plan, with streets radiating from the harbour and intersected by other streets running in a semicircle. The harbour can take vessels of 6,000 tons, and has grain stores dating from 1888-89, built by the Rumanian engineer Anghel Saligny; it is said that in constructing them he used prefabricated concrete panels for the first time in the world.

In recent years the town has been transformed into a considerable industrial centre (metalworking, chemical works, factories producing panels, cement, clothing, etc.), and as a result the town has acquired some fine new architecture and has become more attractive and modern.

The visitor to Brăila must see its *Museum* (collection of history, ethnography and art), the *Greek Church* (built between 1836 and 1872), the **Church of Saints Mihail and Gavril** (a former mosque—the only one in the town—converted into an Orthodox church in 1829), the *Central Municipal Park* (containing a bust of the Emperor Trajan) and the park on the banks of the Danube.

Excursions in the neighbourhood: Lacu Sărat (the Salt Lake), a bathing station where the water has a high salt content, and the Filipoiu Channel in the large "Marsh" of Brăila formed by the Danube to the south of the town.

The inhabitants of this old Danube port and the beauties of the "Marsh" of Brăila are excellently portrayed in the works of Panait Istrati (1884-1935), who came from this area.

Tourist Office: 20, Str. Republicii (tel. 20.48).

Between Brăila and Galați, the other Danube port, the road takes a sudden turn westward, leaving the Danube valley, and then crosses the Siret, which collects the water of most of the rivers of Moldavia and carries it to the Danube.

In the commune of *Sendreni* (km 126–79 miles) the road is joined by D.N. 25 coming from Tecuci along the left bank of the Siret. Rather more than a mile beyond this point is the village of *Barboşi*, where the archaeologists have discovered the remains of a settlement dating from the 6th and 5th centuries B.C.; in the Roman period there was a fortress here, later referred to by the Moldavian chroniclers as the "Fortress of Trajan".

Galați 247 km (154 miles) from Bucharest (187,000 inhabitants), is situated on a plateau surrounded by the Danube, the Siret and Lake Brateş. The eye of the visitor arriving in Galați is caught first by the new housing estates built round the recently established ironworks which has enhanced the industrial character of this busy city. Galați possesses in addition the largest shipyards in the country, a rolling mill producing thin sheet metal, factories producing textiles, foodstuffs, chemicals, etc.

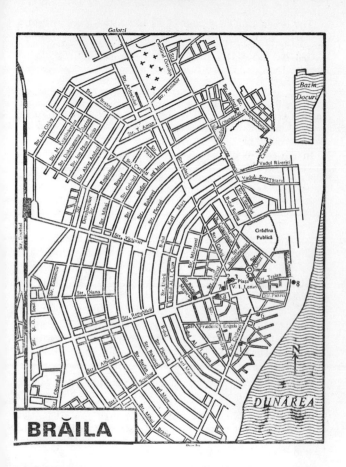

BRĂILA

1 Town hall
2 Museum of Art
3 Historical Museum
4 Hotel Brăila

5 Hotel Republica
6 Post office
7 Tourist Office
8 Landing stage
9 Hotel Traiar

The origin of Galați and of its name has given rise to a variety of theories. One suggestion is that the town was founded by no less a person than Brennus, the leader of the Gauls who passed through this area in the 3rd century B.C. All that is certain, however, is that at the beginning of the 15th century there was a fishing village here, referred to as the "village of Galați"; and at the end of the same century there is documentary evidence for the existence of a river port, the *Schele* of Galați. In later centuries, particularly after the expulsion of the Turks, the port increased in importance; and at the same time a variety of crafts began to flourish.

In the course of the centuries Galați suffered devastation from fires, epidemics and wars. At the end of the second world war the retreating German troops destroyed a large part of the town. As a result of the intensive effort devoted to its rebuilding Galați is now an attractive modern town. It continues to increase in size, extending along the Danube, where a magnificent promenade has been constructed.

The ancient monuments in the town include the fortified *Precista Church* (dedicated to the Virgin), built in the 15th century and rebuilt in the 17th, the *Mavromol Church* (1689), and the *Vovidenia Church* (18th century). Since 1945 Galați has acquired *Museums of Art and History*, which contain some interesting archaeological remains, and a Natural History Museum.

Other sights: the monumental building (architect Ion Mincu) in the traditional Rumanian architectural style which is now the seat of the Regional People's Council; the State Theatre (a building in the classical style); the Mihail Eminescu Park (containing a bust of the poet by K. Storck); and the Public Gardens on the shores of Lake Brateș, the largest fresh-water lake in Rumania (29 square miles).

There are also pleasant excursions to the various fishing areas in the neighbourhood—such as *Crapina*, on the right bank of the Danube, and *Ghimia*, on Lake Brateș—and to the beaches on the shores of the lake and the right bank of the Danube.

Tourist Office: 6, Str. Republicii.

From Galați (or Brăila) the visitor can make the **excursion to the Danube delta**. There are regular services by boat and fast hydrofoil between these towns and **Tulcea** (p. 333).

GALAȚI

1 Museum of Art
2 Museum of the Workers' Movement
3 Museum of History

4 Precista Church
5 Hotel Dunărea
6 Tourist Office
7 Landing stage
8 Main post office

GALAȚI,

27. FROM BUCHAREST
TO CONSTANȚA

Routes to the Black Sea Coast

The distance from Bucharest to the Black Sea coast as the crow flies is about 125 miles, and the regular *air services* cover this in 45 minutes. Travelling by *train*, the tourist passes through the wide fertile plains of the Southern Bărăgan, crosses the Danube on the majestic bridge (2½ miles long, 100 feet high) built in 1890-95 by the Rumanian engineer Anghel Saligny, and then continues over the plateau of the Southern Dobrudja to Constanța. Branches leave the main line at Ciulnița for Călărași (24 km–15 miles) and Slobozia Veche (17 km–10 miles); at Fetești for Făurei (89 km–55 miles), on the Bucharest-Galați line; at Medgidia for Tulcea (144 km–90 miles) and Negru Vodă, the frontier point with Bulgaria (64 km–40 miles); and at Constanța for Eforie Nord (14 km–9 miles) and Mangalia (43 km–27 miles).

The Bucharest-Constanța *road* (266 km-166 miles) first heads north-east as far as Urziceni, and then cuts across the central Bărăgan to Giurgeni. After crossing the Danube it passes over the Dobruja plateau and then descends to the coast to reach Constanța.

Throughout its course this road passes through areas with the lowest recorded cloud cover in Rumania (a mean annual figure of less than 5), and thus with the highest annual sunshine figures (between 2,200 and 2,300 hours). The main road junctions on the way are at Urziceni, for Buzău (54 km–34 miles); at Slobozia, for Călărași (43 km–27 miles) and Brăila (92 km–58 miles); and at Ovidiu, for Tulcea (115 km–72 miles). From Constanța there are roads to Eforie Nord (14 km–9 miles) and Mangalia (43 km–27 miles), to Mamaia (6 km–4 miles), to Negru Vodă, the frontier point with Bulgaria, and to Murfatlar, Adamclisi and Ostrov (125 km–78 miles).

The road to Constanța (D.N. 2) leaves Bucharest by way of Piața 1848, Bd Republicii, Calea Moșilor or Bd Mihai Bravul, and Șos. Armatei Sovietice.

Before leaving the town the road crosses the river Colentina, passing on the left the *Plumbuița Monastery*, built in the 16th century and renovated in the following century by Prince Matei Basarab. Near the exit from the town, on the left of the road, is a new factory producing welded steel tubes.

A little farther on is the *Andronache Forest*, a favourite recreation area for the people of Bucharest. The road then passes through a series of typical communes of the plain country and, at km 51 (32 miles), crosses the River Ialomiţa, which it accompanies almost all the way until it reaches the Danube. After crossing the river the road forks near the small town of *Urziceni* (km 56–35 miles): here D.N. 2 bears left for Buzău (p. 244), a minor road turns back on the left for Ploeşti, and D.N. 2A bears right towards the coast. Beyond Urziceni this road follows an old trade route which linked the passes of the Southern Carpathians with the Danube.

In the middle of the Bărăgan plain the road passes through the town of *Slobozia* (121 km—76 miles—from Bucharest), the centre of the district of the same name and a meeting point of road and rail communications (D.N. 21 to Brăila and Călăraşi; D.N. 2C to Buzău; railway to Călăraşi).

8 km (5 miles) north of Slobozia is the bathing resort of *Amara* (recently enlarged and modernised), on the shores of the lake of the same name. The high mineral content of the water and the mud baths are effective in the treatment of rheumatic conditions, the after-effects of poliomyelitis, etc.

The Danube is crossed by a bridge at *Giurgeni* (km 112–70 miles; 168 km–105 miles—from Bucharest).

Here the waters of the Danube—which have been divided since Călăraşi into two arms, the Borcea and the Dunărea Veche, embracing the extensive "Marsh" of Ialomiţa—come together, only to separate again to the north of the town and enclose the "Marsh" of Brăila. The huge "marshes" are now being reclaimed by the building of dikes which will protect nearly 1,200 square miles of highly fertile arable land against flooding.

On the far side of the Danube the road enters the Dobrudja *(Dobrogea)*.

In the past an extremely backward area, the Dobrudja has in recent years steadily advanced. Factories have been built, its sterile soil has been converted into fields, orchards and vineyards which yield abundant harvests, and its towns and villages have developed.

The first place of any importance is **Hîrşova** (180 km–113 miles–from Bucharest), a small town built on the site of a Roman *castrum (Carsium)* in the year 103 to protect the Danube crossing.

The road, now climbing, now running downhill as it crosses the rolling plateau of the Dobrudja, passes through a series of trim little villages, with houses often decorated with flowers. At *Mihail Kogălniceanu* is an international **airport** used during the summer by aircraft from every country in Europe.

After passing the side road leading to the air-port the road climbs a hill from the top of which the sea can be seen sparkling on the horizon. On the left is the superphosphates factory of Năvodari, on the right the Ovidiu II power station.

Then D.N. 22, coming from the northern Dobrudja (Tulcea), comes in on the left. D.N. 2A passes close to the Ovidiu II power station, is joined on the right by D.N. 22B from Medgidia and Cernavodă, and enters the commune of *Ovidiu*, on the western shore of Lake Siutghiol, 10 km (6 miles) from the centre of *Constanţa*.

28.　　　　CONSTANŢA

Constanţa *(Constantza)*, 266 km (166 miles) from Bucharest, is the administrative, economic and cultural centre of the Dobrudja as well as the principal sea-port of Rumania. Since 1960 the administrative area of the town, which has the status of a region, includes the resorts on the Black Sea coast between Năvodari and Mangalia. Population 181,000.

History

The town of Constanţa was built on the site of the ancient city of *Tomi*. According to an ancient legend the foundation of Tomi was connected with a tragic episode in the expedition of the Argonauts to Colchis, the land of the Golden Fleece. It is said that just to the south of the present town is the place where King Aetes of Colchis buried his young son, who had been hacked into pieces by Jason, the leader of the Argonauts, after the capture of the Golden Fleece; and that some of Aetes' companions remained here and founded a city which they called Tomi.

In fact the establishment of Tomi is probably to be explained by geographical reasons: at this point the land juts out into the sea in a promontory of sufficient height to provide protection for shipping from the northerly and north-westerly winds. We know that the Greek triremes called in here on their voyages to the northern coasts of the Black Sea. Greek settlers from Miletus founded and developed here a trading post subordinate to the city of Histria to the north, also established

---

CONSTANŢA

1 Town hall
2 Tourist Office
3 Hotel Continental
4 Hotel Victoria
5 Hotel Constanţa
6 Casino
7 Archaeological Museum
8 Roman mosaic
9 Archaeological Park
10 Genoese Lighthouse
11 Aquarium
12 Art Museum
13 Mosque
14 Greek church
15 Catholic church
16 Synagogue
17 Post office
18 New lighthouse

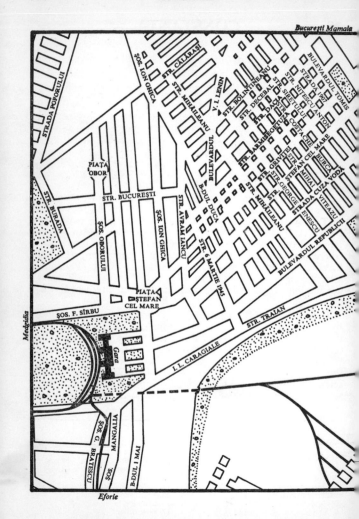

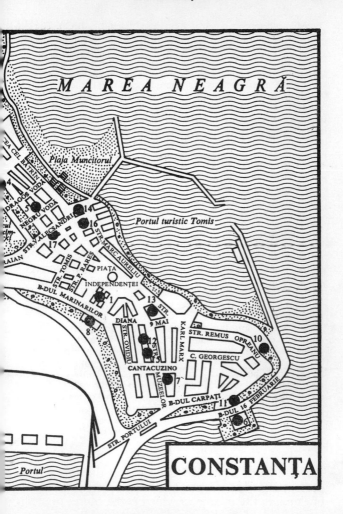

MAREA NEAGRĂ

Plaja Muncitorul

Portul turistic Tomis

PIAŢA
INDEPENDENŢEI

B-DUL MARINARILOR

STR. TOMIS
STR. P. RAREŞ
STR. ALECSANDRI
STR. MARC AURELIU
DRAGOŞ VODĂ
NEGRU VODĂ
TRAIAN

DIANA
STR. OVIDIU
9 MAI
KARL MARX
STR. REMUS OPREANU
STR. MUZEELOR
CANTACUZINO
C. GEORGESCU
B-DUL CARPAŢI
B-DUL 16 FEBRUARIE
STR. PORTULUI

Portul

CONSTANŢA

by Milesian settlers a century earlier (7th century B.C.). The silting up of the port of Histria enabled Tomi to grow into a flourishing city, an active trading and manufacturing centre.

At the beginning of the Christian era the Romans incorporated the Dobrudja—known to them as Scythia Minor—into their Empire. Thereafter Tomi prospered, becoming the metropolis of "Pontus Sinister" (the western coast of the Black Sea). It was adorned with monumental buildings, temples and statues, the remains of which are continually being discovered, adding to the impressive collections of the Archaeological Museum in Constanţa or forming archaeological exhibits in the open air.

Towards the end of the 3rd century Tomi was threatened with invasion by the barbarian peoples. During the 4th century, however, the Emperor Constantine gave it a period of tranquillity, building a new district of the town called *Constantiana* in honour of his sister (hence the present name of the town).

At the end of the 6th century Tomi was destroyed by the Avars. On its ruins a modest fishing port was later established. In spite of the efforts of the Genoese, who tried in the 13th century to restore its trade by building a quay and a lighthouse, the place vegetated throughout the reign of the Wallachian prince Mircea the Old (end of 14th century) and the period of Turkish domination, which was to last until 1877. Thereafter, with the construction of the railway bridge at Cernavodă (1895), the new harbour (1908) and large grain-stores (1909), the town received a fresh lease of life.

At the present day Constanţa has become an important industrial centre, with many modern factories and other enterprises (foodstuffs, metalworks, shipbuilding and repair work). The port has become so busy, not only with Rumania's foreign trade but with the transit trade to the countries of Central Europe, that it has been necessary to build a new harbour of greatly increased capacity. Constanţa also possesses many important modern buildings—a new station, a theatre, a sports stadium, much new housing, schools, shops, etc.

Tour of the Town

The ancient centre of the town is the **Piaţa Independenţei** (Independence Square), formerly the *agora* of Tomi, in the middle of which is the *statue*, in meditative pose, of *Publius Ovidius Naso* (Ovid).

This bronze statue by Ettore Ferrari was erected in 1887 in honour of the great Latin poet who was exiled here by the Emperor Augustus. During the eight years he spent at Tomi Ovid revised his *Metamorphoses*, completed his *Fasti*, and composed the *Tristia* and the *Epistulae ex Ponto*, in which he describes the life of the local people. He died in the year 16 A.D. and was buried with great pomp by the people of Tomi.

In this square is the *People's Council* of the town, occupying an imposing building erected in 1921, notable for its typically Rumanian architecture. It is surrounded by buildings constructed in 1959, with shops on the ground floor.

Behind the People's Council there were discovered in 1959, 16 feet below the present street level, the ruins of a large ancient building with a decorative **mosaic** in six colours. This mosaic — which in size and perfection of workmanship has few rivals in the world — covered the terrace of a commercial building dating from about the 13th century, which then stood opposite the ancient harbour.

Going down towards the sea by the *Str. Karl Marx*, the visitor passes one or two interesting buildings and museums:

The *mosque*, built in 1910 in the Moorish style, with a minaret 160 feet high, from the top of which there is a wide-ranging view over the town, the harbour and the sea.

The *Roman Catholic church*, built in 1885 (architect Romano de Simon), in brightly coloured brick. It is in Romanesque style, with a tall tower.

The *Museum of Plastic Art* (Str. Muzeelor 12) contains more than 200 pictures, works of sculpture and drawings by the greatest Rumanian artists of the 19th and 20th centuries.

The **Archaeological Museum of the Dobrudja** (Str. Muzeelor 23) contains in its 19 rooms an important collection of archaeological material discovered in the Dobrudja.

Note, among other things, a *statue-menhir representing a female deity* (the oldest statue-menhir of this kind discovered in Rumania), a Scythian bronze cauldron, Greek and Roman amphoras, capitals of columns, coins, weights, etc.

In a special room of the Museum are the 24 marble statues and bas-reliefs found in 1962 under the foundations of the old railway station. All the statues except one date from the 2nd and 3rd centuries and represent various divinities. The most interesting are *Fortuna* and *Pontus* (god of the Black Sea), who became the protective divinities of Tomi; *Isis*, an expressive bust; a miniature temple, between the columns of which are two standing figures of the goddess Nemesis; and the "**Snake**", the most striking item in the collection, a fantastic animal with the body of a snake, the muzzle of an animal, and the ears and hair of a man. The figure is carved from bluish white marble and stands 26 inches high. Nothing comparable to it is known anywhere else, and the experts are inclined to see in it an "agathodaimon", a guardian of the sacred places, associated with local divinities.

The Museum also contains a lapidarium, a coin collection and four storerooms for items recently discovered and under examination.

The massive *Orthodox Cathedral*, built between 1884 and 1895, stands near the Museum. It is in typically Rumanian style.

Lower down, on a part of the cliff which has been laid out as a park, is the **Aquarium,** containing characteristic species from the Black Sea, the Danube Delta and the Mediterranean, with a few tropical species.

Nearby are the *Casino*, a building characteristic of the turn of the century, on a terrace jutting out into the sea; a sculptured group, *"The Fishermen"*, by C. Medrea; a *bust of Mihail Eminescu*, whose poems celebrated the beauty of the sea; and the *Genoese lighthouse*, built by Genoese seamen in the 13th century and restored in 1860.

At the north end of the cliff is the *"Tomi" pleasure harbour*, protected by a breakwater. During the summer small passenger boats (hydrobuses) leave here for the various resorts along the coast. Beyond the harbour is a beautiful *beach* (25 acres of fine sand), under a cliff which has been laid out in terraces.

There are two other buildings of interest in this part of the town—the *Hebrew Temple of the Spanish Rite*, built in 1908 in the Gothic style, and the *Greek church*, built in 1867–68 in an unusual style imposed by the donor of the site, Sultan Abdul Aziz, who insisted that the towers of the church should not be higher than the minarets of the mosques in the town of that day.

These two buildings are in the Str. Mircea cel Bătrîn, which leads to the *Park of Culture*. This contains two recent buildings — the *State Theatre* (600 seats), with a neo-classical façade, and the *Palace of Sport*, built 1957–58, with a massive façade decorated with bas-reliefs, containing among other things a hall 118 feet by 66 with 2,500 seats.

At the junction of the Bd Republicii and the Str. Răscoala din 1907 is a kind of open-air museum, the **walls of the city of Tomi.**

Here the visitor can see the remains of the defensive wall built by the Romans in the 2nd century to protect the city to the north and north-west, and of a *tower* erected by the corporation of butchers in the reign of Justinian (6th century), known as the *Butchers' Tower*. The open-air museum also includes an archaeological park, the paths in which are lined with amphoras, columns, friezes, cornices, inscriptions, blocks of stone from ancient buildings, etc. Near the Butchers' Tower is a large marble and ceramic panel showing a *map of the Dobrudja* on which are marked the best known sites of the Greek and Roman periods.

Among the **new buildings of Constanța** must be mentioned, in addition to the blocks of flats with shops on the ground floor, the boldly conceived *railway station*, built in 1959–60 and capable of dealing with 3,000 passengers an hour, complete with waiting rooms and concourses, a restaurant, a bar and a reception room; the *new lighthouse* (completed 1960), a slender structure nearly 200 feet high; and the *"First of May"* Stadium and the park surrounding it, occupying what was formerly a piece of waste ground to the north of the town. The stadium, with tiers of seats in solid limestone like those of the amphitheatres of ancient times, has room for 25,000 spectators.

Tourist Office: 69, Bd Tomis (tel.1.23.42).

29. THE BLACK SEA COAST

To the north and south of Constanţa is a series of important bathing resorts, equipped with ultra-modern facilities and much favoured by foreign visitors.

Their reputation is due not only to the amenities enjoyed by the tourists who are attracted by the beauty of the coast but to a variety of natural advantages. The eastern exposure ensures a long period of sunshine, amounting in the height of summer to 14 hours a day. There are extensive beaches with a deep layer of fine sand. The slope of the beaches is so gentle that children and non-swimmers can enjoy the water without the slightest risk. A further assurance of safety is provided by the absence of tides and currents and by the fact that on most days during the summer (more than 80%) the sea is calm.

The climate is agreeable even in the height of summer, for the sea breezes moderate the heat of the sun.

A. MAMAIA

Mamaia, the principal Rumanian Black Sea resort, lies 6 km (4 miles) north of Constanţa on a tongue of sand between the sea and Lake Siutghiol. It is thus in the unusual position of having the salt water of the sea on its east side and the fresh water of the lake on its west. The lake was originally the mouth of a river but was gradually prevented by the accumulation of sand from discharging its water into the sea. Unlike the other similar lagoons to the south of Constanţa, however, it contains fresh water.

This fresh water seems to have influenced the name of the lake, and of Mamaia itself. The town took its name from a village lying farther north called *Mamakioi* (in Turkish, "the village of butter"). The name of Lake Siutghiol, which is also Turkish, means "the lake of milk". These two names apparently refer to the flocks of sheep who came down from the Carpathians with their shepherds into this southern region with its pasture and abundant supplies of fresh water.

Lake Siutghiol runs along the whole of the western part of Mamaia; at its southern tip is the much smaller Lake Tăbăcăriei, which is fed by the overflow from Lake Siutghiol. On Lake Siutghiol there are a number of boating stations with boats of different kinds. In addition there are many promising places for fishermen throughout its considerable area (8 square miles). In the north of the lake is Ovid's Island, which the great poet is supposed to have frequented during his exile at Tomi; it has a few ancient remains.

There is a modern road from Constanţa to Mamaia, and on this there are two trolleybus lines—N°. 21 from the centre of the town and N°. 22 from the station.

At the entrance to the resort is a thirteen-storey building, the *Parc Hotel*, whose vertical lines are in striking contrast with the horizontal landscape of the beach lying between the lake and the sea. Beyond the hotel a fine *promenade*, gay with flowers, extends along the edge of the beach from south to north of the resort. Motor traffic takes the road along the lake.

MAMAIA

 1 Hotel Victoria
 2 H. Ovidiu
 3 H. Flora
 4 R. Flora
 5 Sulina H.
 6 H. Doina
 7 Doina R.
 8 Delta H.
 9 H. Sirena
10 Neptun H.
11 Dunărea H.
12 Aurora R.
13 Theatre
14 H. and R. Perla
15 Select H.
16 Select R.
17 Dacia H.
18 Lotus H.
19 Delfin H.
20 Pescăruş H.
21 Parc R.
22 Parc.
23 Pelican H. and R.
24 Palas H.
25 Central H.
26 Modern R.
27 Modern H.
28 International H. and R
29 Yalta H.
30 Yalta R.
31 Tomis R.
32 Tomis H.
33 Histria R.
34 Midia H.
35 H. Histria
36 Albatros H. and R.
37 Cazino R.

H = Hotel
R = Restaurant

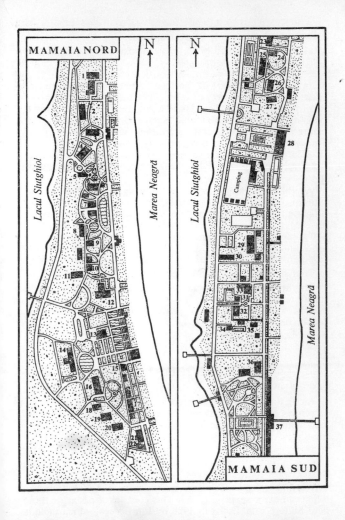

The resort has a total length of 3 miles and a fine beach with an area of more than 100 acres. It faces east and is covered with very fine silver sand formed of finely crushed shells.

In the southern part of the town, apart from the hotels and restaurants, are a variety of other amenities: a sport and amusement park near Lake Tăbăcăriei, a modern shopping centre, the open-air Ovidiu Theatre (1,200 seats) and boating clubs. In the centre are other hotels and restaurants (including one, typically Rumanian, near Lake Siutghiol), two ultra-modern bars, an open-air cinema, and a shopping centre. To the north are camping sites, a group of holiday huts, shops, a landing-stage, sports grounds, etc.

All these buildings—hotels (total capacity 14,000 beds), restaurants, shops, bars, sports facilities, open-air theatre—are in a light and graceful architecture, with many open spaces, which gives Mamaia a most restful atmosphere. There is a park of over 170 acres in which the green lawns are set off by shrubs of all kinds and flower-beds of many colours, and statues are reflected in ornamental lakes of various shapes.

Tourist Office: in the Bucureşti Hotel.

To the north of Mamaia is *Năvodari*, formerly a modest fishing village, which has considerably developed following the establishment of a superphosphates factory. It has a very fine beach, now occupied by a holiday home for school children (capacity 2,000 children).

B. EFORIE NORD

Along the coast to the south of Constanţa are a large number of resorts situated at between 50 and 100 feet above sea level, with their beaches lying at the foot of the cliffs (which have usually been attractively laid out).

These resorts lie along D.N.39 and are served by buses which run regularly between Constanţa and Mangalia and by the railway between these two towns.

The first resort to the south of Constanţa is **Agigea** (km 10—6 miles), near a small salt lake. This contains the Marine Biological Station established in 1926 by Ion Borcea, which includes

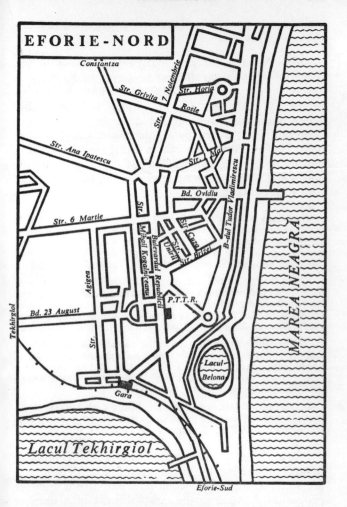

a museum of marine flora and fauna and a nature reserve (bota-nical and zoological).

Eforie Nord is the principal bathing resort to the south of Constanţa. It stands some 50 to 60 feet above the sea, on top of cliffs which have been rein-forced by buttresses of red granite and limestone. Three paths have been cut at different levels in the steep cliff face, linked by flights of steps and flower-beds. Halfway down the cliff is a three storey building containing the Neptune Café, a pâtisserie, a restaurant and a bar; on the lowest level is a terrace decorated with Chinese lanterns.

The **beach** at the foot of the cliff is 100–120 feet wide, and is continually increasing in width as a result of the building of groynes to retain the sand deposited by the sea. A T-shaped breakwater, 600 feet long, serves as a pier for the coastal boats which ply between the various Black Sea resorts.

Along the top of the cliff runs the *Bulevard Tudor Vladimirescu*, lined with attractive villas. At the south end of the boule-vard are a *pleasure lake* covering 15 acres and a beach with room for 2,000 people. The water of the lake, though constantly changed, is between 7° and 10 °C. warmer than the sea.

The most modern hotels are in the north of the town: four- and five-storey buildings set in a park with great areas of grass, flower-beds, ornamental trees and fountains. Not far away is the elegant Perla Mării Restaurant, with seating for 1,000, largely (80%) built of glass.

In the central park is an open-air theatre with 1,800 seats. In the centre of the town are many shops and a large building con-taining the Post Office, the office of the Tarom air line, etc.

Eforie Nord's main attraction is as a relaxing holiday place, but the proximity of lake Techirghiol, the water and mud of which have important curative properties, has led to the establishment of a number of large *therapeutic establishments*.

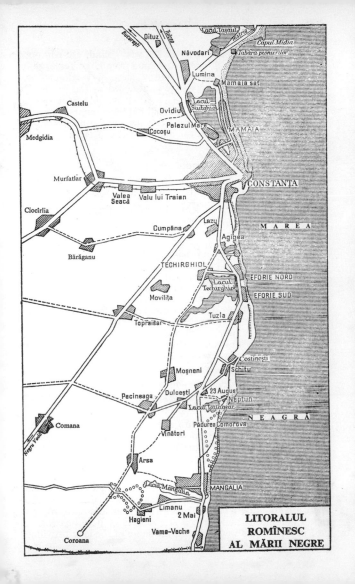

LITORALUL
ROMÎNESC
AL MĂRII NEGRE

The Baths, which are open all the year round, are equipped
to provide hot baths in water and mud from Lake Techirghiol,
mud pack treatment, physiotherapy, aerosol treatment and
medical gymnastics. A polyclinic is attached to the Baths. On
the shore of Lake Techirghiol is a modern establishment for cold
mud baths, equipped with individual cubicles, separate beaches
for men, women and children, a restaurant and other amenities.
There is also a sanatorium for the treatment of the after-effects
of poliomyelitis in children.

Tourist Office: 1, Bd Republicii.

Techirghiol is situated to the north-west of the lake
of the same name, 18 km (11 miles) from Constanţa
and 4 km (2½ miles) from the sea.

The name is of Turkish origin but its meaning is still obscure.
In Turkish *tekir* is a proper name, but it is also an adjective
meaning "salt, bitter". This might be a reference to the lake, for
its water is much more salt than the water of the sea. The water
of the lake (which covers an area of 4 square miles) undoubtedly
possesses curative properties in virtue of its high content (96.663 gr.
per litre) of mineral substances—sodium and magnesium chloride, bromides, sulphates, silicon dioxide, iron oxide, etc. Its
concentration—continually increasing as a result of the high
evaporation rate—is at present seven times that of the Black Sea.

The mud of the lake bottom consists of residues of vegetable,
animal and mineral origin. In addition to mineral salts with curative properties, it contains a whole series of hormone substances
which increase its therapeutic value.

This was the first resort to be established on the Rumanian
coast in 1899. It is situated on a gentle slope surrounded by
hills: a sun-trap in which the water of the lake is maintained
at a constant 22–26 °C. in summer. The mean annual temperature here is higher than on the coast.

The capacity of the resort has increased steadily, and it can
now cater for 5,000 visitors, compared with 2,000 in 1950.
There are specialised establishments for rheumatic and gynaecological conditions and for the after-effects of poliomyelitis. In
1961 new premises were built on the shore of the lake providing
cold baths for 1,000 people.

There is a regular bus service between Eforie Nord and Constanţa, and a service of motor launches between Eforie Nord and Eforie Sud.

C. EFORIE SUD

The resort of Eforie Sud, 5 km (3 miles) from Eforie Nord and 19 km (12 miles) from Constanţa, is situated on a *cliff* 100 feet high between the sea and Lake Techirghiol. The cliff face has been consolidated and properly laid out, and there are steps leading down to the *beach*. This is of considerable length but narrow, with groynes which should gradually increase its width. There is a jetty which provides landing places for the coastal boat services.

The resort, which is in process of rapid development, can cater for up to 11,000 visitors at the same time. The proximity of Lake Techirghiol makes it also a *treatment centre*, with sanatoria, baths, a polyclinic, etc.

The luxuriant growth of vegetation (trees, lawns and flower-beds, formal gardens) gives Eforie Sud a park-like atmosphere. There is an open-air theatre (2,000 seats) and an open-air cinema (700 seats).

A small **archaeological museum** (Bd Republicii) contains interesting ancient remains discovered in the town or the surrounding area. (The Greek city of *Stratonis* is thought to have been situated at Tuzla, to the south of Eforie Sud.) The material includes objects dating from the Neolithic period, amphoras and oil lamps of the Greek and Roman period, a gold pendant of the Roman period, bas-reliefs in marble and limestone, fragments of columns, capitals and stone slabs with inscriptions found at Tuzla.

There is a regular bus service between Eforie Sud and Constanţa.

Tourist Office: 1, Str. Dorului.

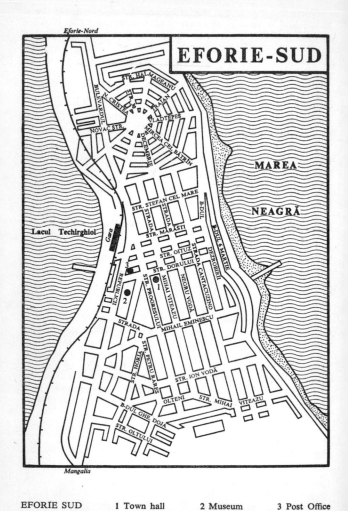

EFORIE SUD   1 Town hall   2 Museum   3 Post Office

D. MANGALIA

A number of new resorts have developed on the southern part of the coast, taking advantage of wide and easily accessible beaches.

The small resort of *Costineşti*, 32 km (20 miles) from Constanţa, has a beach rather more than a mile long and 200–230 feet wide, in the shelter of Cape Tuzla, with a sanatorium for young people and a summer camp for students.

Farther south is *Neptun*, opened in 1960, on a tongue of sand between the sea and Lake Tatlageac. Between Neptun and Mangalia are the recently established resorts of *Jupiter*, *Venus* and *Saturn*, which are now accepted as being the finest resort developments one the Rumanian Black Sea coast.

Mangalia, 43 km (27 miles) from Constanţa, is the most southerly resort on the Rumanian coast. It occupies a favoured situation on the south-eastern tip of the Dobrudja plateau (65 feet above sea level), sheltered on the north by the *forest of Comorova* (containing roe-deer, grouse, and a pheasant rearing farm) and flanked on the south by *Lake Mangalia*, occupying the bed of an old river now blocked by sand from the sea. The lake is 3 km (2 miles) from the town; on the side nearest the town are radioactive sulphurous hot springs (22½-23½ °C.) which are recommended for the treatment of chronic rheumatism, lumbago, sciatica, dermatoses, and chronic conditions of the liver and kidneys.

The beach of Mangalia, which extends to some 7 acres, is covered with siliceous sand. The climate is particularly mild, recalling that of the Mediterranean.

Mangalia is situated on the ruins of an ancient city founded by the Greeks in the 6th century B.C. It was known as *Callatis* both in the Greek and Roman period. From the 13th century it appears on maps under the name of *Pangalia* or Pangala. In 1593 it took the name of *Mangalia*, which it has retained until the present day.

Since 1958 Mangalia has developed into a modern resort with comfortable hotels, shops, restaurants, an open-air theatre, a sports stadium and a fine House of Culture. A children's sanatorium and another for adults, equipped with a spacious covered pool, make it possible to provide treatment throughout the year. Like other places along the coast, the town has some attractive parks. The cliffs descends in a series of broad ledges to the **beach,** where a long jetty provides landing-places for the coastal boats.

In a small villa overlooking the sea (Str. V. Pârvan) is an **archaeological museum** containing remains of the past found in the area: amphoras, urns, inscriptions, statuettes, bas-reliefs, Greek and Roman coins, including some from the city of Callatis, marble capitals and a fine *statue of Aphrodite* in marble (3rd century A.D.).

There are also the **remains of the ancient Greek city** and ruins of the Roman period, including a majestic building with marble columns lying to the north of the sports park and an **ancient tomb** (4th century A.D.) in the centre of a stone enclosure 50 feet in diameter. The tomb, built of large sandstone slabs, contained the skeleton of a man, a crown of gilded bronze and the remains of a papyrus written in Greek. The papyrus was so damaged that only a fragment could be read, indicating that the dead man was a high dignitary.

To the south of the town is a building in Oriental style, the *Mosque of Esmahan Sultan*, erected by the Turks in the 15th century.

Tourist Office: 2, Şos. Constanţa.

The road continues south of Mangalia to Vama Veche, 8 km (5 miles) away, the frontier point with Bulgaria.

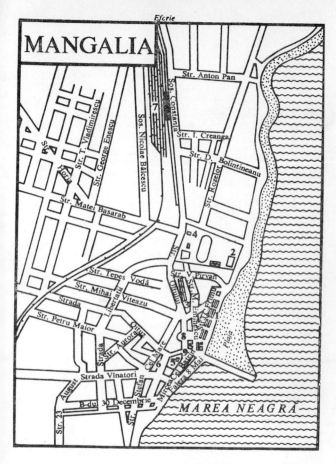

MANGALIA

1 Town hall
2 Museum
3 Walls of Callatis
4 Ancient
5 Mosque
6 Post office
7 Station
8 Piața Victoriei
9 Piața Lenin

D.N. 38, which runs from Constanţa to *Negru Vodă*
on the Bulgarian frontier (54 km–34 miles), links
up with the roads from Sofia and the Bulgarian
coast. It offers no particular interest.

A. MURFATLAR, ADAMCLISI, OSTROV
(133 km–83 miles)

D.N. 3 runs from Constanţa to **Murfatlar** (19 km–
12 miles), whose limestone hills support not only
a famous *vineyard* producing sweet and luscious
wines of high quality (many gold medals in international competitions), but also rare plants and animals,
which have led to the area being designated as a
nature reserve.

The commune of Murfatlar contains a horticultural and viticultural research station and modern stores capable of taking
800 waggon-loads of wine. Near here, under a chalk hill, were
discovered three small *churches* built one on top of the other,
several underground passages, tombs, Cyrillic inscriptions, tools,
pottery, etc. dating from the 10th century.

On the same road, 64 km (40 miles) from Constanţa, is **Adamclisi,** with one of the most imposing
ancient monuments in Rumania: the **Tropaeum
Trajani,** which was built on the orders of the Emperor
Trajan to glorify the Romans' victories over the
peoples of Scythia Minor (the present-day Dobrudja).

The monument, which dates from the 2nd century A.D., is
circular in shape (102 feet in diameter, 131 feet high) and is surrounded by a staircase of seven steps. It consisted of a large
cylindrical plinth, in the form of truncated cone, with an external
facing of stone slabs; and on top of this were two superimposed
hexagonal structures supporting the trophy-statue. On two sides

of the upper hexagonal structure is an inscription, Trajan's dedication of the monument to Mars Ultor.

The cylindrical plinth was decorated with 54 **metopes,** of which 49 remain, representing a variety of incidents from the Roman campaigns in the Danube area. Among the most interesting scenes are a legionary fighting with two Dacians, the Emperor acclaimed by his troops, a horseman, a fight on a chariot, two prisoners being brought before the Emperor, trumpeters, standard-bearers, a Dacian family offering submission, a flock of sheep, etc.

There are also some interesting fragments of sculpture (fragments from the topmost storey representing a barbarian prisoner, geometric patterns, broken pieces of a frieze, the head of a Medusa, etc.).

Four different theories have been put forward about the original appearance of the monument. Recent studies have suggested that it was planned on two axes of symmetry corresponding to two inscriptions on the upper hexagonal structure and to a terminal trophy with two faces.

A pattern based on multiples of six can also be seen in the arrangement of the 54 bas-reliefs on historical subjects. There are six groups of nine scenes each; and each group is concerned with a particular theme, with a representation of the Emperor in the central scene of the group. The six groups consist of two parallel cycles of three, each comprising a marching scene, a fighting scene and a scene representing the victory over the enemy. Thus in the first cycle we see a march and a cavalry clash, a fight over a fortified "laager" of chariots, and the surrender of prisoners and the civilian population. The second cycle showed infantry on the march, infantry fighting, and the acclamation of the Emperor. Each group was divided by the figure of the Emperor into two series of four scenes, and these smaller groups were in turn formed of two pairs of scenes almost identical with each other.

This symmetrical arrangement is exactly comparable with the succession of scenes XXXVI–XLII on Trajan's Column.

Not far from the monument were discovered the remains of a mausoleum dedicated to the Roman soldiers killed in the fighting and the remains of a city founded by Trajan, bearing the same name as the monument.

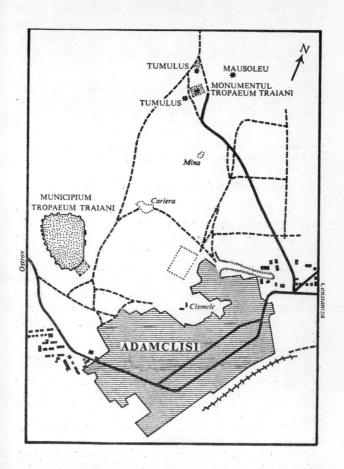

133 km (83 miles) from Constanţa is the small
town of *Ostrov*, on the banks of the Danube. Here
there is a wine-making establishment where the
grapes from the vineyards on the surrounding hills
are pressed.

Near Ostrov, on one of the picturesque islands in the middle
of the Danube called *"Păcuiul lui Soare"*, were discovered the
remains of a powerful Byzantine city of the 10th century, which
continued to exist until the 13th or 14th century.

At Ostrov the Danube can be crossed by ferry to reach
Călăraşi, which is connected with Bucharest by D.N.3 (127 km
—79 miles) and by railway (via Ciulniţa).

B. HISTRIA (66 km–41 miles)

D.N. 22, now completely resurfaced, follows the
Constanţa-Hîrşova road as far as the "Ovidiu II"
power station, and then turns off to the right towards
the northern Dobrudja. It crosses the valley of the river
Casimcea, passing near Lake Taşaul; then at Tariverde
(50 km–31 miles — from Constanţa) a road goes off
on the right. This passes through the commune of
Nuntaşi and in 16 km (10 miles) comes to **Histria,**
in a bare landscape which has a certain grandeur
of its own.

At Histria are the ruins of the most ancient city in Rumania,
founded in the 7th century B.C. by Greek settlers from Miletus.
At this period Histria was actually on the coast, and its harbour
did a flourishing transit trade in the 6th and 5th centuries B.C.
Goods from Athens, Corinth, Rhodes, Miletus and other cities
passed through Histria into the Danube area and travelled as far
as the Carpathians. In return Histria sent cereals, honey, fish
and slaves to Greece and Asia Minor.

Then the bay on which the city was built gradually silted up,
and it passed through a period of stagnation in the 3rd and
2nd centuries B.C. In the Roman period (1st–2nd centuries A.D.)
Histria enjoyed administrative autonomy and achieved a measure of prosperity, as is shown by the erection of a number of

temples and other large buildings. Destroyed by the Goths in the year 248, Histria was rebuilt (end of 3rd century), but finally declined in the 7th century when the Byzantine Empire gave up the line of the Danube.

We can see at Histria the remains of a number of cities built on top of one another in the course of twelve centuries. Buildings of the Roman period, for example, were erected on the foundations, 13 feet thick, of the **city walls** of the Greek period.

The massive wall enclosing the city, built at the end of the 3rd century, strengthened and enlarged in the 4th–6th centuries, is a repository of broken columns, for it contains fragments of columns, architraves and cornices from buildings of ancient Histria destroyed by the Goths. On the west side the wall was flanked by three great *towers* and five *bastions*, and the main gate was defended by two external and two internal towers. Near the main tower of the fortress is a stone staircase leading up on to the wall, from which there is a wide view over the city and Lake Sinoe.

Behind the main gate was a spacious paved **square**, on the south side of which was a *basilica* (5th–6th centuries). The walls of this building still stand to a height of some 6 feet. From this square a well paved street runs south, passing the ruins of two *basilicas*, the second of which is the largest in Histria (82 feet by 41 feet). Opposite this was a commercial building, a kind of *market* divided into shops *(tabernae)* selling different types of goods. The two buildings date from the 6th and 7th centuries.

The **Roman Baths,** built in the 3rd century but restored several times during the 3rd and 4th centuries, occupied a huge building, of which there remain three cubicles, formerly part of the main hall, decorated with *coloured mosaics* in geometric and floral patterns. Behind the Baths was a *commercial and industrial district* in which a metal-worker's shop, a bakery and cereal stores have been identified.

From the Baths one of the main streets of the town of the late Roman period, running eastward, led to one of the *aristocratic districts* of the city. This is proved by the discovery in this area of a spacious house with a pillared patio and a public building containing many rooms (6th century).

To the north-east of the city must have been the **sacred area** of the town in the Greek period, as is shown by the discovery of *two Greek temples* and an altar. One of the temples, dating from the 5th century B.C. and built in limestone blocks, was apparently dedicated to *Aphrodite;* the second, according to the dedicatory inscription, was sacred to the *"great god"* and dates from the 3th century B.C.

C. THE NORTHERN DOBRUDJA

Returning to D.N. 22 and continuing northward, the traveller passes through *Baia*, near *Hamangia* station (on the Medgidia-Tulcea line), where important remains dating from the Middle Neolithic period have been discovered.

Among these is a statue, the "Thinker", representing a man sitting in a meditative pose with his chin supported in his hands. The "Hamangia culture" is noted for its fine sculptures of human figures, usually women, indicating the existence of a fertility cult.

89 km (55 miles) from Constanţa, the road passes through **Babadag,** surrounded by hills covered with woods, vineyards and meadows.

The remains of the Roman period discovered here bear witness to the long history of the area. The town retains a few monuments from its past: the *mosque*, built in 1373, and the *Calaigi Fountain* close by.

From the highest hill in the surrounding area (Koiumbaba, 873 feet) there is a picturesque view of Babadag, and also of Lake Razelm to the east with the ruins of the old fortress of *Heracleia*. A country road (8 km — 5 miles) runs from Babadag to the commune of Enisala, lying just under the ruins of Heracleia. In the ruins were discovered coins and pottery dating from the time of the Wallachian prince Mircea the Old, who called himself "Prince reigning as far as the Great Sea".

Some ten miles to the south of Enisala is the picturesque fishing village of *Jurilovca* (sturgeon, sea and lake fish, etc., preparation of caviare); in the neighbourhood — at Doloşman, on the peninsula of Bisericouţa, and at Slava Rusă — are the ruins of Byzantine citadels.

Beyond Babadag D.N. 22 comes to Tulcea, passing through the foothills of the *Măcin Mountains*, a chain of Palaeozoic date, worn down by erosion, which are the oldest mountains in Rumania. There are many flourishing vineyards in this area, particularly in the north near the village of Niculițel. From **Tulcea** (123 km–77 miles–from Constanța) a road runs to Isaccea, on the south bank of the Danube, and to 23 August, from which there is a ferry to Galați (p. 290); and another road runs south from this road to Măcin, where there is a ferry to Brăila (p. 289).

31.   THE DANUBE DELTA

Beyond Galaţi the Danube, which up to this point has been flowing from north to south, changes course and turns firmly east, reaching the Black Sea in 150 km (95 miles). Thousands of years ago, in the prehistoric period, this final stretch of the Danube's course was only half its present length, for the sea then extended inland in a large bay. Gradually the Danube filled this bay with its alluvium (almost 70 million tons a year) and created the Delta, the youngest part of Rumanian territory. By a freak of nature this area lies close to the most ancient mountains in Rumania, the Măcin Mountains, which are contemporary with the Vosges in France and the Black Forest in Germany. Seen from the Danube, these mountains, 1,532 feet high, have retained something of the majesty of the old Hercynian chain.

The Delta

The Danube begins to spread out into a fan shape to the north-east of Tulcea, at *Ceatalul Chiliei* (Ceatal=fork), where the northern arm of the Delta—*Chilia*, some 60 miles long and accounting for 70% of the total volume of the river—branches off. Ten miles east of Tulcea the Danube again divides into two arms: *Sulina*, the main watercourse of the Delta, 40 miles long, which has been made a navigable channel for sea-going ships, and *Sf. Gheorghe*, the southern arm, which winds tortuously about and has a length of 70 miles. These three arms divide the Delta into three large areas—Letea in the north, Sf. Gheorghe in the middle, and Dranov between Sf. Gheorghe and Lake Razelm. These areas, amounting to some 1,700 square miles in all, are broken up by a multitude of secondary streams, linked with a complex pattern of lagoons and marshes. Only a few "grinds" (tongues of land), representing 9% of the total area, remain permanently above water. The climate is not subject to much variation and the Delta can be visited throughout the year.

The Delta can be regarded as a large natural laboratory, in which the landscape is continually being modified by erosion and the deposit of alluvium. The "grinds" and the bottoms of the pools are continually being raised, the streams silt up and the Delta gains steadily at the expense of the sea, particularly at the mouth of the Chilia (260 feet a year).

This new land, sodden with water, is covered with *luxuriant vegetation* which gives it a strange charm. A considerable area is occupied by reeds—some 1000 square miles, including 400 square miles of "plaurs", floating islands of reeds from which fragments are constantly breaking loose and drifting about on their own, producing unexpected changes in the geography of the Delta. The lakes of the Delta are gay with water plants, resplendent white or yellow water-lilies. On the banks of the streams are forests of oak, willow and poplar, twined round with all kinds of climbing plants, with something of the appearance of a tropical mangrove swamp.

The forest on the "grind" of Letea, with its rich variety of trees, shrubs and other plants, is of particular interest. The corner of the forest known as the "Garden of Omar" is remarkable for the luxuriance of its vegetation and the vigorous growth of lianas on its trees. The south-eastern and northern parts of the Letea forest are an important natural monument. From Letea the visitor can reach another similar area, the forest of Caraorman.

The *fauna* of the Danube delta is one of the richest in Europe. It provides 50% of the fresh-water fish of Rumania, and is frequented by migrating sea fish like the sturgeon, the source of the famous caviare.

The Delta has rightly been called the "paradise of birds", for in addition to the millions of migrants which halt here on their journey from the south in spring and their return to the south in autumn more than 300 species of birds live in the luxuriant vegetation of the Delta (wild ducks and geese, swans, cormorants, woodcock, etc.). Some species of larger birds, such as the pelican, the egret and little egret, the spoonbill, and the black and white wild duck, have been declared protected species and occupy large reserves. The mammals of the Delta include boars, wolves, foxes, minks, otters, etc.

The economic importance of the Delta is not confined to its fish: in recent years the reeds have provided raw material for considerable quantities of cellulose, paper, artificial fibres, etc.

In order to avoid upsetting the biological balance of the Delta the gathering of the reeds is carried out systematically in the more accessible areas.

Most of the **tourist excursions in the Delta** start from *Tulcea,* which is known as the "gateway to the Delta". It can be reached by bus (from Constanța or the resorts along the coast), air (from Bucharest or Constanța), train (by a branch which leaves the Bucharest–Constanța line at Medgidia) or boat (from Brăila–Galați).

Tulcea (35,500 inhabitants), situated within a circle of hills, has a history going back two thousand years.

The ancient port, mentioned by Herodotus, played an important part in the exchange of goods between the Greeks from Miletus who had settled at Histria, Tomi, etc., and the native Geto-Dacian population. Ovid refers to the old and powerful city of *Aegyssus,* as it was called by the Romans. The town was first mentioned under its present name in the 17th century.

Today Tulcea is an important centre of the fishing industry (canning and fish flour factories, modern refrigerated stores). The town also contains a modern plant for processing non-ferrous metals, factories manufacturing food products, a factory producing reed boards and a small shipyard. Tulcea possesses a fine promenade along the quays on the Danube, a hotel complex, a park on the shores of Lake Ciuperca and the *Azizir Mosque.* Other places of interest are a *museum* containing archaeological material discovered in the area, an aquarium and a reference library. To the east of the town, on a hill overlooking the river, is an obelisk commemorating the return of the Dobrudja to Rumania.

Excursions in the Delta

a) On the Chilia arm (Tulcea–Periprava 103 km–64 miles). The sites of tourist interest on this arm of the Danube, which forms the frontier with the U.S.S.R., are:

Ceatalchioi; Pardina, a centre for reed-gathering and the starting point for Pardina Island (nesting place of wild geese, colonies of pelicans and spoonbills) and Lake Tatanir (abounding with fish; fishing village with fish store); *Chilia Veche* (on the site of the Greek city of *Achillea,* founded in the 5th century B.C.), a fishing centre, connected by a small channel to the Sulina; *Peri-*

DELTA DUNĂRII

0   10 km

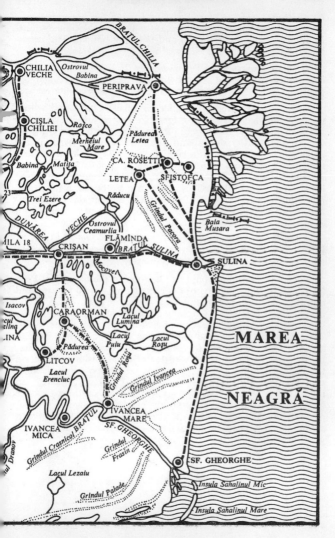

prava, the starting point for the Letea Forest (oaks, surrounded by a thick growth of shrubs and climbing plants). The neighbouring lagoons are the haunt of wild geese and pelicans.

b) On the Sulina arm (Tulcea–Sulina 71 km–45 miles). This is the most frequented arm of the Danube, with a channel cut to give access to sea-going ships. The sites of tourist interest are:

Ilgani (tourist chalet); **Maliuc,** a village established within the last few decades, with a research centre and museum of the reed industry; *Gorgova* (a fishing village, with Lake Gorgova just to the south; ducks and colonies of egrets nest in the neighbourhood); *Mila 23* (a large fishing village with a modern fish store); *Crişan* (an important fishing centre, starting point for the Caraorman Forest); **Sulina,** an old Byzantine port used by the Genoese and the Turks, with a good beach, a hotel and a holiday village. The life of this port in former days is described by the Rumanian writer E. Botez (literary pseudonym Jean Bart) in his novel "Europolis".

c) On the Sf. Gheorghe arm (Tulcea–Sf. Gheorghe 113 km–71 miles). This winding arm of the Danube is rarely used for ordinary navigation. The places of tourist interest are:

Nufăru (a commune built on the ruins of the old city of Prislava; nearby are the ruins of the ramparts of an old fortress and a bridge); *Victoria* (a fishing village where the picturesque Litcov channel branches off to the Sulina); **Mahmudia** (built on the site of the Roman–Byzantine city of *Salsovia;* nearby is the hill of *Beştepe,* with a wide-ranging view over the Delta, Lake Razelm and the sea); *Murighiol* (a fishing village with a camping site; nearby, remains of ancient walls); *Calinova* (a fishing village, on the right of which a channel branches off to the south, leading to Lake Razelm); *Ivancea* (two fishing villages; nearby an important ·breeding area for cranes; to the south-east is the beginning of the reserve for swans, egrets, herons, spoonbills); *Sf. Gheorghe* (fishing centre, particularly famed for the sturgeon fishing and the preparation of caviare; new houses and stores; good beach).

Practical
Information

RUMANIA

CONTENTS

WHERE TO GET INFORMATION ABOUT TRAVEL IN RUMANIA

Outside Rumania, information can be obtained from the National Tourist Office (Carpaţi) at the following addresses:

Austria: Opernring 1, Vienna.

Belgium: 26 Place de Brouckère, Brussels.

Denmark: Vesterbrogade 55 A, Copenhagen.

France: 38 Avenue de l'Opéra, Paris.

Germany (Democratic Republic): Frankfurter Tor 5, Berlin.

Germany (Federal Republic): Corneliusstr. 16, Düsseldorf; Neue Mainzer Str. 1, Frankfurt/Main; Klopstockstr. 8, Munich.

Hungary: 72 Tököly Utca, Budapest.

Israel: 97 Ben Jehuda Street, Tel Aviv.

Italy: Via Albrici 10, Milan; Via Torino 100, Rome.

Netherlands: 17-19 Kleine Gartmanplantsoen, Amsterdam.

Spain: 157 Avenida Alfonso XIII, Madrid.

Sweden: Gamla Brogatan 33, Stockholm.

Switzerland: Talstrasse 58, Berne.

United Kingdom: 98-99 Jermyn Street, London SW..1.

U.S.A.: Flat 328, 500 Fifth Avenue, New York.

Within Rumania, information can be obtained either from the National Tourist Office or from regional tourist offices in the chief towns of the various regions. Addresses are given below.

National Tourist Office

National Tourist Office (Carpaţi), 7, Bd Magheru, Bucharest, tel. 14.51.60, telex 270-278-279, telegraphic address Carpatourist.

National Tourist Office (Carpaţi), 22, Str. 7 Noiembrie, Braşov, tel. 921.12840, telex 012228.

National Tourist Office (Litoral), Hotel Bucureşti B, Mamaia, tel. 916.31152, telex 014221.

Regional Tourist Offices

Region	Address	Tel.	Telex
Alba	Alba Iulia - 3, Str. Republicii	1238	031530

Arad	Arad - 78, Str. Republicii	11440	036
Argeş	Pitesti - 2, Str. Plevnei	14561	018221
Bacău	Bacău - 10, Calea Mărăşeşti	11681	021227
Bihor	Oradea - 1, Aleea Strandului	14878	034214
Bistriţa-Năsăud	Bistriţa - 1, Piaţa Centrală	1056	038
Botoşani	Botoşani - 1, Piaţa 1907	12784	1827
Braşov	Predeal - 74, Str. Gh. Gheorghiu-Dej	11095	012219
Braïla	Braïla - 20, Str. Republicii	13626	0118538
Buzău	Buzău - 176, Str. Unirii	2535	01184
Caraş-Severin	Reşiţa - 2, Bd. Lenin	1066	013516
Cluj	Cluj - 2, Str. Gh. Sincai	13778	031286
Covasna	Sf. Gheorghe - 2, Str. Ciucului	1953	0128
Dîmbovita	Tîrgovişte - 11, Piaţa Libertăţii	1889	01188
Dolj	Craiova - 9, Str. Al. I. Cuza	13763	016262
Galaţi	Galaţi - 6, Str. Republicii	14436	015226
Gorj	Tg. Jiu - 6, Str. Eroilor	2758	016513
Harghita	Miercurea Ciuc, - 1, Str. Petöfi	1675	021421
Hunedo-ara	Deva - 1, Piaţa Unirii	12026	032277
Ialomiţa	Slobozia - 136, Str. Matei Basarab	1060	01182
Iaşi	Iaşi - 18, Piaţa Unirii	12356	022216
Ilfov	Bucharest - 1, Str. Ilfov	164545	—
Mara-mureş	Baia Mare - 9, Str. Pietrosului	14177	033225
Mehedinţi	Turnu Severin - 64, Str. Traian	12627	016415
Mureş	Tg. Mureş - Piaţa Trandafirilor	30289	035224
Neamţ	Piatra Neamţ - 1, Str. Karl Marx	13090	021611
Olt	Slatina - Str. Revoluţia din Octombrie	1922	018325
Prahova	Ploieşti - 6, Str. 16 Februarie	21808	019210
Satu Mare	Satu Mare - 14, Bd Eliberării	12272	033421
Sălaj	Zalău - 11, Piaţa Libertăţii	1889	037

Sibiu	Sibiu - 4, Piaţa Unirii	14063	012731
Suceava	Suceava - Str. N. Bălcescu Bl. I A	10503	023210
Teleorman	Alexandria - 273, Piaţa Libertăţii	1918	0118115
Timiş	Timişoara - 3, Str. Piatra Craiului	12929	013242
Vaslui	Vaslui - 66, Str. Stefan cel Mare	1748	0217
Vîlcea	Rm. Vîlcea - 30, Str. Argeş	2327	018414
Vrancea	Focşani - 109, Str. Mare e Unirii	2144	0118931
Bucha-rest	Bucharest - 2, Str. Mihai Vodă	164760	—

I. WHEN TO GO AND WHERE TO GO

Blessed by nature with countless beauties, to which have been added throughout the centuries the monuments erected by successive generations of men, Rumania offers every attraction to the visitor.

Its physical configuration covers a wide range of different forms, from the sandy beaches of the coast to the rocky summits of the Carpathians. The country rises in a series of concentric "steps" of roughly the same size, giving a peculiar harmony and symmetry to the landscape; and each of these "steps" has its own particular attractions.

On the Black Sea coast, with its eastern exposure, summer visitors find a generous sun, large beaches of fine sand, and a series of modern resorts—Mamaia, Eforie Nord, Eforie Sud, etc.—in addition to the various remains of ancient civilisation such as the ruins of Histria (founded by Greek settlers seven centuries before our era), the Roman mosaic at Constanţa (3rd century), the fine collections of the Constanţa Archaeological Museum, and the Adamclisi monument. At the northern tip of the coast is an extraordinary area with has not its like in Europe— the Danube Delta, with its network of waterways, its forests overgrown with lianas, and its vast reed-beds which provide a home for pelicans and all kinds of other birds and wild animals.

The fringes of Rumanian territory consist for the most part of a ring of plains; but these plains do not create the impression of uniformity which one might expect, for each has its own characteristic features. Their fertile soil favours the growth of cereals, particularly in Moldavia and Wallachia. Along the rivers, at the junction of ancient lines of communication, are a series of large towns, in which the remains of past centuries rub shoulders with the buildings of the present day. Half way between the Danube and the Carpathians is Bucharest, the capital of Rumania, a city of gardens and museums, with all the dignity conferred by more than five hundred years of existence but also with the youth and charm of the more recent parts of the town. Farther north, in a kind of bay formed by the plain in the hills of the Subcarpathians, is Ploeşti, the "town of black gold". In the north-east of the country, on the banks of the Bahlui, is Iaşi (Jassy), the former capital of Moldavia, with its four or five century old churches, its modern buildings and its industrial enterprises. In the west is the Timiş plain, with Timişoara nestling in its verdant landscape; and farther north, on the banks of the Criş Repede in the Criş plain, is Oradea, with its old Baroque houses flanked by new buildings in contemporary style.

Then comes the ring of the Subcarpathian hills, their slopes covered with flourishing orchards of fruit trees of all kinds (apples, pears, quinces, apricots, cherries, plums, etc.). On the sunny slopes of the hills, too, there are large vineyards producing excellent wines, particularly round Panciu-Odobeşti (between Adjud and Rîmnicul Sărat), Dealul Mare (between Buzău and Ploieşti), Drăgăşani (in the Olt valley) and Miniş (to the south-west of the Apuseni Mountains). Nor must we forget the underground wealth hidden in these hills (oil, salt, coal), as a result of which the whole area is coverd with forests of oil derricks, and with large petrochemical factories (Brazi, Borzeşti, etc.)—huge alignments of modern buildings which are crowned at night with a diadem of scintillating lights.

Scattered about among the hills are smiling villages, their houses straggling up the hillsides, and old cities with long histories like Suceava, capital of the Voivodes of Moldavia from the 14th to the 16th century and now a town in process of rapid development, a convenient centre for the tourists who come to see the famous monasteries with their façades covered with painting (Humor, Voroneţ, Suceviţa, etc.). Travelling southward, the visitor will come to Tîrgu Neamţ with the ruins of the citadel of Neamţ (14th century) and, in the Humuleşti district, the modest house in which the great Rumanian story-teller Ion Creangă (1837–89) was born. On the banks of the Bistriţa are Piatra Neamţ, surrounded by picturesque forest-covered hills, and the resort of Slănic Moldova where the tourist can relax from his exertions. In the hills which fringe the Southern Carpathians is Cîmpina, in the Prahova valley, where visitors stop to see the house in which Nicolae Grigorescu (1838–1907) spent the closing years of his life. Then the traveller comes to Curtea de Argeş, the capital of Wallachia in the 14th century, or to Tîrgu Jiu in northern Oltenia, where Constantin Brâncuşi (1876–1957), one of the founders of contemporary sculpture, has left the imprint of his genius in a series of works displayed in the town park.

Finally, in the centre of Rumania, covering nearly a third of its total area, we come to the majestic mountain mass of the Carpathians. With their depressions nestling between the steep rock faces, their valleys carved out by the rushing torrents, their slopes almost everywhere clad with an evergreen mantle of conifers, their wide upland meadows and their lofty peaks, the Carpathians form a world of their own with its own particular charm.

The Carpathian valleys offer the visitor the wild beauty of the Bicaz Gorges (Eastern Carpathians), of the Prahova valley or the Olt valley (Southern Carpathians). On the high tops he can enjoy wide-ranging views, and finds rocks carved by nature into a variety of strange forms– the Panaghia, the Tower of Budu and the Doric Column in the Ceahlău range, the Pietrele Doamnei in the Rarău Mountains, the Towers of Zăgan or Mîna Dracului (the Devil's Hand) in the Ciucaş Mountains, the Sphinx and the Babele (the Old Women) in the Bucegi range, and many others round which popular fancy has woven a variety of poetic legends.

Throughout the ages human settlement in the valleys of the Carpathians has taken on many different forms —villages of shepherds or woodmen, halting places on the roads which linked the communities on either side of the mountains. Some of these settlements developed into centres of woodworking or milk production; others possessed mineral springs —like Herculane, whose radioactive waters were known to the Romans. The mountains of Rumania contain over a hundred health resorts known for their mineral waters or their bracing air, including— to mention only the most important —Borsec, Călimăneşti, Căciulata, Felix, Herculane, Lacu Roşu, Olăneşti, Predeal, Sinaia, Sovata, Vatra Dornei and 1 Mai.

In winter the mountains are the haunt of skiers. The most popular areas are Sinaia and Predeal (Prahova valley), Poiana Braşov (on Postăvarul), Păltiniş (in the Cibin Mountains), the Bîlea valley (Făgăraş Mountains, for spring skiing), Mount Semenic, Stîna de Vale (in the Western Carpathians), and Borşa (in the Rodna Mountains). A network of tracks and over 150 huts are there to serve the purposes of ski trekkers and mountain walkers (p. 380).

A characteristic feature of the mountains of Rumania is the large number of depressions in between the areas of high ground. Sometimes these are of considerable extent and are given the name of "countries". It is here that the creations of folk art are found in their purest state: not only material things like architecture, dress and domestic implements but spiritual creations (folk songs, poems and dances and traditional customs). In the north are the Oaş Country and the Maramureş Country; in the Eastern Carpathians, the Dorne Country; round Braşov, the Bîrsa Country; at the foot of the main range of the Southern Carpathians, straddling the River Olt, the Loviştea Country (the "Country of Hunting"); to the north of the Retezat range, the Haţeg Country; in the south-east of the Banat, the Almaj Country; and in the Western Carpathians, the Motzi Country. Each of these areas has its own important and personal contribution to make to the immense wealth of Rumanian folk art.

The main tourist routes run through some of these "countries" (the Bîrsa, Loviştea and Haţeg Countries). Other easily accessible areas are the villages in the Bran-Cîmpulung corridor and in the Cibin Mountains, which likewise possess an abundant folklore and interesting national costumes.

After this rapid survey of the girdle of the Carpathians let us now descend into the country of Transylvania which it encloses. We discover first, on the fringe of this area, a number of picturesque depressions, like the Făgăraş Country (between the River Olt and the Făgăraş Mountains) or the Praid depression with the important thermal resort of Sovata. The Transylvanian plateau is dotted throughout its length with hills—some of them almost small mountains, others gentle rounded hills, like the hills of Tîrnave in the centre of the plateau whose sunny slopes bear the celebrated vineyards of that name.

As he crosses this plateau the visitor encounters a series of places of great interest. There are the villages of southern Transylvania with their old fortified churches and their wealth of folklore; there are the health resorts; and above all there are the towns: Cluj (Gothic and Baroque buildings, Ethnographical Museum, Botanic Gardens); Braşov (mediaeval buildings); Sibiu and Sighişoara (mediaeval districts); Tîrgu Mureş (old buildings, museum); Alba Iulia (Roman remains).

We have cited only a selection of the many tourist attractions of Rumania. To these must be added a varied range of fine scenery, interesting caves, historical and artistic monuments, the immense scope which the country offers those interested in shooting or fishing, and—not last—the attractive new buildings of recent years and the friendly atmosphere created by traditional Rumanian hospitality, today no less than in the past.

It is usual, in discussing the tourist attractions of a country, to suggest the best time of year to visit it. In Rumania, with its temperate continental climate, each season is different, and each has something of interest to offer the visitor. In spring he finds the country covered with a luxuriant mantle of green and gay with flowers; in summer he is drawn by its sunny beaches; in autumn he can enjoy all the varieties of fresh fruit then in season; and in winter he can ski, or relax amid magnificent mountain scenery, or see the interesting traditional festivities which mark the New Year. Since Rumania enjoys very long and very fine autumns, and since as a rule spring comes rapidly on the heels of winter, it is fair to say that for all practical purposes the only times of year which are less suitable for visitors are the very short periods between the end of October and mid December and between the end of February and mid April.

Planning a Trip

The programme of a visit to Rumania will differ according to the mode of transport. Many visitors will have their own car; others will prefer to fly in and hire a car, with or without driver, through a tourist agency; while for those without a car the wide range of excursions offered by the National Tourist Office open up the wealth of Rumania's tourist attractions.

Organised trips

The National Tourist Office (Carpați) organises many different types of trip in association with travel agencies in other countries, Tarom (the Rumanian national airline) and foreign airlines:

1. *Package tours*, either in summer (to the coastal resorts or to other places of interest) or in winter (skiing holidays or stays in mountain resorts like Poiana Brașov, Predeal or Sinaia). It is possible alto to have two-centre holidays, spending part of the time on the coast and part inland.

2. *Cruises on the Danube*. During the summer there are cruises on the Danube from Vienna to Giurgiu or Hîrșova on the modern cruise ships "Oltenița" and "Carpați", calling in for sightseeing at Bratislava, Budapest and Belgrade, and also at Drobeta-Turnu Severin (for the resort of Băile Herculane and the remains of the Roman camp of Drobeta) and

Giurgiu (for a trip to Bucharest). These cruises are combined with a return flight to Vienna either from Bucharest or from Constanța; in the latter case it is possible to round off the trip with a stay at one of the Rumanian Black Sea resorts.

3. *Cruises in the Black Sea and the Mediterranean* on the luxury liner "Transilvania".

4. *Car trips*. For the various possibilities (package tours, fly-drive, etc.) see the section on *Motoring* below, p. 359.

5. *Study and special interest trips*. Special trips are organised for those with interests in particular fields (history, art, ethnography, speleology, botany, ornithology, etc.). For example:

— *archaeology and history:* remains of ancient cities like Histria (7th century B.C.), Tomi (now Constanța: 6th century B.C.), Callatis (now Mangalia: 6th century B.C.), Drobeta (now Drobeta-Turnu Severin: 1st-2nd centuries), Sarmizegethusa (Ulpia Traiana: 2nd century), the Dacian settlements of Costești, Blidaru and Grădiștea de Munte, etc.

— *Byzantine art:* the painted monasteries of northern Moldavia (Voroneț, Moldovița, Sucevița) and the monasteries of Putna, Agapia, Sinaia, Cozia, Arnota, Tismana, etc.

— *ethnography and folk traditions:* northern Moldavia, the Maramureș, the Oaș country, Vrancea, the Hațeg country, etc.

— *ornithology:* the Danube delta - one enormous bird reserve, frequented by some 350 species.

— *botany:* the nature reserves in of Bucegi, Retezat, Mount Domogled, the ancient forest of Slătioara, the Turda gorges, etc.

— *speleology*. Rumania, homeland of Emil Racovița, founder of the science of bio-speleology, has large numbers of caves and karstic features of great interest, like Topolnița, Comarnic, Scărișoara, Meziad, etc.

6. *Trade fairs, exhibitions and congresses*. Businessmen and others attending trade fairs, exhibitions and congresses in Rumania can apply to the National Tourist Office in Bucharest or its branches in other countries for room reservations, car-hire, the services of a guide-interpreter or other facilities (city tours, excursions, etc.).

Individual holidays

Many people prefer to take their holidays on their own, and arrangements to meet their particular requirements can readily be made through the various tourist offices in Rumania. They can apply, either direct or through a travel agency, to:

— The *National Tourist Office (Carpaţi)*, 7, Bd Magheru, Bucharest (tel. 14.51.60, telex 270-278-279).

— The *National Tourist Office (Litoral)*, Municipal Offices, Constanţa-Mamaia (tel. 917/31152, telex 014.221 or 014.266), which, in association with foreign travel agencies, organises restful holidays at the coastal resorts of Mamaia, Eforie Nord, Eforie Sud, Mangalia, Neptun, Jupiter, Saturn, Venus, Olimp and Costineşti.

— The *National Tourist Office (Carpaţi)*, 22, Str. 7 Noiembrie, Braşov (tel. 921/12840, telex 012.228), which organises holidays at any time of year, or special winter sports holidays in mountain resorts of international reputation like Poiana Braşov and Predeal.

— The various *regional tourist offices* (see list on p. 339), which organise holidays with full or part board and provide other tourist services.

— The *Rumanian Automobile Club (A.C.R.)*, 27, Str. Nikos Beloiannis, Bucharest (tel. 13.42.60, telex Autoclub Bucureşti 001.373).

Geriatric treatment

The Bucharest Geriatric Institute, directed by Dr Ana Aslan (who produced the well-known preparations Gerovital H_3 and Aslavital), provides treatment throughout the year for people seeking to alleviate conditions associated with ageing and to revitalise their organism. Treatment is carried out either at the Institute in Bucharest, in geriatric sanatoria at Otopeni and Snagov or at the resorts of Băile Herculane or Eforie Nord. It is also possible to have outpatient treatment at the Institute, staying at a hotel in Bucharest.

Prospective patients should write in advance to the Institute, at 9, Str. Mănăstirea Cădăruşani, Bucharest.

Visitors undergoing geriatric treatment are entitled to all the facilities granted to tourists.

Holidays for retired people

Older people can have out-of-season holidays in Rumania at very reasonable rates — either a restful holiday at a mountain or seaside resort or a period of treatment at a health resort or one equipped with facilities for geriatric treatment. With its mild climate and long sunny autumn, Rumania is very pleasant even out of season; and the resorts are then less crowded and the charges lower.

Holidays for young people

A variety of different types of holiday are available for members of youth and student organisations, sports clubs, etc.: *summer holidays in the country* (Săliște, Bran, Rucăr, Putna, Poiana Mărului); *summer holidays in the mountains* (Păltiniş, Pîrîul Rece, Buşteni); *winter holidays* (Păltiniş, Predeal, Semenic, Muntele Mic, with facilities for skiing); *tour of Rumania* (a 13-day trip, taking in the main tourist centres, with accommodation and full board in students' residences); *special interest holidays* (the painted monasteries of northern Moldavia; ethnography; archaeology, the Dacian and Roman sites); *mountain treks* (in the Bucegi Mountains; stays at Sinaia and Poiana Braşov); in the Făgăraş Mountains); *boat trips* (on the Olt or the Danube).

II. HEALTH RESORTS

Thanks to the varied pattern of its geography, its climate and its abundance of mineral springs, Rumania possesses a large number of thermal and climatic resorts (more than a hundred altogether).

The Institute of Balneology and Physiotherapy in Bucharest plays an important part in the organisation of medical treatment and in the study of the resources offered by the country's mineral springs. The specialists attached to the Institute, in collaboration with those in the various resorts, have reviewed and improved the methods of treatment and reorganised the operation of the sanatoria. The resorts now have the latest equipment, enabling the most complex treatments to be carried out, and specialised medical staffs.

In addition most of the resorts are important holiday centres, providing starting points for a great variety of excursions.

A course of treatment lasts from 12 to 20 days. Between 1 October and 30 April there are reduced charges at all resorts.

The Rumanian Black Sea coast has a total length of 150 miles. In the height of summer the sun shines here, on average, 12 hours a day. The hotels and other buildings at Mamaia, Eforie Nord, Eforie Sud, Neptun, Jupiter, Venus, Saturn and Mangalia are all modern. These resorts are recommended for the treatment of the nervous system and of gynaecological and dermatological conditions. Excursions can be made from here to the remains of important ancient cities (Callatis, Tomi, Histria, Tropaeum Trajani, etc.). Near Constanța, in the commune of Murfatlar, is a nature reserve containing unique or very rare specimens of fauna and flora. Also at Murfatlar is the Department of Viticultural Research, which has the most modern wine storage facilities in the whole country.

Călimănești-Căciulata. In the Olt valley. Altitude 920 feet. Many springs, recommended for the treatment of affections of the digestive passages and associated glands, the kidneys and urinary tract, and the locomotor and peripheral nervous systems, and for industrial diseases. Excursions to Cozia Monastery, Rîmnicu Vîlcea, the hermitage of Ostrov, Turnu Monastery.

Băile Herculane. In the Cerna valley at the western end of the Southern Carpathians. Altitude 425 feet. Many springs of sulphurous water discovered by the Romans, and recommended for the treatment of rheumatic conditions, affections of the peripheral nervous system, skin diseases, chronic intoxications, industrial diseases, etc. Excursions to the Cross of Ghizela, in the Cerna valley and to Mount Domogled.

Sovata. On the southern slope of the Gurghiul Mountains. Altitude 1,740 feet. Salt lakes — Aluniș, Negru (rich in mud containing mainly chlorides), Roșu and Ursu (warm water). This resort is recommended for the treatment of various gynaecological conditions, rheumatic diseases, and affections of the peripheral nervous system. Excursions in the Sebeș valley and to Mount Saca.

Vatra Dornei. Situated in a mountainous area at the junction of the Dorna and the Bistrița. Altitude 2,625 feet. Recommended for the treatment of affections of the cardiovascular, locomotor and peripheral nervous systems. Excursions in the Bistrița valley, to the Giumalău range, to the Pietrele Doamnei. Skiing in winter.

Băile Felix and *1 Mai*. 5 miles south-east of Oradea. These resorts are recommended for the treatment of various diseases of the locomotor and peripheral nervous systems, affections of the digestive passages and associated glands. At 1 Mai is found a variety of water lily not known anywhere else in the world, *Nymphaea lotus L.* Excursions to Oradea, to the cave of Hula Bradului, to Stîna de Vale.

Lacu Roşu. 16 miles from Gheorgheni. Altitude 3,215 feet. Recommended for the treatment of nervous asthenia and for physical and mental exhaustion. Many excursions—to Mounts Suhardul Mare, Suhardul Mic and Hăşmaşul Mare, and to the Bicaz Gorges.

Tuşnad. At the foot of the western slope of Mount Harghita. Altitude 2,130 feet. Carbo-gaseous baths, recommended for the treatment of cardiovascular conditions, peripheral circulatory disturbances, affections of the central nervous system and asthenic neurosis. Excursions to Lake Sf. Ana and Stîna Şoimilor.

Other important resorts are Amara, Borsec, Buziaş, Govora, Olăneşti, Predeal and Sinaia.

III. PASSPORTS AND CUSTOMS

Passport. Every visitor to Rumania must possess a valid passport with a Rumanian visa.

A tourist visa is granted immediately and free of charge. It is obtainable on application to the diplomatic and consular offices of the Socialist Republic of Rumania (see list below), or at any of the frontier points open for the admission of travellers coming by road, rail, air, river or sea.

A tourist visa is issued on the spot to all visitors to Rumania travelling under arrangements made by a Rumanian or foreign travel agency and to those travelling on their own.

Visitors who have come to Rumania on business and want to see something of the country after the expiry of their normal visa can also obtain a tourist visa, as can visitors in transit through Rumania.

Tourist visas are issued by diplomatic and consular offices of the Socialist Republic of Rumania and at frontier points open for passenger traffic.

The tourist visa is issued for a period of between 3 and 60 days, but can be extended for up to 120 days. Application for an extension should be made, before the expiry of the original visa, to the Inspectorate of Militia in Bucharest or the chief town of a region. Regional tourist offices will assist visitors who require an extension.

Rumanian Embassies and Consulates

Albania: Tirana, Druga Th., Gèrmenji 222.

Algeria: Algiers, 24, rue Si-Arezki (Hydra).

Argentina: Buenos Aires, Calle Arroyo 970.

Austria: 60 Vienna, Prinz-Eugenstrasse 60.

Belgium: Brussels 18, 105, rue Gabrielle.

Brazil : Brasília, D. F., Shi-Sul QL 2/2, Casa 6, Península 6.

Bulgaria: Sofia, 10, Dimităr Poljanov.

Burma: Rangoon, 71 Mission Road.

Canada : Ottawa, 473-475 Milbrod Street.

Central African Republic : Bangui, Quartier N'G aragba.

Chile : Santiago, Calle Benjamin 2949-55 Lac Condes.

China: Peking, Fan Ti Lu 13.

Cuba: Havana, Calle 21, N° 37E/HEI (Vedado).

Cyprus: Nicosia, Katsonis 8.

Czechoslovakia: Prague I, Mala Strana, Nerudova 5.

Denmark: Copenhagen, Stradagervej 27, Hellerup.

Egypt : Cairo, 6 El Kamel Mohamed, Zamalek.

Finland: Helsinki, Stenbäckinkatu 24.

France: Paris 7e, 5-7, rue de l'Exposition.

Germany (Democratic Republic): Berlin-Pankow, Parkstrasse 23.

Germany (Federal Republic): Köln-Bayenthal, Oberlander Ufer 68.

Ghana: Accra, House N°. C 119-3, Ferrar Avenue, P.O. Box M 112.

Great Britain: London W. 8, 4 Palace Green, Kensington.

Greece: Athens, 14 Ravine.

Guinea: Conakry, 9 Carrefour Bd - Présidence (Trésorerie Nationale).

Hungary: Budapest XIX, Thököly ut. 72.

Iceland: Residence: London W. 8, 4 Palace Green, Kensington.

India: New Delhi, 9 Tees January Marg.

Indonesia: Jakarta, Djalan Teuku Umar 45.

Irak: Baghdad, 52 5 35 Masbah.

Iran: Teheran, Av. Fakhr Abad 12.

Israel: Tel Aviv, 27 Rehov Adam Hachoen.

Italy: Rome, Nicolo Tartaglia 36, Via Parioli.

Japan: Tokyo, Meguro-ku-Tokyo 2, 3-1, Aobadai.

Lebanon: 1173, Badaro St., Kfouri Forest.

Luxemburg: Residence: Brussels 18, 105, rue Gabrielle.

Mongolia: Residence, Ulan Bator, Ul. Mira.

Morocco: Rabat, 10, rue d'Ouezzane.

Netherlands: The Hague, Catsheuvelstr. 55/4.

North Korea: Pyong Yang, Di-sen-don (Phenian).

North Vietnam: Hanoi, 5, Le-Hong-Phong.

Norway: Residence: Stockholm, Fulgiavägen 2, Lidingö 1.

Pakistan: Islamabad, House 10, 90th Street.

Peru: Lima, 690 Orantia, San Isidoro.

Poland: Warswa, Szopena 10.

Spain: Madrid, 17 Alfonso XIII.

Sudan: Khartoum, New Extension, Plot 20, Block 9A/E, Street 3.

Sweden: Stockholm, Ostermalmsgatan 36.

Switzerland: Berne, Kirchenfeldstrasse 78.

Syria: Damascus, 32, Av. Al Jala'a, Rue J. Hanaro.

Tanzania: Dar es Salaam, 11 Ocean Road.

Tunisia: Tunis, 6 rue Magon.

Turkey: Ankara, Yesilyurt Sokaği 4, Kavaklidere.

Uruguay: Montevideo, Avenida Lord Ponsonby 2550.

U.S.A.: Washington D.C., 1601 23 rd Street, N.W.

U.S.S.R.: Moscow, Mosfilmovskaya 64.

Venezuela: Caracas, Avenida Principal de la Castellana 42, La Castellana.

Yugoslavia: Belgrade, Kneza Milosa 70.

Zaire: Kinshasa, 5 Avenue de l'Ouganda, Gombe.

Customs. Rumania operates, with some supplementary concessions, the provisions of the Customs Convention and the additional Protocol (New York, 4 June 1954). This means that visitors entering or leaving Rumania can take with them, without special authority or payment of duty, personal effects, foodstuffs and medicines required during their stay.

In addition to clothing, personal effects include the following items, provided that they are for the visitor's own personal use: personal jewellery, two cameras with 24 films, a small ciné camera with two reels of film, a pair of field-glasses, a portable tape-recorder, a portable radio, a portable typewriter, a child's pram or push-chair, a tent and other camping equipment, two shotguns with 100 cartridges, fishing equipment, a bicycle, a kayak or canoe not more than 5.50 m long, a pair of skis, two tennis rackets or similar articles, medicines required while in Rumania and foodstuffs (including 2 litres of spirits, 5 litres of wine and 300 cigarettes).

Visitors can take into Rumania, tax-free, presents for friends and relatives up to a total value of 2000 lei. On leaving the country they can take with them goods bought with currency officially changed in Rumania together with any gifts they have received, up to a value of 1000 lei. Goods brought into Rumania or taken out of Rumania of a value exceeding these limits are subject to the appropriate customs duties.

Visitors in transit through Rumania can bring in any goods belonging to them on condition that they take them out again when they leave the country. It is a penal offence to bring in goods for sale or to sell personal effects.

On entering Rumania visitors are required to declare in writing to the customs authorities any gold coins or medals, objects made of precious metal, and precious stones, whether mounted or unmounted, which they have in their possession. The following items may not be taken into or out of Rumania: narcotic drugs, firearms and ammunition (other than sporting guns), explosives and homing pigeons.

Valuable art objects and rare books of scientific or artistic value can be taken out of Rumania only with the approval of the competent authorities and an exit visa issued by the customs.

Cars and motor-cycles can be taken into Rumania with a full tank of petrol and any oil and grease required. Spare parts can be taken into the country provided that they are taken out when leaving.

IV. CURRENCY AND EXCHANGE

Currency. The basic unit of currency in Rumania is the *leu* (plural *lei*), which is divided into 100 *bani*. There are notes issued by the Rumanian National Bank with a value of 1, 3, 5, 10, 25 and 100 lei, and coins with a value of 1 and 3 lei and 5, 10, 15 and 25 bani.

Exchange. Foreign currency may be brought into Rumania without limit and in any form (traveller's cheques, bank drafts, letters of credit, etc.).

Visitors with a tourist visa are granted an exchange premium of 189.33% on all convertible currency.

Important. Unused cash and traveller's cheques in lei can be changed back when leaving Rumania on production of the receipt issued when changing foreign currency.

Foreign currency can be changed at branches of the National Bank of Rumania; at branches of the Rumanian Bank of Foreign Trade in Bucharest; and at special exchange offices at frontier points and international airports and in certain hotels, restaurants, bars and shops. Any exchange of currency except at these authorised banks and exchange offices is a penal offence.

Credit cards (Access, American Express, Barclaycard, Diner's Club, Eurocard, Carte Blanche) can be used in Rumania.

V. HOW TO GET TO RUMANIA

By Air

The Rumanian Airline, TAROM, and a number of foreign lines (AUA, Aeroflot, Air France, British Aiways, Lufthansa, Swissair, Sabena, etc.) provide regular connections between Bucharest and the principal cities of Europe.

Bucharest-Vienna-Frankfurt.

Bucharest-Zurich-Paris.

Bucharest-Prague-Berlin.

Bucharest-Brussels-London.

Bucharest-Rome.

Bucharest-Moscow.

Bucharest-Athens-Cairo.

Bucharest-Budapest-Warsaw.

During the summer there are direct services between a number of European towns (Copenhagen, Stockholm, Brussels, Frankfurt on Main, Cologne, London, Paris, Vienna, Zurich, etc.) and the Rumanian Black Sea coast.

Addresses of TAROM

Central office: Bucharest-Băneasa airport (tel. 33.00.30).

Commercial service: tel. 33.30.45.

Reservations: Bd Republicii 16 (tel. 16.33.46 and 14.74.33).

Amsterdam: K.L.M., 1-3 Leidseplein (tel. 49.91.23 and 43.42.42).

Athens: M. J. Allalouf & Co., 20 Venizelos Ave (tel. 62.48.08).

Beirut: Fouad A. Khayat, rue de Phénicie, Hôtel Martinez (tel. 22.20.47).

Berlin: Interflug (DDR) Alexanderplatz 5-102 (tel. 53.01.46).

Brussels: TAROM, 26 Place de Brouckère (tel. 18.00.79).

Budapest: Malev, Dorottya utca 2 (tel. 186.805).

Cairo: TAROM, 12 B Mahmoud Azmi St., Zamalek (tel. 81.82.45).

Copenhagen: TAROM, Vesterbrogade 55 A (tel. EVA 6129).

Frankfurt: TAROM, Neue Mainzer Strasse 1 (tel. 28.82.51).

Istanbul: Türk Hava Yollari, Meşrutiyet Cad. 30, Sişhane (tel. 44.47.00-7).

London: TAROM, 98-99 Jermyn Street S.W.1. (tel. 930 8812).

Moscow: TAROM, Mosfilmskaya 40 (tel. 14.32.640).

Paris: TAROM, 1 rue Daunou (tel. Richelieu 3132-3); Air France, 119 Champs-Elysées, 8e (tel. Balzac 7050 and 5029).

Prague: TAROM, Letiste Ružyne (tel. 34.10.86); CSA, Revolucni 3 (tel. 65.74.19).

Rome: TAROM, via Torino 100-101 (tel. 482.983 and 460.267).

Sofia: Balcan, Pl. Narodno Sobranie 12 (tel. 87.01.82 and 88.45.94).

Tel Aviv: TAROM, 13-5 Zeitlin St. (tel. 26.38.25).

Vienna: TAROM, Opernring 1 (tel. 57.77.02).

Warsaw: TAROM, Okecie Airport.

Zurich: TAROM, Talstrasse 59 (tel. 27.17.30).

By Rail

Bucharest is connected with the principal European cities by daily through trains, with sleeping and restaurant cars.

Orient Express: Paris-Strasbourg-Munich-Salzburg-Vienna-Budapest-Bucharest. Though carriages Paris-Bucharest, 1st and 2nd class, and through sleeping cars Paris-Bucharest four times a week.

Wiener Walzer: Basle-Zurich-Buchs-Innsbruck-Salzburg-Vienna-Budapest-Curtici (Rumanian frontier)-Braşov-Bucharest. Connections with the principal European expresses: Vienna-Ostend Express (Vienna-Frankfurt on Main-Bonn-Brussels-London); Austria-Italy Express (Vienna-Venice-Bologna-Rome); Zurich-Berne-Geneva; Express 42 (Basle-Belfort-Paris). The *Wiener Walzer* has through carriages, 1st and 2nd class, between Bucharest and Basle and sleeping cars between Bucharest and Vienna and between Vienna and Basle.

Balt-Orient-Express: Berlin Ostbhf-Prague-Brno-Bratislava-Budapest-Episcopia Bihor (Rumanian frontier)-Oradea-Cluj-Braşov-Bucharest. Connection at Berlin with the Sassnitz Express (Malmö-Stockholm, Malmö-Oslo) and the Ostsee Express (Warnemünde-Copenhagen). Through carriages, 1st and 2nd class, and sleeping cars between Bucharest and Berlin.

Nord-Orient-Express Warsaw-Katowice-Zilina-Budapest-Episcopia Bihor (Rumanian frontier)-Oradea-Cluj-Braşov-Bucharest. In summer there are daily through carriages Warsaw-Constanţa, Prague-Constanţa and Budapest-Constanţa. Through carriages (1st and 2nd class and sleepers) between Bucharest and Warsaw.

Carpaţi Express: Warsaw-Lvov-Vicşani (Rumanian frontier)-Suceava-Bacău-Bucharest. Through sleeping cars Bucharest-Warsaw-Bucharest,

Danubius Express: Moscow-Kiev-Ungheni (Rumanian frontier)-Iaşi-Bîrlad-Bucharest-Sofia. Through sleeping cars between Bucharest and Moscow and between Sofia and Moscow.

Belgrade-Bucharest: Belgrade-Vrset-Stamora (Rumanian frontier)-Timişoara-Craiova-Bucharest. Connection at Belgrade with the Direct Orient Express (Zagreb-Venice-Milan-Lausanne-Paris-London), the Hellas Express (Nish-Skopje-Salonica-Athens) and the Zagreb-Ljubljana-Venice-Bologna-Rome train.

Bucharest Express : Rijeka-Zagreb-Jimbolia (Rumanian frontier) - Bucharest-Nord. Connections for Milan, Rome, Paris and London.

Mamaia Express : Warsaw-Prague-Budapest-Episcopia Bihor (Rumanian frontier)-Cluj-Bucharest-Constanţa. Runs June-September.

Varna Express : Warsaw-Lvov-Vicşani (Rumanian frontier)-Bacău-Constanţa-Mangalia. Runs in summer.

Transdanubium : Prague-Bratislava-Budapest-Curtici (Rumanian frontier)-Bucharest. Runs in summer.

By Boat

Rumania can be reached either by sea (Mediterranean-Aegean-Sea of Marmara-Black Sea), arriving at Constanţa, or by way of the Danube, taking the Rumanian ships "Olteniţa" and "Carpaţi" which provide a regular connection in summer between Vienna and Giurgiu (37 miles from Bucharest) and Hîrşova (57 miles from Constanţa).

By Car

A network of modern roads makes it easy to reach Rumania either by car or bus, using the frontier points at Borş and Nădlac (coming from Hungary), Moraviţa (coming from Yugoslavia), Giurgiu, Varna Veche and Negru Vodă (coming from Bulgaria), and Albiţa, Siret and Halmeu (coming from the U.S.S.R.).

VI. Communications within Rumania

By air. The Rumanian air line TAROM provides one or more services daily between Bucharest and a number of Rumanian towns (Constanţa, Tulcea, Bacău, Iaşi, Suceava, Tîrgu Mureş, Sibiu, Cluj, Baia Mare, Satu Mare, Oradea, Deva, Arad, Craiova, Timişoara). Examples of fares are: Bucharest-Constanţa 82 lei, Bucharest-Iaşi 140 lei, Bucharest-Timişoara 166 lei, Bucharest-Oradea 172 lei.

By rail. Rumania has a considerable network of railways. Seats must be reserved on express and fast long distance trains. In summer there are special services to the Black Sea coast and the main tourist areas. All trains have 1st and 2nd class carriages, and long distance trains have restaurant and sleeping cars.

Fares (in lei) between certain frontier points and the principal towns in Rumania:

	1st cl.	2nd cl.
Curtici-Arad (17 km)	8 lei	5 lei
-Deva (165 km)	56	37
-Braşov (476 km)	114	76
-Bucharest (642 km)	149	99
Stamora-Timişoara (56 km)	20	13
-Craiova (380 km)	96	64
-Bucharest (589 km)	131	87
Ungheni-Iaşi (21 km)	11	7
-Ploieşti (345 km)	87	58
-Bucharest (404 km)	114	76
Vicşani-Suceava (39 km)	14	9
-Bacău (186 km)	62	41
-Bucharest (488 km)	114	76
Episcopia Bihor-Oradea (6 km)	5	3
-Cluj (158 km)	50	33
-Braşov (489 km)	114	76
-Bucharest (655 km)	149	99

The fares indicated are for ordinary trains. For express trains add a supplement of 6 lei (1st class) or 4 lei (2nd class) up to 250 km, and of 12 lei (1st class) or 8 lei (2nd class) beyond 250 km; for fast trains add a supplement of 10 lei (1st class) or 8 lei (2nd class) up to 250 km. The supplement for a couchette (sleeper) is about 11 lei per 100 km.

By road. There are passenger bus services throughout the country, and during most of the year there are coach excursions on the main tourist routes (Prahova valley, Olt valley, monasteries of northern Moldavia, Lacu Roşu, Bicaz Gorges, etc.).

Taxis. Taxis are continuously available in all the towns and the main health resorts. Fares are at the rate of 3 lei plus 0.50 lei for every 300 metres. Tips have been officially abolished.

By river. There are regular passenger services on the Danube between the following towns: Brăila-Sulina; Brăila-Chilia Veche; Tulcea-Sf. Gheorghe; Brăila-Oltina; Orşova-Moldova Veche. Fares: Brăila-Sulina 54 lei (1st class), 41 lei (2nd class); Brăila-Galaţi 8 lei (1st class), 6 lei (2nd class); Orşova-Moldova Veche 31 lei (1st class), 23 lei (2nd class).

In summer there are regular trips from Constanţa along the Black Sea coast. Fares from Constanţa (Tomis tourist harbour): Eforie Nord 7 lei, Eforie Sud 8 lei, Mangalia 16 lei. In addition there are excursions and regular services on the Bicaz reservoir (Eastern Carpathians) and the Bega Canal which links the town of Timişoara to the Danube. During the summer there are pleasure trips in motor launches on the Bucharest lakes and on Lake Snagov (25 miles from Bucharest).

VII. MOTORING

Visitors arriving in Rumania by car have no particular formalities to go through at the frontier and no customs or other taxes to pay. All that is required is an international driving licence.

Letters of credit issued by motoring clubs and associations affiliated to the F.I.A. or the A.I.T. are honoured in Rumania.

International insurance certificates ("green cards" and "blue cards") are valid. Visitors arriving without an internationl certificate must take out insurance with the state insurance organisation (ADAS).

(a) *Points of entry into Rumania*

From HUNGARY: (i) international highway E 15, via Artand, Borş (frontier point) and Arad; (ii) Szeged - Mako - Nădlac (frontier point) - Arad; (iii) Bekescsaba - Gyula - Vărşand (frontier point) - Arad.

From YUGOSLAVIA: (i) international highway E 94, via Vatin, Moraviţa (frontier point) and Timişoara; (ii) Zrenjanin - Nova Crnja - Jimbolia (frontier point) - Timişoara; (iii) International highway E 94, via Kladovo and Drobeta-Turnu Severin (over the Iron Gates dam) (frontier point).

From BULGARIA : (i) international highway E 20, via Ruse, Giurgiu (frontier point) and Bucharest; (ii) international highway E 95, via Varna, Vama Veche (frontier point), Mangalia and Constanţa; (iii) Kardan - Negru Vodă (frontier point - Constanţa.

From the SOVIET UNION : (i) international highway E 20, via Porubnoe, Siret (frontier point) and Suceava; (ii) Leuşeni - Albiţa (frontier point) - Huşi.

At all frontier points customs and tourist information offices are open at all times; at Albiţa and Siret they are open from 8 a.m. to 8 p.m.

PECO petrol stations are open from 7 a.m. to 10 p.m.; in the larger towns some stations are open all the time.

(b) Driving in Rumania

Road markings and signs in Rumania are in accordance with the Geneval International Convention (1949). The highway code is similar to that of other European countries.

Speed limits : in built-up areas, 60 km per hour (37 ½ m.p.h.) for private cars and 40 km per hour (25 m.p.h.) for other vehicles; outside built-up areas, 100 km per hour (62 ½ m.p.h.) for private cars, 80 km per hour (50 m.p.h.) for buses, 70 km per hour (44 m.p.h.) for minibuses and 60 km per hour (37 ½ m.p.h.) for motor-cycles.

The use of the horn is prohibited in towns and health and holiday resorts.

It is absolutely forbidden to drive after consuming any alcoholic drinks.

(c) The Rumanian Automobile Club

The Rumanian Automobile Club (A.C.R.), 27 Str. Nikos Beloiannis, Bucharest (tel. 13.42.60, 13.42.68 and 15.41.85, telex 011.323), with branches in the principal Rumanian towns, provides the following services:

— a free breakdown service on the road, subject to a maximum of 30 minutes;

— free towing up to a maximum distance of 30 km (19 miles);

— the return home of the car and its passengers on the basis of a motoring club's letter of credit;

— legal assistance and health care on the basis of a letter of credit;

— information on road conditions and weather;

— information and assistance on technical matters and travel arrangements (accommodation, etc.).

Breakdown help on the road is provided by the patrol vehicles of the A.C.R., which operate on all the important trunk roads.

Branches of the A.C.R., as well as tourist offices throughout the country, issue petrol coupons giving a reduction in price of 15% when payment is made in convertible currency.

The A.C.R. also organises various forms of individual and group excursion.

(d) Travel arrangements and facilities offered by the A.C.R.

(i) Package tours

For visitors travelling with their own car the A.C.R. provides "package" arrangements on very favourable terms, with full board in the best (luxury class) hotels, free technical assistance and 200 free litres of petrol (premium grade). Packages of this kind cover a holiday of 15 to 18 days, either in the visitors' own car or in a hired car (with or without driver).

(ii) Fly-drive

This arrangement covers the flight to and from Rumania and the use of a car, together with accommodation and meals in the best hotels and restaurants and free technical assistance.

(iii) Hotel coupons

These coupons, which can be bought in any European country, entitle the traveller to dinner, bed and breakfast in a first-class hotel and restaurant, together with 5 free litres of petrol (premium grade). Any number of coupons can be purchased.

(iv) Camping/caravanning coupons

These entitle the visitor to the use of camping and caravanning sites at reduced rates, together with 5 free litres of petrol (premium grade) per day.

(v) Rent-a-car

Cars can be hired, with or without driver, at any tourist office in Rumania or at any branch of the A.C.R. The hirer must have held a driving licence for not less than a year and must lodge a sum by way of security which is repaid when the car is returned.

Among the models available are the Volkswagen 1300 and 1600, the Dacia 1100 and 1300, the Fiat 124 and the Mercedes 220 and 220 automatic.

VIII. FOREIGN EMBASSIES

Albania: 18, Str. Ştefan Gheorghiu, Bucharest.

Argentina: 11, Str. Drobeta, Bucharest.

Austria: 7, Str. Dumbrava Roşie, Bucharest.

Belgium: 32, Bd Dacia, Bucharest.

Brazil: 1, Str. Praga, Bucharest.

Bulgaria: 5, Aleea Modrogan, Bucharest.

Central African Republic: 18, Str. Zborului, Bucharest.

Chile: 44, Str. Eminescu, Bucharest.

China: 8, Str. Polona, Bucharest.

Cuba: 14, Intrarea Armaşului, Bucharest.

Czechoslovakia: 11, Str. I. Ghica, Bucharest.

Denmark: 20, Aleea Modrogan, Bucharest.

Egypt: 21, Bd Dacia, Bucharest.

Ethiopia: 13, Str. 29 Novembra, Bucharest.

Finland: 16, Bd Dacia, Bucharest.

France: 13-15, Str. Biserica Amzei, Bucharest.

Germany (Democratic Republic): 6-8, Dumbrava Roşie, Bucharest.

Germany (Federal Republic): 12, Aleea Modrogan, Bucharest.

Great Britain: 24, Str. Jules Michelet, Bucharest.

Greece: 85, Bd Republicii, Bucharest.

Hungary: 65, Str. Al. Sahia, Bucharest.

India: 16, Str. Stefan Gheorghiu, Bucharest.

Indonesia: 18, Str. Popa Chiţu, Bucharest.

Irak: 18, Br Dr P. Groza, Bucharest.

Iran: 8, Str. Praga, Bucharest.

Israel: 5, Str. Dr C. Burghelea, Bucharest.

Italy: 7, Str. I.C. Frimu, Bucharest.

Japan: 8, Bd Ana Ipătescu, Bucharest.

Mongolia: 6, Str. Fagaruş, Bucharest.

Netherlands: 18, Aleea Zoe, Bucharest.

North Korea: 63, Str. Dionisie Lupu, Bucharest.

North Vietnam: 86, Str. Grigore Alexandrescu, Bucharest.

Norway : 19, Tolstojeva, Belgrade.

Pakistan : 18, Str. Victor Mirea, Bucharest.

Peru : 19A, Str. Paris, Bucharest.

Poland : 23, Aleea Alexandru, Bucharest.

Spain (Consulate): 34, Str. Paris, Bucharest.

Sweden : 13, Şos. Kiseleff, Bucharest.

Switzerland : 12, Str. Pitar Moş, Bucharest.

Turkey : 72, Calea Dorobanţi, Bucharest.

Uruguay : 8, Str. Brâncuşi, Bucharest.

U.S.A. : 7-9, Str. T. Arghezi, Bucharest.

U.S.S.R. : 8, Şos. Kiseleff, Bucharest.

Venezuela : 7, Str. Duiliu Zamfirescu, Bucharest.

Yugoslavia : 34, Calea Dorobanţi, Bucharest.

Zaire : 41, Aleea Alexandru, Bucharest.

IX. THE ARTS; ENTERTAINMENTS

The increasing contribution being made by Rumania in all spheres of contemporary life is demonstrated by the number of international congresses, conferences and symposia held there each year.

At present, too, the International Association of South-Eastern European Studies, the General Secretariat of the Balkan Medical Union and the editorial offices of the journal (published in French) "Archives de l'Union Médicale Balkanique" are based in Bucharest.

Among Rumanian cultural and artistic activities the following may be particularly mentioned:

—the George Enescu International Festival and Competition for violinists, pianists and singers, held at Bucharest every three years in memory of the great Rumanian musician. The last three competitions brought a number of promising young musicians to the fore and attracted famous conductors and soloists (Sir John Barbirolli, Herbert von Karajan, David Oistrakh, Yehudi Menuhin, Artur Rubinstein, etc.).

— the Rumanian Film Festival (for selected entries in all genres — artistic, documentary, reportage, cartoons), held at Mamaia in the second half of June.

—the summer courses in Rumanian language, literature, history and art organised at Sinaia in August of each year by the University of Bucharest.

Displays of folk art and music are very popular. Among the most important occasions of this type is the Festival of Rumanian Folk Singing, Dancing and Costume, which is held at the beginning of August each year at Mamaia and Sinaia and attracts the best individual performers and groups from every part of the country.

On the Sunday nearest to 20th July a very ancient and picturesque traditional occasion takes place on Mount Găina, in the Western Carpathians. This is the "Găina Fair", to which villagers flock in their thousands from all over the Western Carpathians to take part in the celebrations, which constitute a regular festival of folk singing and dancing.

Bucharest also has a special theatre, open all the year round, for performances of folk art; and the principal towns of Rumania have their own folk groups who give most attractive performances. There are many folk music orchestras, including in particular the "Barbu Lăutaru" section of the Philharmonic Orchestra of Bucharest, which has carried out a number of successful foreign tours.

Performances of opera and ballet are given both in Bucharest and in the large provincial towns (Cluj, Iaşi, Timişoara, Braşov, etc.). The repertoire includes works by the great masters of opera and ballet as well as by Rumanian composers.

Music lovers have also a choice of interesting concerts devoted both to the great classical composers and to the most noted representatives of contemporary music. Bucharest alone has three symphony orchestras—the George Enescu Philharmonic Orchestra, the Rumanian Radio and Television Orchestra and the Orchestra of the Ciprian Porumbescu Conservatoire. There are 14 other symphony orchestras in Rumania, as well as a whole galaxy of talented solo players. Altogether the country possesses 42 theatres, 5 opera houses, 13 operetta and variety theatres, 22 puppet theatres, 17 symphony orchestras, 19 folk music orchestras and 8 folk art groups run by the State.

Sports enthusiasts are catered for by national and international competitions in a great variety of different sports. Various international championships take place regularly in Bucharest and other Rumanian towns. These include table tennis championships (February), skiing (February, at Poiana Braşov), volleyball (June, in Bucharest), wrestling both classical and catch-as-catch-can (July, Bucharest), kayaking and canoeing

(July, Snagov), the Victory Cup for yachting (July, Mamaia), water polo (August, Bucharest), the Snagov Regatta (rowing–September) and athletics (September, Bucharest).

The section on entertainments would not be complete without mentioning the cafés, with variety turns and dance bands, to be found in Bucharest, the large towns and the holiday resorts.

X. POSTAL SERVICES AND TELEPHONES

Letters for foreign countries cost 2.75 lei (up to 20 grammes—1/10 oz); a registered letter costs 3.45 lei, an express letter 9.15 lei. Picture postcards cost 1.85 lei.

Letters sent by *air* to foreign countries pay additional charges according to country—0.85 leu for countries in Europe, 5.70 lei for the United States.

A telephone conversation costs 14 lei a minute to Austria, 16.00 lei a minute to West Germany, 21.30 lei a minute to France, 23.60 lei a minute to Great Britain and 22.45 lei a minute to Sweden.

XI. SHOPPING

Visitors can bring back from Rumania a wide range of products (textiles, knitted goods, shoes, cosmetics, perfumes, drinks, cigarettes, works of art, records, books, icons, etc.) and interesting examples of local crafts (carpets, items of clothing, etc.).

These articles can be paid for with tourist cheques issued by the National Bank of Rumania, in lei obtained by the exchange of convertible currency, or in foreign currency in special "shopping centres" In 'Comturist' shops, in certain handicraft shops and in the duty-free shops at Bucharest and Constanţa airports.

XII. FOOD AND DRINK

Rumania has a particularly rich and varied cuisine. But though it is legitimate to talk of a specifically Moldavian or Wallachian or Transylvanian cuisine, each with its own regional specialties, there is also a purely Rumanian cuisine, with a variety of characteristic and tasty dishes which the visitor can enjoy all over the country.

Among these dishes may be mentioned a whole series of soups —
soup with forced-meat balls (the finest of Rumanian soups),
paysanne soup (meat soup containing all kinds of vegetables)
borshch of lamb (flavoured with lovage), giblet soup (made
from giblets of fowl, and thought to be of value as a restorative,
so that it is usually served at the end of a long banquet) and
fish soup (a kind of bouillabaisse). With some exceptions
Rumanian soups tend to be on the acid side, and are generally
served with eggs or cream.

Another Rumanian speciality is poached eggs, served floating
in butter on a layer of *mamaliga* (a kind of polenta). *Mamaliga*
is also used in many other dishes, for example in *balmuş*, large
balls of *mamaliga* stuffed with ewe's milk cheese, coated with
fat and baked in an oven.

Mamaliga is also used as an accompaniment to certain other
dishes. The famous *sarmale* (bitter cabbage leaves stuffed with
meat), one of the most characteristic Rumanian dishes, are
usually served along with *mamaliga*. Although the ingredients
are generally the same, *sarmale* are not cooked the same way in
Moldavia and Transylvania. Vine leaves soaked in boiling
borshch are sometimes used instead of cabbage leaves, and the
sarmale are then served with cream or yoghourt. The Rumanian
tocane (a kind of stew) are made from pork, beef or mutton
with a strong flavouring of onions, and are also served with
mamaliga. The meat and vegetable stew called *ghiveciu* — or
the variety known as "monks' *ghiveciu*", made without meat,
cooked in oil, and served cold — contains more than twenty
kinds of vegetable. Another typically Rumanian dish is the
Moldavian *pîrjoala*, a kind of large flat rissole of strongly
spiced minced meat, served with a great variety of different
garnishings.

Grills occupy a place of honour in Rumanian cooking. They
are found in great variety, but the most popular are *mititei*
(meat balls rolled into cylindrical shape) and *patricieni* (sausages)
which for aroma and flavour are quite unrivalled.

There are, too, all sorts of characteristic dishes made with
game and fish, which are found in such abundance in Rumania.
Among these may be mentioned in particular carp on the spit,
a typical local speciality of the fishermen of the Danube Delta.
Among Rumanian cakes one or two deserve special mention,
for example the *plăcinte* (a kind of turnover), the Moldavian
cozonac (a bun or brioche), the *pasca* (Easter cake), and a
whole series of other cakes — the *baclava* (made of nuts and

honey), the *cataif* (made with whipped cream), etc.—which no doubt go back to remote Oriental origins but have long since been taken over into the Rumanian cuisine.

The entrée is accompanied by the traditional glass of *ţuica*, a type of plum brandy which varies in strength and flavour according to district (Piteşti, Vîlcea, Argeş or Buzău).

As for wines, there is an embarrassment of choice. They come from all parts of the country, ranging from dry to sweet, from red to white. Some of them are of ancient renown, like the famous *Feteasca* or the *Grasa* of Cotnari. Others have long enjoyed a considerable reputation: for example the *Riesling*, the *Muscat*, the *Pinot* and the *Chardonnay* of Murfatlar, the *Băbeasca* of Niculitel, the white *Feteasca*, the *Pinot gris* and the *Aligoté* of Jassy, the *Plăvaia*, the *Galbena*, the *Furmint*, the "black" *Băbeasca* and the *Frîncuşa* of Coteşti, Odobeşti, Panciu and Nicoreşti, the wines of Valea Călugărească, Drăgăşani and Tîrnave—and this is far from exhausting the list. In addition the Rumanian vineyards produce excellent table wines which—though perhaps not in the category of *appellations contrôlées*—have won many gold medals. Nor is Rumanian "champagne" to be despised: its delicate flavour can best be appreciated if it is drunk at the end of a good meal.

XIII. SHOOTING AND FISHING

Visitors going to Rumania to shoot or fish obtain an entry visa in the same way as any other visitor. If you are taking a gun this must be entered on your passport (make, calibre, serial number). Guns and ammunition must also be entered on the customs declaration form on arrival in Rumania.

Visitors are normally allowed to take in two sporting guns and 100 cartridges; but where the arrangements are made through the National Tourist Office the number of cartridges may be increased, on the basis of a confirmation issued by the N.T.O.; the permitted number will vary according to the type of game and the duration of stay.

Hunting dogs can also be taken into Rumania, provided that the owner produces at the frontier point a veterinary certificate confirming that the dog has had an anti-rabies vaccination not less than one month and not more than five months before the date of travel, and that no case of rabies has been reported in the area of origin within the preceding two months.

Shooting and fishing seasons

Larger game: Carpathian deer, 1 September to 30 November; fallow deer, 1 September to 30 November; roe-deer, 15 May to 31 October; chamois, 1 September to 30 November; bear, 1 March to 15 January; wild pig, 1 October to 28 February; black and red grouse, 1 April to 15 May; bustard, 10 April to 15 May.

Smaller game: hare, pheasant, 1 October to 31 January; pigeon, turtledove, 1 August to 21 March; hazel grouse, 15 September to 15 December; quail, 15 August to 30 November; woodcock, 1 September to 30 April.

The following may be shot throughout the year: marten, fox, wild cat, lynx (with a special permit), badger, otter, mink.

Water game. The Danube Delta offers sportsmen a great range of waterfowl and water animals. The following may be shot between 15 August and 20 March: snipe, duck, goose, coot, ibis, cormorant, heron, crane. Pelicans, bustards and swans may be shot only with a special permit.

Fishing in mountain waters: native trout, 1 May to 15 September; rainbow trout, 1 November to 28 February. Charges vary according to the size of the catch.

Fishing in hill waters: various species of fish may be taken between 15 June and 30 April.

XIV. USEFUL ADDRESSES IN BUCHAREST

Miscellaneous

National Tourist Office (Carpaţi), 7, Bd Magheru (tel. 14.19.22); Băneasa Airport (tel. 17.65.37); Nord Railway Station (tel. 17.05.78).

Rumanian Bank of Foreign Trade, 22, Calea Victoriei (tel. 16.35.52).

Tarom, 16, Bd Republicii (tel. 16.33.46).

C.F.R. Travel Agency No. 1, 2, Calea Victoriei.

C.F.R. Travel Agency No. 2, 130, Calea Griviţei.

Rumanian Automobile Club, 27, Str. N. Beloiannis (tel. 13.75.36).

Airlines

Aeroflot, 35, Bd Bălcescu (tel. 16.74.31).

Air France, 35, Bd Bălcescu (tel. 13.95.52).

Alitalia, 41, Bd Magheru (tel. 12.11.75).

AUA, 7, Bd Bălcescu (tel. 14.12.21).

British Airways, Intercontinental Hotel, 4, Bd Bălcescu (tel. 16.30.22 and 16.32.60).

CSA, 5, Str. Batistei (tel. 14.80.59).

EL AL, 5, Str. Batiştei (tel. 14.61.01).

Interflug, 31, Şos. Kiseleff (tel. 33.23.62).

Lot, 41, Bd Magheru (tel. 12.29.71).

Lufthansa, 18, Bd Magheru (tel. 12.99.50).

Panamerican, Hotel Intercontinental (tel. 13.63.60).

Sabena, 22, Bd Bălcescu (tel. 15.12.26).

SAS, 5, Str. Batiştei (tel. 15.15.51).

Swissair, 18, Bd Magheru (tel. 13.66.76).

Hotels

Intercontinental, 4, Bd Bălcescu (tel. 14.04.00 and 13.70.40). Luxury hotel (421 rooms), with every comfort and amenity: restaurants, brasseries, conference room, reception rooms, underground parking (c. 1000 cars), exchange office.

Athénée-Palace, 1, Str. Episcopiei (tel. 14.08.99; telex 162-163 Bucharest). Luxury hotel (300 rooms) with every comfort. On the ground floor are a restaurant (summer garden), café, brasserie, bar, reception room, hairdresser, florist, tobacco kiosk, exchange office, space for parking.

Lido, 5-7, Bd Magheru (tel. 16.00.00; telex 161 Bucharest). Luxury category (250 rooms and suites). On the ground floor are a restaurant with open terrace (orchestra, dancing), bar, self-service buffet, hairdresser, tobacco kiosk, exchange office, parking space, swimming pool.

Ambasador, 8, Bd Magheru (tel. 11.04.40; telex 160 Bucharest). Luxury category (400 beds). On the ground floor are a restaurant (orchestra, dancing), brasserie, hairdresser, tobacco kiosk.

Nord, 143, Cal. Griviţei (tel. 16.41.40). Luxury category (504 beds).

24

Restaurants and bars

In addition to the restaurants in the five hotels listed the following may be mentioned:

Pescăruş, summer terrace (orchestra, dancing), in an extremely picturesque situation in the Herăstrău Park, on the shores of the lake of the same name; Rumanian and Continental cuisine. Tel. 17.09.83.

Băneasa-Parc, a typically Rumanian restaurant on the fringe of the Băneasa woods; Rumanian cuisine, folk orchestra. Tel. 17.05.96.

Bucureşti, 36, Calea Victoriei (tel. 13.44.82). Long established reputation for its cooking; Continental cuisine.

Carul cu Bere, 5, Str. Stavropoleos; typically Rumanian cuisine; one of the oldest restaurants in Bucharest.

Melody Bar, 12-14 Bd Magheru: night club, open until 6 a.m. Cabaret; dancing.

Continental Bar, 3, Str. Colonadelor (tel. 15.79.82). Night club, open until 6 a.m. Cabaret; dancing. Closed on Mondays.

There are many cafés, brasseries and snack bars throughout the town.

Theatres and concert halls

National Theatre (the I.L. Caragiale Theatre): Comédia Theatre, 42-44, Calea Victoriei; Studio Theatre, 13, Piaţa Amzei.

Athenaeum, 2, Str. Constantin Esarco: headquarters of the George Enescu Philharmonic Orchestra.

Radio and Television Concert Hall, 62, Str. Nuferilor.

State Operetta Theatre, 1, Splaiul Independenţei.

Satirical and Musical Theatre (the C. Tănase Theatre): Savoy Theatre, 33-35, Calea Victoriei; Victoria Theatre, 174, Calea Victoriei.

Ţăndărică Puppet Theatre, 18, Str. Academiei and 48-50, Calea Victoriei.

In summer there are many performances of plays, operas, folk singing and dancing, variety, etc.

Shops

Eve (women's clothing and other articles), 9, Bd Magheru.

Adam (men's clothing and other articles), 27, Str. 13 Decembrie.

Victoria (department store), 17, Calea Victoriei.

Caleidoscop (a group of shops selling jewellery, perfume, fancy goods, handicrafts, textiles), 1-3, Bd Magheru.

Bucureşti (department store), 2, Str. Bărătiei.

Farmec (cosmetics), 63, Calea Victoriei.

Gioconda (silk), 95, Calea Victoriei.

Romarta (textiles, fancy goods for men and women, shoes, silk), 60, Calea Victoriei.

Romarta Copiilor (articles for children), 36, Calea Victoriei.

Servicing and repair of cars

Garage, 85, Calea Dorobanţi (tel. 12.28.56): washing, greasing, oil change, adjustments, repairs.

Ciclop Garage, 6, Bd Magheru: washing, greasing, oil change, repairs.

Many PECO service stations, for the supply of petrol and oil, throughout the town.

Postal and telephone services

Post Offices: Central Post Office, 37, Calea Victoriei (6 a.m. to midnight); Otopeni Airport; Hotel Athénée-Palace; Hotel Lido; Northern Station.

Telephone: local calls 25 bani. Many public telephones in all main streets, in shops, restaurants, cafés, tobacco kiosks, etc. International calls: Paris 63.90 lei, Rome 50.25 lei, London 70.80 lei, New York 218.10 lei (3 minutes).

Telegrams (per word): Paris 2.10 lei, London 3.15 lei, New York 7.50 lei, Rome 2.40 lei.

Telex (3 minutes): Great Britain 22.50 lei, France 23.40 lei, Western Germany 18 lei, Sweden 23.40 lei,

Medical services

Medical services are provided for visitors in hotels by qualified specialists. Meals prepared under medical direction are served in patients' rooms. Full medical services are available to patients from specialised clinics.

Museums

Museum of the History of the Socialist Republic of Rumania, 12 Calea Victoriei. 10 a.m. to 6 p. m. Closed Monday.

Aman Museum, 8, Str. Rosetti (tel. 14.58.12). 2 to 8 p.m. Closed Monday.

Anthropological Museum, Bd Petru-Groza (tel. 13.91.) 9 a.m. to 2 p.m. Closed Sunday. Specialists only.

Art Museum, 1, Str. Ştirbei Vodă (tel. 13.30.30). 11 a.m. to 6 p.m. Closed Monday.

Avachian Collection, 10, Str. S. Cihoski (tel. 12.17.25). Tuesday, Thursday and Saturday, 10 a.m. to 1 p.m. and 5 to 8 p.m.; Sunday 10 a.m. to 1 p.m.

Băneasa Zoo, 9 a.m. to 7 p.m. Closed Monday.

Botanic Gardens. 7 a.m. to 7 p.m.; hot-houses Thursday and Sunday 7 a.m. to 2 p.m.

Bucharest Historical Museum, 2, Bd 1848 (tel. 13.40.33). 11 a.m. to 8 p.m. Closed Monday.

Central Military Museum, 137, Str. Izvor (tel. 15.40.10). 10 a.m. to 6 p.m. Closed Tuesday.

Coandă Scientific Museum, 28 ,Bd Ana Ipătescu. Daily, except Monday, 11 a.m. to 1 p.m. and 5 to 7 p.m.; Sunday 11 a.m. to 3 p.m.

Collection of Comparative Art, 3, Str. Obedenaru. Tuesday and Thursday 9 a.m. to 1 p.m.; Friday and Saturday 3 to 8 p.m.; Sunday 10 a.m. to 6 p.m.

Dona Collection, 12, Str. Dr Dona (tel. 13.76.54). Tuesday, Thursday, Sunday, 10 a.m. to 1 p.m. and 4 to 7 p.m.

Fire Service Museum, 33, Bd Dimitrov. 12 noon to 8 p.m.; closed Monday.

Folk Museum, 1, Str. Dr Minovici (tel. 17.15.05). 10 a.m. to 1 p.m. and 4 to 6 p.m. Closed Monday.

George Enescu Museum, 141, Calea Victoriei. 10 a.m. to 1 p.m. and 5 to 7 p.m. Closed Monday.

Iser Collection, 9, Bd Bălcescu. Tuesday 4.30 to 7.30 p.m.; Sunday 10.30 a.m. to 12 noon.

Karadja Collection, 31, Str. Gr. Mora (tel. 17.90.77). Thursday, 10 a.m. to 1 p.m.

Medrea Museum, 16, Str. Budişteanu (tel. 15.74.83). 2 to 8 p.m. daily.

Minulescu Collection, 19, Bd Gh. Marinescu (tel. 14.31.32). Sunday 11 a.m. to 1 p.m.

Mogoşoaia Museum (tel. 18.03.12). 10 a.m. to 4 p.m. Closed Monday and Tuesday.

Museum of Rumanian Astronomy, 21, Bd Ana Ipătescu (tel. 12.93.89). Wednesday and Friday 9 a.m. to 1 p.m.; Tuesday, Thursday, Saturday, Sunday 5 to 8 p.m. Closed Monday.

Museum of Feudal Art, 3, Str. Dr Minovici (tel. 17.15.05). 10 a.m. to 1 p.m. and 5 to 7 p.m. Closed Sunday afternoon and Monday.

Museum of Folk Art, 107, Calea Victoriei (tel. 16.42.94). 11 a.m. to 6 p.m. Closed Monday.

Museum of the History of the Communist Party and of the Revolutionary and Democratic Movement in Rumania, 3, Şos, Kiseleff. Daily, except Monday, 10 a.m. tp 7 o.m.; Saturday 10 a.m. to 2 p.m.

Museum of Literature, 4, Str. Fundaţiei. Tuesday and Friday 10 a.m. to 2 p.m.; Thursday and Saturday 4 to 8 p.m.; Sunday 10 a.m. to 2 p.m. and 4 to 8 p.m.

Museum of the State Archives, 2, Str. Arhivelor. Monday, Wednesday, Friday 8 a.m. to 2 p.m. and 5 to 8 p.m.; Tuesday, Thursday, Saturday 8 a.m. to 2 p.m.

Natural History Museum, 1, Şos. Kiseleff (tel. 15.34.73): 10 a.m. to 2 p.m. and 4 to 7 p.m.; Sunday 10 a.m. to 8 p.m. Closed Monday.

Nottara House, 51, Bd Dacia. Tuesday, Thursday, Saturday, Sunday 10 a.m. to 1 p.m. and 4 to 7 p.m.

Numismatic Exhibition, 133, Calea Victoriei (tel. 16.01.70). 8 a.m. to 3 p.m. Closed Sunday.

Oprescu Collection, 16, Str. Dr Clunet (tel. 14.90.12). Sunday 3 to 5 p.m.

Railway Museum, 193 B, Calea Griviţei. 9 a.m. to 2 p.m. (Sunday 1 p.m.). Closed Monday.

Simu Museum, 5-7, Str. Biserica Amzei. 1 a.m. to 7 p.m.; closed Monday.

Severeanu Collection, 26, Str. I.C. Frimu (tel. 12.94.82). 11 a.m. to 7 p.m. Closed Monday.

Storck Museum, 16, Str. V. Alexandri (Tel. 11.78.89). Tuesday, Friday, Sunday 10 a.m. to 1 p.m.; Thursday 4 to 7 p.m.

Tattarescu Museum, 7, Str. Domniţa Anastasia (tel. 14.10.06). As for Storck Museum.

Technical Museum, Park of Liberty (tel. 23.93.90). Thursday 7 a.m. to 5 p.m.; Sunday 9 a.m. to 12 noon.

Village Museum, 20, Şos. Kiseleff (tel. 18.61.91). 10 a.m. to 6 p.m. Closed Monday.

Weinberg Collection, 36, Str. Al. Sahia (tel. 16.66.86). Thursday and Sunday 4 to 6 p.m.

Zambaccian Museum (tel. 11.23.66). 11 a.m. to 7 p.m. Closed Monday.

HOTELS

Visitors have a wide range of hotels in different categories in Bucharest, other towns in Rumania, and the main health, bathing and winter sports resorts.

Most hotels have restaurants attached to them.

As a rule hotel staffs speak foreign languages..

The charges for rooms and suites vary according to the standard of comfort of the hotels.

Place	Name and address of hotel	Category
Alba Iulia	*Apulum*, 1 Piaţa 1 Mai	I
	Transilvania, 10 Piaţa 1 Mai	I
Arad	*Astoria*, 79 Bd Republicii	I
	Mureşul, 88 Bd Republicii	I
Bacău	*Decebal*, 6 Str. 6 Martie	I
	Bistriţa, 3 Calea Mărăşeşti	I
Bicaz	*Ceahlău*, 8 Str. Centrală	II
Bistriţa	*Cerbul*, 7 Str. N. Titulescu	II
Baia Mare	*Bucureşti*, Piaţa Victoriei	I
Bucharest	*Intercontinental*, 4 Bd Bălcescu	Luxury
	Athénée Palace, 1-3 Str. Episcopiei	Luxury
	Lido, 5 Bd Magheru	Luxury
	Ambasador, 6-8 Bd Magheru	Luxury
	Nord, 143 Calea Griviţei	Luxury
	Union, 6 Str. 13 Decembrie	I
	Muntenia, 21 Str. Academiei	I

Place	Name and Address of Hotel	Category
	Cişmigiu, 18 Bd 6 Martie	I
	Victoria, 15 Calea Victoriei	I
	Dunărea, 140 Calea Griviţei	II
	Bucegi, 2 Str. Witting	II
	Cerna, 29 Bd Dinicu Golescu	II
Băile Herculane	*Cerna*	I
Brăila	*Traian*, I Piaţa Lenin	I
	Delta, 58 Str. Republicii	II
Braşov	*Carpaţi*, 9 Bd Carpaţi	Luxury
	Postăvarul, 2 Str. Grigorescu	I
Poiana Braşov	*Bradul*	I
	Poiana	I
	Sport	I
Cluj	*Napoca*, 1 Str. Iosza Bela	I
	Continental, 1 Str. Napoca	I
	Siesta, 6 Str. Sincai	I
	Astoria, 3 Str. Horia	II
	Central, 29 Piaţa Libertăţii	II
Constanţa	*Continental*, 20 Bd Republicii	I
	Palas, 11 Str. R. Opreanu	I
Craiova	*Jiul*, 1-3 Calea Bucureşti	I
	Minerva, 1 Str. Kogălniceanu	I
Deva	*Dacia*, 3 Piaţa Unirii	II
Drobeta-Turnu Severin	*Parc*, 2 Bd Republicii	I
	Traian, 1 Str. Karl Marx	II
Eforie Nord	*Europa, Carmen, Cupidon*	Luxury
	Apolo, Atlas, Argeş, Arta, Azur, Belona, Bucegi, Bega, Belvedere, Diana, Felix, Fortuna, Jupiter, Lira, Selena, Union, Venus	I
	Putna, Sirius, Uranus	II

Place	Name and Address of Hotel	Category
Eforie Sud	*Cosmos, Ancora, Flamingo, Gloria,*	
	Excelsior, Parc, Riviera, Oltenia	I
	Făgăraş, Ciobănas, Suceava, Turist	II
	Amurg, Jiul, Mureş, Sirena	III
Galaţi	*Galati,* 1 Str. Republicii	I
Iaşi (Jassy)	*Continental,* 4 Str. Cuza Vodă	I
	Unirea, 5 Piaţa Unirii	I
Jupiter	*Cozia, Scoica, Delta, Cometa,*	
	Meteor, Olimpic, Atlas, Capitol	I
	Iris, Nalba, Violeta	II
Mamaia	*International*	Luxury
	Parc, Perla, Aurora, Sirena,	
	Doina, Flora, Victoria, Albatros,	
	Modern, Central, Palas, Pelican,	
	Bucureşti, Pescăruş, Dacia, Delfin,	
	Lotus, Select, Dunărea, Neptun,	
	Delta, Sulina, Ovidiu, Midia,	
	Tomis, Histria	I
Mangalia	*Scala, Zefir*	I
	Astra, Orion, Zenit	II
Mediaş	*Central,* Str. Rosmarinului	I
Miercurea Ciuc	*Harghita,* Str. Lenin	I
Odorheiu Secuiesc	*Tîrnave,* 2 Piaţa 23 August	I
Oradea	*Dacia,* 1 Aleea Strandului	I
	Transilvania, 2 Str. Teatrului	I
	Park, 3 Str. Republicii	II
Ploieşti	*Piatra Neamt Ceahlăul,* 1 Piaţa Karl Marx	Luxury
	Berbec, 1 Str. Republicii	I and II
Predeal	*Carmen*	I and II
	Rosmarin	I

Place	Name and Address of Hotel	Category
Piteşti	*Argeş*, 19 Bd 7 Noiembrie	I and II
Putna	*Putna*. Str. Mănăstirii	II
Rădăuţi	*Rădăuţi*, 9 Str. Stefan cel Mare	I
Reşiţa	*Semenic*, 2 Bd Lenin	I
Rîmnicu Vîlcea	*Alutus*, Piaţa Maxim Gorki	I
Satu Mare	*Dacia*, 12 Piaţa Libertăţii	I
Saturn	*Diana, Atena, Alfa, Beta, Aida, Semiramis, Siret, Gama, Narcis, Cerna, Cleopatra, Tosca, Prahova*	I
Sfîntu Gheorghe	*Sfîntu Gheorghe*	I
Sighişoara	*Steana*, 12 Bd Gh. Gheorghiu-Dej	I
Sibiu	*Impăratul Romanilor*, 4 Str. Bălcescu	I
	Bulevard, 10 Piaţa Unirii	I
Sighetu Marmaţiei	*Gutinul*, Piaţa Gării	I
Sinaia	*Palas*, 30 Str. 13 Decembrie	I and II
	Alpin, Cota 1400	I
Suceava	*Balada*, 7 Str. Lenin	I
	Arcaşul, 6 Str. Mihai Viteazul	I
Timişoara	*Bonatul*, 5 Bd Republicii	I
	Carpati, 4 Str. Piatra Craiului	I
	Timişoara, 47 Str. 13 Decembrie	I
Timişul de Jos	*Dîmbul Morii*	I
Tîrgu Mureş	*Transilvania*, 43 Piaţa Trandafirilor	I
Venus	*Anca, Dana, Irina, Carmen, Nina, Lidia, Corina, Egreta, Ileana, Felicia, Rodica, Cocorul, Pajura, Veronica*	I

It is wise to book in advance, particularly in the busier towns and resorts. Arrangements for this purpose can be made through any travel agency approved by the National Tourist Office.

CAMPING SITES

The number of camping sites in Rumania is steadily increasing. The following is a selection of sites lying on or near main roads (the location being indicated by the distance along the road, with the distance from the road in brackets):

D.N.   1: Km 10.3 (1 km), Băneasa (with holiday bungalows)

        km 35 (7 km), Snagov Park (with bungalows)

        km 68.5 (3 km), Păuleşti-Ploieşti

        Km 80, Paralela 45 - Băicoi (with bungalows)

        Km 117, Popasul Izvorul Rece - Sinaia (with bungalows)

        Km 310 (4 km), Dumbrava Sibiului (with bungalows)

        Km 349.5, Băile Miercurea (with bungalows)

        Km 446 (2 km), Turda-Băi (with bungalows)

        Km 473 (1.7 km), Făget-Cluj (with bungalows)

        Km 58 (20.5 km), Popasul Băile Balvanyos (with bungalows)

D.N. 12: Km 45.5 (1 km), Popasul Moara la Făgădău- Tuşnad (with bungalows)

D.N. 12B: Km 18 (2.5 km), Slănic-Moldova (with bungalows)

        Km 26, Popasul Lacu Roşu (with bungalows)

D.N. 14: Km 87.5, Hula Daneşului

D.N. 15: Km 76 (1 km), Tîrgu Mureş (with bungalows)

        Km 277, Potoci-Bicaz (with bungalows)

        Km 372,1, Gherăeşti-Băcau (with bungalows)

        Km 146, Runcu Vatra Dornei (with bungalows)

        Km 233.3, Popasul Ilieşti (with bungalows)

        Km 3 (7.5 km), Firiza (with bungalows)

        Km 31, Popasul Sineşti (with bungalows)

D.N. 2A: Km 205 (10 km), Mamaia-Sat

        Km 177 (39 km), Pelican-Murighiol (with bungalows)

D.N. 24: Km 183.2, Bucium-Iaşi

D.N.   3: Km 58.3, Popasul Hanul din Salcîmi (with bungalows)

D.N. 39: Km 12.5 (1 km), Eforie Nord

Km 16.7 (1 km), Eforie Sud

Km 27 (3 km), Costineşti

Km 36.1 (2 km), Neptun

Km 38 (2 km), Jupiter

Km 38.1 (1 km), Venus

Km 64, Vama-Giurgiu

Km 338 (4 km), Popasul Parc Crihala - Drobeta-Turnu Severin (with bungalows)

Km 555.5, Pădurea Verde - Timişoara

D.N. 65: Km 72 (0.5 km), Popasul Scorniceşti (with bungalows)

D.N. 66: Km 67.5, Debarcader - Tîrgu Jiu

Km 81.8, Popasul Castrul Roman - Bumbeşti (with bungalows)

D.N. 67: Km 152, Stejării-Horezu (with bungalows).

D.N. 68B: Km 13 (13,5 km), Cinciş - Lacul Teliuc (with bungalows).

D.N. 7: Km 63, Popasul Mătăsaru-Găeşti (with bungalows).

Km 114,5 (2 km), Trivale-Piteşti (with bungalows).

Km 123, Popasul Valea Ursului (with bungalows).

Km 157, Popasul Topologu (with bungalows).

Km 235, Popasul Rîul Vadului - Cîineni (with biungalows).

D.N. 76: Km 181, Băile 1 Mai.

The camping sites usually have an area of about 3½ acres and accommodate 50 to 60 tents. Except at Mamaia the surface is grass. The sites are connected with the neighbouring towns by regular bus services.

The sites are situated near restaurants or have camp shops. They are provided with all necessary facilities—lighting (220 volts), sanitation, ablution blocks. No special formality or permit is required for camping.

TOURIST HUTS

The mountains of Rumania are well provided with huts and other accommodation for tourists—shelters, ordinary huts, hutted hotels and groups of huts. Altogether there are more than 150, most of them being in the Southern Carpathians.

The Bucegi range, at the eastern tip of the Southern Carpathians, contains 15 huts, a shelter used by climbers ascending the eastern face, and a comfortable hotel (the Alpin, at an altitude of 4,600 feet).

The huts are in three main areas: on the eastern slopes (above the Prahova valley, from which many paths lead up into the mountains), on the plateau, and in the upper Ialomiţa valley which cuts through the range.

In the Făgăraş Mountains there are 10 huts and a group of 9 houses in the Sîmbăta valley, one of the approach routes to these mountains. The picturesquely situated Bîlea hut, on a promontory in Lake Bîlea, is an important centre for skiing in spring (as late as the month of May). The Negoiul Hotel, a hut recently built just under the summit of Serbota, offers a fine view of Mount Negoiu (8,300 feet).

The Banat Mountains are particularly well provided with huts. Although not very high, these mountains are very popular with skiers. There are three main groups of huts: a) at Crivaia (7 huts with accommodation for 240); b) on the plateau on the summit of Mount Semenic, at a height of 4,600 feet (19 huts with accommodation for 325; the skiing slopes are equipped with chair-lift and ski-lift); and c) a group under the summit of Mount Mic, at 5,000 feet (9 huts with accommodation for 411).

Among the huts of the Western Carpathians may be mentioned Stîna de Vale (with ski slopes in the neighbourhood), Padiş (in the Cetăţile Ponorului, an area rich in karstic features), Scărişoara (near caves containing a glacier of the Quaternary period) and Vadul Crişului (near the cave of the same name).

In the mountains of northern Rumania is the resort of Borşa, on the northern slope of the Rodna Mountains, with a tourist hotel and an easily accessible hut. This resort, on the road linking northern Moldavia with the Maramureş, is popular with skiers on account of the good skiing slopes nearby.

The Eastern Carpathians, to the west of which runs a chain of volcanic hills, have been steadily increasing the accommodation they offer tourists. Those who are attracted by picturesque scenery will certainly want to visit the huts at Rarău (at the foot of the impressive limestone towers known as the Pietrele Doamnei), Dochia (summit of Mount Ceahlău), Cheile Bicazului (in the middle of a defile of striking beauty), Ana (to the north of a lake formed in the crater of a volcano), Ciucaş (in the mountains of the same name), etc.

Most of the huts contain a snack bar or a restaurant and have electric light. Some of them have running water; the others are near supplies of drinking water.

VOCABULARY

English	*Rumanian*
Good morning	Bună dimineaţa
Good day	Bună ziua
Good evening	Bună seara
Goodnight	Noapte bună
Good journey!	Drum bun
Good appetite!	Poftă bună
May I...?	Permiteţi
Please	Vă rog
Thank you	Mulţumesc
Goodbye	La revedere
Yes	Da
No	Nu
Where is...?	Unde este...?
...Street	Strada...
...Hotel	Hotelul...
...Restaurant	Restaurantul...
Tea-shop	Cofetăria
Station	Gara
Port, harbour	Portul
Airport	Aeroportul
Bus stop	Staţia de autobus
Trolley-bus stop	Staţia de troleibus
Tram stop	Staţia de tramvai
Taxi rank	Staţia de taxiuri
Post office	Poşta
Embassy	Ambasada
Legation	Legaţia
Sports ground, stadium	Stadionau
A bookshop	O librărie
A chemist's	O farmacie
A hospital	Un spital
A doctor	Un medic
A garage	Un garaj
Telephone office	Oficiul de telefoane
How much is...?	Cît costă...?
Bread	Pîinea
Meat	Carnea
Wine	Vinul
Beer	Berea
Butter	Untul

Fish	Peştele
Cake	Prăjitura
Fruit	Fructele
A packet of cigarettes	Un pachet de ţigări
A box of matches	O cutie de chibrituri
Newspaper	Ziarul
Book	Cartea
Gramophone record	Discul
Tram ticket	Biletul de tramvai
Bus ticket	Biletul de autobus
Railway ticket	Biletul de tren
Air ticket	Biletul de avion
Boat ticket	Biletul de vapor
What time is it?	Cît e ceasul?
What is the weather like?	Cum e vremea?
When does the train go?	Cînd pleacă trenul?
When does the train arrive?	Cînd soseste trenul?
One	Un, una
Two	Doi
Three	Trei
Four	Patru
Five	Cinci
Six	Sase
Seven	Sapte
Eight	Opt
Nine	Nouă
Ten	Zece
Eleven	Unsprezece
Twelve	Doisprezece
White	Alb
Red	Roşu
Yellow	Galben
Green	Verde
Blue	Albastru
Black	Negru
Purple, violet	Violet
To the right	La dreapta
To the left	La stînga
Stop!	Opreşte!
Beautiful	Frumos
Ugly	Urît
Big	Mare
Small	Mic
Bill, check	Plata

My name is...	Mă numesc...
My address is...	Adresa mea este...
What is your name?	Cum vă numi'i?
What is your address?	Ce adresă aveţi?
Leu, a leu (monetary unit)	Leu, un leu
Lei (pl.), ten lei	Lei, zece lei
Friendship	Prietenie

Pronunciation

The following indications are only approximate:

Vowels. a=*ah;* e as in *pen;* i=*ee;* final unstressed i is very short, like a consonantal *y;* o as in *short;* u=*oo;* ă like the second syllable in *father;* î a little like the u in *hut.*

Consonants. ş=*sh;* ţ=*ts;* j=*zh* (as in French *j*); c before e or i=*ch;* c before other vowels=*k;* ch before e or i=*k;* g before e or i=*j;* g before other vowels=hard g as in *good;* gh before e or i=hard g as in *good;* r is rolled; other consonants roughly as in English.

	Bucharest	Arad	Bacău	Baia Mare	Brașov	Craiova	Constanța	Cluj	Deva	Galaț	Iași
Buch.		555	285	589	172	236	265	483	401	247	413
Arad			604	312	425	508	820	264	154	742	732
Bacău				497	179	435	550	459	179	179	128
Baia Mare					459	539	899	151	324	776	515
Brașov						256	440	308	271	317	307
Craiova							501	388	250	436	563
Constanța								748	666	222	467
Cluj									173	638	553
Deva										588	785
Galați											245
Iași											

between the principal towns

Oradea	Ploiești	Pitești	Suceava	Sibiu	Tg. Mureș	Timișoara	Giurgiu	Miercurea Ciuc	Tulcea	V. Dornei
635	60	114	434	272	400	607	64	272	391	543
112	540	444	581	283	369	52	619	522	838	472
611	240	313	149	321	354	656	349	201	275	258
200	574	475	348	317	256	364	653	409	1025	239
460	115	134	328	142	270	477	239	97	413	437
540	234	122	584	222	350	332	300	353	627	513
900	325	379	699	537	665	872	329	537	126	808
152	423	324	317	166	105	334	547	258	734	208
226	386	287	599	129	257	161	465	368	792	381
790	202	314	328	459	533	794	311	380	96	437
705	368	480	167	449	448	784	477	295	341	276
Orad.	575	476	469	318	257	164	699	410	873	360
Ploiești		112	389	257	385	592	124	212	298	498
Pitești			501	158	286	493	178	231	410	571
Suceava				400	272	805	498	253	424	109
Sibiu					128	290	336	239	555	291
Tg. Mureș						418	464	153	524	163
Timișoara							632	574	890	542
Giurgiu								336	455	607
Miercurea-Ciuc									371	316
Tulcea										533

INDEX

This guide has been printed by Nagel Publishers and Printers
in Geneva (Switzerland)

Legal Deposit N°. 738

Printed in Switzerland

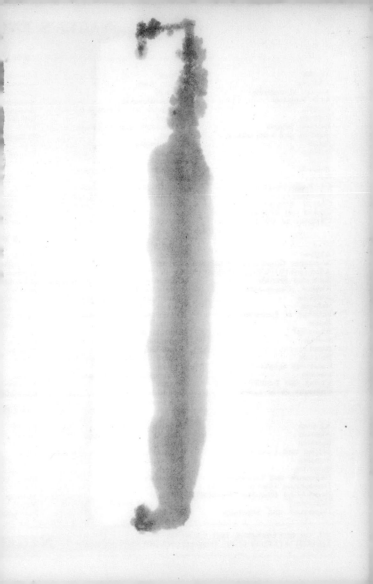

Algeria	China	Greenlar
Andorra	Costa Rica	Guatema
Angkor (Cambodia)	Cyprus	Holland
Arab Emirates	Czechoslovakia	Hondura
Austria	Denmark and Greenland	Hungary
Bahrain	Düsseldorf	Iceland
Balearic Islands	Düsseldorf and Duisburg	India ar
Belgium and Luxemburg	Egypt	Indonesi
Belize	El Salvador	Iran
Bolivia	Europe	Ireland
Brazil	Finland	Israel
Bulgaria	Florence and its environs	Italy
Burma*	France*	Ivory Co
Cambodia (Angkor)	French and Italian Riviera	Japan
Canada	Germany (Federal Republic)	Kuwait
Central America	Germany (Democratic Republic)*	Leningra
Ceylon (Sri Lanka)	Great Britain	Liechten
Châteaux of the Loire	Greece	Luxembu

Algérie	Chine	Grèce
Allemagne (République Fédérale)	Chypre	Groënlar
Allemagne (République Démocr.)*	Costa Rica	Guatema
Amérique centrale	Côte d'Azur et Riviera italienne	Hollande
Angkor (Cambodge)	Côte d'Ivoire*	Hondura
Autriche	Danemark et Groënland	Hongrie
Bahrein	Düsseldorf	Iles Balé
Belgique et Luxembourg	Düsseldorf et Duisbourg	Inde et
Belize	Egypte	Indonési
Birmanie*	Emirats du Golfe	Iran
Bolivie	Espagne	Irlande
Brésil	Etats-Unis	Islande
Bulgarie	Fédération des Emirats Unis	Israël
Cambodge (Angkor)	Finlande	Italie
Canada	Florence et ses environs	Japon
Ceylan (Sri Lanka)	France	Koweit
Châteaux de la Loire	Grande-Bretagne	Leningra

Ägypten	Finnland	Island
Algerien	Florenz und Umgebung	Israel
Balearen	Frankreich	Italien
Belgien und Luxemburg	Französische und Italienische	Japan
Brasilien	Riviera	Jugoslaw
Bulgarien	Griechenland	Leningra
Dänemark und Grönland	Grönland	Marokko
Deutschland (Bundesrepublik)	Großbritannien*	Der Mo
Deutschland (Demokr. Republik)	Holland	Moskau
Düsseldorf	Indien und Nepal	Nepal
Düsseldorf und Duisburg	Irland	Norwege

5-7, rue de l'Orangerie, 1211 GENEVA 7
Tel. (022) 34 17 30/34 17 39 - Telegram: NAGELEDIT-GENÈVE